MUSLIM REFORMIST POLITICAL THOUGHT

CENTRAL ASIA RESEARCH FORUM
Series Editor: Shirin Akiner
School of Oriental and African Studies, University of London

Other titles in the series:

MUSLIM REFORMIST POLITICAL THOUGHT

Revivalists, modernists and free will

Sarfraz Khan

Routledge
Taylor & Francis Group

LONDON AND NEW YORK

First published 2003
by Routledge
2 Park Square, Milton Park, Abingdon, Oxon, OX14 4RN

Simultaneously published in the USA and Canada
by Routledge
270 Madison Ave, New York NY 10016

Routledge is an imprint of the Taylor & Francis Group

Transferred to Digital Printing 2010

© 2003 Sarfraz Khan

Typeset in Sabon by LaserScript Ltd, Mitcham, Surrey

British Library Cataloguing in Publication Data
A catalogue record for this book is available from the British Library

Library of Congress Cataloging in Publication Data
A catalog record for this book has been requested

ISBN10: 0–700–71237–2 (hbk)
ISBN10: 0–415–59139–2 (pbk)

ISBN13: 978–0–700–71237–3 (hbk)
ISBN13: 978–0–415–59139–3 (pbk)

Publisher's Note
The publisher has gone to great lengths to ensure the quality of this reprint
but points out that some imperfections in the original may be apparent.

Contents

Acknowledgements

Now that this work finally comes to an end, I feel ever more obliged to all those without whose sincere and selfless cooperation this work would not have been accomplished. They are numerous, and everyone in his or her own way helped me with grace and generosity. The constraints of space seem unkind to them, but I don't have to be. My eternal gratitude goes to all of them individually, whether their names appear here or not, with a submission that they equally share what will presumably be regarded as my accomplishment.

I owe very special thanks to my learned supervisor, Dr. Shirin Akiner, for her unfailing encouragement and wise guidance, from which I have greatly benefited. She allowed me the necessary independence to develop my own ideas, while at the same time, her timely interventions saved me from many unnecessary excursions into uncharted territory.

I have fond regards for my friend and colleague from Peshawar University, (currently the Vice Chancellor) Dr Zulfiqar Gilani, who, while staying in Brighton, voluntarily undertook to review the initial draft of this thesis and offered valuable suggestions. My friend Dr Zahid Mushtaq helped me a great deal in translating Russian material into English; Manochehr, Akhtar Jan, Ahsan Wahga and Farida Garnett are those whose assistance in translating the Persian and Tajiki references deserves special mention.

I am extremely grateful to Professor Thomas Trevor for his kind perusal of my final draft and for his valued approval of the same, which provided me with welcome required reassurance. It would be an act of disloyalty not to acknowledge the kindness of my friend Jonathan Hay, who invariably responded to my requests positively. I must also mention my elder brother, Dr Zaheerullah Khan, who supplied promptly whatever literature I needed from the former Soviet Union.

How can one ignore those friends whom one can trustingly call on in moments of stress and pain, which have never been scarce? I proudly recall my friend, Dr Shahdin Malik, who would often instruct me like a guru to overcome my novicehood in the realm of computers. Then, lengthy discussions with my compatriot friend Abdul Wasey both enhanced our insight into the Islamic perspectives of our theses and helped us to release our tension. In the latter part of my work, I have been lucky to have Ishtiaq's friendship, who has made my life easier in many respects.

I would also like to take this opportunity to express my gratitude to the Commonwealth Scholarship Commission for granting me a Fellowship to come to Britain to study, and also for generously extending the award at a time when I desperately needed it. I have greatly benefited from the Commission's efficiency and supportive attitude.

And no one deserves my admiration more than my beloved wife, Dr Riffat Aziz, who has stunningly proven her once-made vow of putting up with me through thick and thin. She has endured all the anxiety with great grace and perseverance, and at times also had to bear with the sensitivity of my temper. My daughters, Bela Khan, seven, and Malala Khan, four, although their tender age would not have let them realise the state their parents were in, often their ambivalent and questioning eyes would sadden me. But I hope and pray that this first experience will add to their confidence.

Note on Transliteration

In a study using a variety of languages and scripts it is almost impossible to be consistent in transliteration. The simplest and least ambiguous forms of transliteration have been used. Russian has been transliterated according to the Library of Congress system. The use of diacritics, and of single inverted comma to indicate a glottal stop have been avoided. Apparent inconsistency in the transcription of the sound 'j' (as in 'John') arises from the fact that it is rendered as 'j' in words of Arabic, Persian (Tajiki) and Uzbeki origin but as 'dzh' in words of Russian origin.

Introduction

MUSLIM REFORMIST TRENDS: AN OVERVIEW

Orthodox Muslims consider Islam to be a complete and consummate religion. They argue that changes or reforms are neither possible nor tolerable and regard any attempt at introducing change as an intolerable intrusion into a divinely revealed religion, hence apostasy. However, the existence of various sects, throughout the history of Islam, testifies to the presence of acute disagreements in the Muslim community. These religious sectarian movements have expressed spontaneous discontent with the existing order, and represented the aspirations of Muslim people for social change.[1]

The need to adapt Islam to modern times mounted in the nineteenth century when the Muslim world in general realised its weakness and backwardness in relation to the militarily and technologically powerful West. Some representatives of the Muslim intelligentsia began actively advocating reform in religious and other practices and structures (educational, political, cultural and social) to make Islam more relevant to the demands of contemporary society. This approach, which attempts to forge changes in religion and society, may be termed 'reformist'. It is a complex process, one which requires not just a superficial adaptation of practices, but a fundamental alteration of the religious system of values, in order to bring Islam into line with the changing circumstances of a new age.

In the Christian world the term 'Reformation' refers to the struggle which took place in the first half of the sixteenth century against the Church as an institution. Some of the reformers invoked the doctrine of predestination, namely, that man's fate is divinely determined in advance, as an argument against the Church's claim that man's salvation depended on the kindly deeds and chaste exploits of the holy fathers. Martin Luther (1483–1546) renounced the Catholic concept of 'merit', deeming it a blasphemous haggling with God, and instead put forward the idea of salvation through faith.[2] John Calvin (1509–1564) went further, maintaining that divine predestination was eternal and unchanging; some people were destined to salvation, and others to eternal damnation. Jesus Christ sacrificed himself not for the sake of everybody, but for those who have been chosen by God. Evidence of being chosen lay in man's conduct. Thus, a Christian could regard himself as being endowed with divine blessing and could proclaim his actions as those of the 'broom of God'. This interpretation of the idea of predestination was used as a religious foundation for individual activity and liberation from the control of the Church.

Muslim reformist movements have inevitably followed a different path from the analogous Christian trends because Islam has neither an organised institution such as the Church, nor an officially ordained clergy. Functions similar to those of the Christian clergy are discharged by the *ulama* (the collective term for all religious functionaries, including teachers and interpreters of the sacred law). The foundation of their temporal power was (and in some societies still is) the exclusive right to interpret the word of God. Thus, ordinary believers had no right to exercise *ijtihad* (systematic original thinking). Most of the *ulama* have traditionally defended the 'purity' and fundamental nature of the laws that have been transmitted to them through the centuries. The *ulama* have used the doctrine of predetermination to sustain the existing social and political structure, promoting the idea that these were ordained by God. These attitudes impede freedom of thought and action, and encourage passive subordination to the prestige of the *ulama* and the rulers. In order to break free of the domination of the *ulama* it has been essential to revise the doctrine of predetermination. Muslim reformists, therefore, in contrast to the Christian Protestants, put greater emphasis on the doctrine of freedom of will. Reformist Islamic teaching presents a new understanding and interpretation of the entire complex of religious, ethical, political and economic problems. New interpretations are offered regarding the ontological and epistemological aspects of the problem of relations between God and man, which sanction the freedom of the will.

Muslim reformist movements, like their Christian counterparts, are based on an understanding of a personal relationship between man and God; they seek to abolish, or at least minimise, the mediating role of the clergy in this relationship. In both religions, the reformist movements introduced a more democratic attitude in religious institutions and rituals. In Islam, this has encouraged such developments as the translation of the Quran into the vernacular, the offering of prayers in indigenous languages, and the simplification of the *Haj* ritual. A key feature of Muslim reformist movements is humanism, based on a rationalistic critique of the medieval world outlook. More precisely, it represents an affirmation of human dignity, of man's right to freedom of thought and action and of his multifarious development as an individual.

An important feature of Muslim reform movements has been their anti-colonial bias. The reason for this is historical. These movements first

2

emerged in the nineteenth century when the Muslim world was suffering under various forms of foreign colonial rule. The fight for liberation from the oppression of alien colonial masters soon merged with the struggle against the religious oppression of the orthodox *ulama*.

Two specific trends may be distinguished in Muslim reformist movements: 'Modernism' and 'Revivalism'. Modernism generally implies 'Europeanisation' or 'Westernisation' and is expressed in the adoption of European/Western standards. This is mostly justified by recourse to the doctrine of *ijtihad* (systematic original thinking): the argument is that such changes are compatible with Islamic principles and dogmas. In most cases, the reformist approach to Islam is characteristic of the intelligentsia and bourgeoisie who have experienced a European education and had contact with the Western way of life. However, European standards and institutions are often not applicable to local conditions, and are alien to ordinary Muslims. Therefore, even today, modernists mostly represent a tiny minority within their own countries. They are often accused of apostasy by the orthodox, and are distrusted or misunderstood by the population at large.

In the political theory of the modernist reformists the idea of the supremacy of religious law is rejected. Instead, they tend to advocate modern, Western-style legislative practices. They denounce outdated canons and standards, arguing for the revision of *fiqh* and the recognition of the right to *ijtihad* for every Muslim, or for a democratically elected legislative body (*majlis*). They reject the need for a spiritual 'Vicegerent' (Caliph); some support instead the call for an elected, secular head of state who has no religious powers.

In the socio-economic sphere they often interpret Islamic teachings as sanctioning Western-style capitalism, although they try to combine this with concepts of a welfare state and Islamic socialism. In the field of education, Muslim reformists advocate the restructuring of the system, with particular emphasis on the need for the inclusion of modern sciences in the curricula. They are also in favour of the acquisition of modern technology.

The second, more popular trend presents reformist ideas in the form of revival of the ideals of early Islam. The revivalist approach was sometimes rooted in opposition to colonial rule, glorifying Muslim achievements in the past, but it soon acquired a broader intellectual base. Islam is regarded by this group as the absolute, divine truth, and any deviation from the established precepts is considered *bida* ('innovation'). They differ from the orthodox in the fact that they do not accept as authoritative the whole range of traditional beliefs and practices that have developed over the centuries amongst Muslims, but wish instead to go back to the practices of early Islam. They agree with the modernists in opposing blind acceptance of the authority (*taqlid*) of medieval schools. But the revivalists wish essentially to re-enact the past, whereas the modernist reformists talk of

3

reinterpretation. Thus, reformist thinkers have either had to discard the traditionalists' rejection of innovation by advocating the need for *ijtihad* ('modernist' reformism), or, on the contrary, have had to maintain that the modifications they suggest are aimed at ridding Islam of corrupt forms of *bida* ('revivalist' reformism). Reformists have sometimes gravitated towards Westernism, and sometimes drifted towards revivalism.

The various ideological trends, orthodox, modernist and revivalist, should not be taken as reflecting merely religious differences amongst Muslims. Rather they represent the fundamental contradictions that are to be found in modern and early modern Muslim societies. The actions of the reformist Muslim intelligentsia have shaped the development of political and social thought in their respective countries, but beneath the surface, there has generally been a strong, albeit often silent, orthodox opposition. This has frequently re-emerged in times of stress.

PURPOSE OF THIS WORK

Muslim reformist movements in Asia and Africa have been the focus of much scholarly attention. Analogous developments in Central Asia, however, have been largely neglected. So far as Western scholars are concerned, this was largely because, until very recently, much of the relevant material was inaccessible, held in regional libraries and archive funds in the Soviet Union which foreigners were rarely permitted to visit. Soviet scholars were inhibited by ideological constraints: religious reformism was scarcely a permissible topic. Since the collapse of the Soviet Union in 1991, the situation has begun to change. There has been an upsurge of interest in the socio-political thought of the Central Asian reformists at the turn of the century. Access to primary sources is gradually becoming easier. Much fundamental research, however, remains to be done.

The present work focuses on the development of Muslim reformist (*jadid*) political thought in the Emirate of Bukhara in the period 1870–1924, with particular reference to the writings of Ahmad Donish and Abdal Rauf Fitrat. In the early twentieth century a movement to establish schools using more modern methods of instruction (*usul-i-jadid*, from Arabic, 'new method') took root in Bukhara. Later, the adherents of this movement began to demand political and administrative reform. The followers of this movement were subsequently known as *jadid* (from Arabic, lit. 'new', reformist/modern) and their ideology *Jadidism* (reformism/modernism).

This work aims to utilise as much original literature as possible in order to examine the development of the socio-political thought of the Muslim reformist thinkers of the Emirate of Bukhara under the impact of the radical socio-economic changes which took place in the second half of the nineteenth and early twentieth centuries (1870–1924). The socio-political thought of the two most influential and prolific writers, Ahmad Donish and

Abdal Rauf Fitrat, is examined in detail and an attempt is made to analyse their work within the broader context of Muslim reformist thought. Donish, an original thinker and the precursor of Muslim reformism in Bukhara, and Fitrat, the last exponent of this reformist tradition, represent two critical stages in the development of political thought in late nineteenth–early twentieth-century Bukhara. They are therefore of special interest to students of the evolution of political reformism in the region. During Fitrat's lifetime, conflict with the orthodox *ulama* and rulers became so intense that he and his fellow reformists had to flee from the Emirate to Russian-governed Turkistan. There, a more radical frame of reference gradually began taking root. This was eventually to lead to revolution in Bukhara, the liquidation of the Emirate, and ultimately the destruction of the reformist movement.

PREVIOUS WORK ON THE SUBJECT

Very little specific work is available on Muslim reformist political thought in Bukhara. The writings of Sadradin Aini and Faizulla Khodzhaev, both themselves pro-reform activists in the 1920s, provide most of the first-hand information. The first serious account of *Jadidism* in Bukhara is given by Sadradin Aini in his book *Tarikh-i Emiran-i Manghitia Bukhara* ('History of the Manghit Emirs of Bukhara'),[3] written in Tajiki and published in 1923. His book *Bukhara Inqilab-i Uchun Materiallar* ('Materials on the History of Revolution in Bukhara'),[4] written in Uzbeki and published in 1926, also discusses the role of the *jadid* in the Bukharan revolution. In order to defend the *jadid* movement he interpreted it as a revolutionary movement, and even attempted to treat *Jadidism* and Bolshevism as inseparably linked.[5] Faizulla Khodzhaev attempts to portray reformist activities in Bukhara as a prelude to the revolutionary movement in Bukhara.[6] Both S. Aini and F. Khodzhaev give a positive evaluation of the role of *Jadidism* in Bukhara.[7]

Some very useful information regarding the struggle of Bukharan reformists for the establishment of new-method schools can be found in I. Umnyakov's article 'K Istorii Novo-Metodnoi Shkoly v Bukhare' ('History of the New-Method School in Bukhara'),[8] published in 1927.

An eminent Russian orientalist, Evgenii Edvardovich Bertels (1890–1957), in his 21 page article describing the manuscripts of Ahmad Donish's works, written in 1933 and published in 1936,[9] argued that the works created by the Central Asian urban bourgeoisie in the middle of the nineteenth century marked a significant move forward, leading, in the twentieth century, to the emergence of the so-called *jadid* school; this analysis underlines the importance of beginning the study of *Jadidism* from the mid-nineteenth century.[10] Though the intention of Bertels's article is only to introduce Donish's manuscripts *Navadir-ul-Voqai* ('Rare Events') and *Risala Mukhtasari az Tarikh-i Sultanat-i Khonadon-i Manghitia* ('A Short Treatise on the History of the House of the Manghit Emirs'), he perceptively comments that Donish's ideas on reform and the state are of great importance for the history of *Jadidism* because they encapsulate the chief goals of the *jadid*.[11]

Later, Soviet/Russian scholars, both before World War II and subsequently, devoted some attention to the socio-political thought of Muslim Central Asia in the colonial period, but they adopted a highly negative attitude to the Muslim reformist movement (*Jadidism*), dubbing it,

the ideology of anti-revolutionary, anti-people, bourgeois nationalists.

Since the Soviet establishment of the time feared the revival of Islam and nationalism in Central Asia, scholars either did not mention the *jadid*, or alluded to them in a negative manner.

The works written by Soviet scholars between 1940 and 1970 show a strong political bias and portray the *jadid* movement in an unfavourable light. They accuse them of limiting their activities to the cultural field. However, they try to make a distinction between 'enlighteners' and the *jadid*. 'Enlighteners' such as Ahmad Donish are praised for their criticism of the despotic nature of the Emir's rule and for spreading enlightened and revolutionary ideas, while other reformists ('*jadid*') are condemned for opposing revolution, advocating constitutional monarchy and for being representatives of various types of bourgeoisie.

B. Gafurov and N. Prokhorov, in *Padenie Bukharskogo Emirata*[12] ('The Fall of the Emirate of Bukhara'), published in 1940, wrote

The bourgeois nationalist party of the Young Bukharan-Jadids was only the expression of the nationalist bourgeoisie to capture power; they were ready to make compromises with the Emir and limited their activities only to the cultural field.[13]

In his book *Istoriya Tadzhikskogo Naroda*[14] ('History of the Tajik Nation'), published in 1949, B. Gafurov devoted 11 pages to the reformist movement, depicting reform activists as representatives of the emerging bourgeoisie and advocates of a constitutional monarchy in Bukhara. I. Braginskii briefly deals with reformist literature in his book *Ocherki iz Istorii Tadzhikskoi Literaturi*[15] ('Sketches from the History of Tajik Literature'), published in 1956. Some factual information about the reformists is given in the first part of the first volume of *Istoriya Uzbekskoi SSR*[16] ('History of the Uzbek SSR'), published in 1956. All these commentaries follow the official line. In 1957, Z. Radzhabov, in *Iz Istorii Obshchestvenno-Politicheskoi Mysli Tadzhikskogo Naroda vo Vtoroi Polovine XIX i v Nachale XX Vekov*[17] ('From the History of the Socio-Political Thought of the Tajik People in the Second half of the 19th and Beginning of the 20th Century'), devotes a full chapter to *Jadidism* in

Central Asia. Criticising the reformers in ruthless and censorious terms, he blames them for trying to cut Central Asia off from Russia. Later, the subject of *Jadidism* was touched upon by Ishanov in 1969,[18] Iskandarov in 1970,[19] and a number of others, but they followed an almost identical line.

Amongst Western writers, P. Etherton's *In the Heart of Asia*,[20] published in 1925, narrates the events of the Bolshevik advances in Turkistan and Bukhara, and mentions that the Young Bukharan Party was liberally financed by the Bolsheviks so that they could strike the first blow against Bukhara. He sees the whole issue of the *jadid* struggle against the Emir of Bukhara in the context of 'the great game'. Alexander Park, in *Bolshevism in Turkistan*,[21] published in 1957, argues that

> the *jadid* movement in Bukhara emerged in the inspirational glow of the 1905 revolution and the Young Turk rebellion of 1908, ... [it] appeared first as an extension of the jadid movement, which among Russia's Islamic peoples was the counterpart of Eastern Slavdom's own westernizing movement.[22]

He also reports some post-October revolution events affecting the *jadid*.[23] In 1960, Richard Pierce devotes one page to 'Dzhadidism' while referring to 'The Rise of Native National Consciousness' in Central Asia.[24] Geoffrey Wheeler in 1964 limits his description of pre-revolutionary *Jadidism* to

merely a Muslim reformist movement with no separatist aims.[25]

Alexander Bennigsen and Chantal Lemercier-Quelquejay have devoted two pages to *Jadidim* in Central Asia.[26]

Seymour Becker's work *Russia's Protectorates in Central Asia: Bukhara and Khiva, 1865–1924*,[27] published in 1968, is an important contribution to the history of the Central Asian Khanates. It examines the motives and methods for the extension of Russian control over the Khanates, the post-conquest policies of imperial Russia towards the Bukharan and Khivan states, the reasons for those policies, and finally, the fate of Bukhara. Becker analyses the manner in which the traditional societies of Bukhara and Khiva were brought, through the agency of the Russian state, into the orbit of the modern Western world. The work remains a valuable basic textbook for students of Central Asia, offering perceptive insights into the events that influenced developments in Bukhara and Khiva. He argues that these states, having had no contact with the modern West, lacked the basis for a nationalist, anti-colonial movement.[28] Although the book touches upon the native reform movement in Bukhara, it does not deal in detail with reformist thought or with thinkers such as Ahmad Donish and Abdal Rauf Fitrat.

Another major contribution to this field is H. Carrere d'Encausse's book, *Islam and the Russian Empire Reform and Revolution in Central Asia*,[29] published in French in 1966, in English in 1988. She rightly identifies the crisis of Bukharan Muslims in the early twentieth century as part of the general crisis of Islam at that time. Some light is shed on the efforts of earlier Muslim thinkers in other parts of the Russian empire to bring about a reform of Islamic belief and practice. However, she, too, fails to analyse in depth the political thought of Bukharan thinkers, probably because of lack of access to the main sources, such as Donish's *Navadir-ul-Voqai*[30] and Fitrat's *Rahbar-i-Najat*[31] ('The Guide to Salvation'). Edward Allworth's *The Modern Uzbeks*,[32] published in 1990, provides significant insights into the literary activity of some of the Bukharan reformist thinkers, especially Fitrat. Some useful information about Bukharan reformists, especially Fitrat, is given by Hisao Komatsu in *The Evolution of Group Identity among Bukharan Intellectuals in 1911–1928: An Overview*, published in 1989.[33]

Dr Khalid Adeeb in his PhD dissertation, *The Politics of Muslim Cultural Reform: Jadidism in Tsarist Central Asia*, provides a comprehensive account of *Jadidism* in Turkistan.[34] He addresses the problem of the emergence of modern intellectuals as a new social category in an agrarian society. He ably describes and analyses *Jadidism* in Turkistan and focuses on social reproduction of reformist ideas. However, Bukharan *jadid*, except Fitrat, have not been dealt by him thoroughly and one of Fitrat's most important works *Rahbar-i-Najat* was not available to him.[35]

METHODOLOGY

The present work aims firstly to chart and secondly to analyse the main trends of Muslim reformist political thought in Bukhara. It makes extensive use of previously inaccessible, often as yet unpublished material in a variety of languages. It consists of an introduction, four chapters and a conclusion. The first chapter deals with the historical background to *Jadidism* paying special attention to the socio-political, economic, cultural and religious organisation of the Emirate of Bukhara during the second half of the nineteenth and early twentieth centuries. It examines the impact of the penetration of Russian investment into the Emirate and the construction of the railway line, and the subsequent local socio-economic changes which contributed to the emergence of *jadid* political thought.

The life and thought of Ahmad Donish, the forerunner of reformist thought in the Emirate of Bukhara, is covered in the second chapter. His three visits to Russia are discussed and an exposition of his ideas and reform proposals is given, based on his manuscript *Navadir-ul-Voqai*.

The third chapter describes the background of reformism in Islam in general, and then examines the history of the reformist movement in Bukhara in the late nineteenth and early twentieth centuries, the emergence of the first pro-reform organisations and the Young Bukharan Party. Chapter Three also covers some of the events that occurred in Russia and Turkistan during the Russian revolutions, and explains their effect upon the supporters of reform in Bukhara. It traces the attempts of the *jadid* to reform the system, by persuasion as well as by direct action, and the history of the Bolshevik-backed revolution in Bukhara.

The life, works and socio-political thought of the most influential thinker of the movement, namely, Abdal Rauf Fitrat, is examined in the fourth chapter, plentifully illustrated by direct translations from his writings, most of which are still inaccessible to Western scholars. His works *Munazara* ('The Dispute'), *Bayanat-i-Sayyah-i-Hindi* ('The Tales of an Indian Traveller') and *Rahbar-i-Najat* ('The Guide to Salvation') are consulted and an attempt is made to explain coherently his philosophical and political thought. The concluding chapter assesses the significance of the reformist political thought of Donish, Fitrat and the *jadid* movement, and sets it in the broader context of reformist political thought in the Muslim world.

Chapter One

The Emirate of Bukhara (1870–1924)

HISTORICAL BACKGROUND

Early History

Around 1000 BC, the inhabitants of the Central Asian river valleys are known to have been mostly cultivators and to have achieved an advanced level of civilisation. By contrast, the people living in the mountains and arid steppe regions were nomads and cattle-breeders.[1] Archaeological evidence indicates that they were of Iranian origin. The area remained mostly under Achaemenian domination until 330 BC, when Alexander the Great, during his Persian campaigns, captured Bactria and Sogdiana (339–334 BC). The city of Maracanda (present Samarkand) in Sogdiana was destroyed. Central Asia maintained its political and economic links with the Greeks even after the death of Alexander, remaining under Greek influence until the second century BC. The Scythians conquered Sogdiana in 159 BC. Subsequently, the Kushans ruled the area in the first and second centuries AD, and formed what was probably the largest union of nomadic tribes in Central Asia. At the peak of their rule the Kushans controlled eastern Turkistan, Sogdiana, Bactria, Afghanistan and part of northern India. In the fifth century the Ephthalites (White Huns) occupied Central Asia. Their capital, Paikent, was 40 kilometres away from the present city of Bukhara. In the sixth century Turkic tribes began to occupy the region.

The Arabs conquered the area in the seventh century AD. However, Bukhara was not captured until 709 and Samarkand not until 713. The Arab conquest of Central Asia was completed by the middle of the eighth century and *Mawra al-Nahr* (lit. 'beyond the river'), the lands to the north of the Amu Darya (Oxus), which included the territories of Khwarezm and Bukhara, became part of the Arab Caliphate. The Arabs settled some of their own people in the area but mostly ruled through local governors. Under Qutaiba ibn Muslim, the governor of Khorasan (705–714 AD), a major effort was initiated to convert the local population to Islam. At the beginning of the eighth century the Quran was translated into Persian in Bukhara.[2] In 776 AD an uprising led by Muqanna, a native of Merv, broke out against the Arabs. After some initial success the movement was finally crushed in 783 AD. At first the new Muslim religion was imposed by force, sometimes with great brutality and the wholesale destruction of the monuments and the cult objects of other faiths, especially those of Zoroastrianism. Later, however, more moderate policies prevailed. The incorporation of Transoxiana into the Caliphate strengthened administrative and political links as well as cultural and commercial contacts with the Muslim world, which led to the spread of the new faith. By the beginning of the ninth century the region had been integrated into the Muslim world to such an extent that Caliph Mamun from AD 813 to 817 made Merv his capital instead of Baghdad.[3]

In the ninth century Ismail-Ibn-Ahmad (848–907 AD), founder of the Samanid dynasty, succeeded in establishing himself as ruler of the region and made Bukhara his capital. He embellished Bukhara with many fine buildings, mosques, *madrasa* and palaces, and the city was celebrated for its learning and culture. Bukhara achieved an intellectual and cultural refinement in this period as a result of intense cultivation of Sunni theology with some admixture of the sciences such as astronomy, astrology, mathematics and medical art.[4] Towards the end of the tenth century the Samanid state was destroyed by the Karakhanids, Turks from the valleys of the Rivers Ili and Chu, and by Ghaznavids, Turks from the south of the Amu Darya. The Seljuqs, originally from the Turkmen steppes, ruled over Central Asia in the eleventh and twelfth centuries. They were followed by the Karakitais and in the Aral region, by the Khwarezmshahs. As a result of the efforts of Arabs and local Muslim converts Islam was firmly established in the main urban centres by mid-ninth century, and the institutional infrastructure, such as mosques, *madrasa* (lit. 'lesson-giving place', college), libraries and trained religious functionaries, was set in place. A tradition of Muslim higher education was established. Central Asian, especially Bukharan, institutions of higher learning played a very important role in Muslim civilisation. Schools known as Nizamiya were founded by Nizam-ul-Mulk, a grand *vazir* of the Seljuq rulers, in the later half of the eleventh century at Baghdad (1065) Nishapur, Balkh and Herat. These are often considered to be the first *madrasa*. However, the town of Merv (modern Mary, in Turkmenistan) in Central Asia is believed to have had a similar school that provided accommodation, a library and scholarships to students as early as the tenth century. In Bukhara the first such school is believed to have been founded in 937.[5]

The Samanid and Seljuq periods (eighth–twelfth centuries) have been known as Golden Age of Islam. Scholars of that period were well acquainted with scholarly works translated from Greek, Hebrew and Hindi into Arabic. Though most of this translation took place in Baghdad,

Bukhara became the centre for translation from Arabic into Farsi/Tajiki. The interpretation and application of these works became part of the Central Asian and Bukharan intellectual legacy. Men like al-Farabi (870–950 AD), Ibn Sina (980–1037 AD), Al-Biruni (973–1048), al-Khwarizmi (d. 840 AD), al-Ghazali (d. 1111 AD) and many others produced a wealth of knowledge in various fields including science and theology.[6]

At the beginning of the thirteenth century, Mongols under Genghiz Khan attacked Central Asia. Bukhara was captured in 1220 and ransacked. Despite profound damage to cities and irrigation system caused by the invaders, Islamic learning and culture survived the Mongol conquest, though not unbruised. The Mongols soon converted to Islam and became increasingly Turkicised. In 1370 Tamerlane (1336–1398), a Turkicised Mongol of the Barlas tribe, emerged as ruler of the area and went on to form a mighty empire. During the reign of Ulugh Beg, grandson of Tamerlane, three *madrasa*, at Bukhara, Ghijduvan and Samarkand, and an astronomical observatory near Samarkand were constructed.[7]

Emergence of the Khanate (subsequently Emirate) of Bukhara

At the beginning of the sixteenth century (1506), Uzbek tribes under Sheibani Khan (r. 1500–1510), a descendant of Genghiz Khan, occupied Central Asia and founded the Sheibanid dynasty. As nomads, the Uzbeks regarded their lands as the property of the whole ruling family and divided them into smaller principalities, ruled by various princes of the royal house. Samarkand remained the capital and residence of the *Khan* ('oldest member of the ruling house'). After his death in 1511, the successors of Sheibani Khan founded two Khanates on the ruins of his conquests – Bukhara and Khwarezm. During the reigns of Ubaidallah (r. 1512–1539) and Abdullah Khan (r. 1557–1598), the capital was shifted from Samarkand to Bukhara. The title *Khanate of Bukhara* emerged during this period.[8] Khwarezm became known as Khiva in the seventeenth century after its capital was transferred from Kunya-Urgench to Khiva.[9] In spite of many destructive invasions and revolts, by the sixteenth century Bukhara had grown into an important political, cultural and religious centre.

By the end of the century the Sheibanids had been replaced by the Janid or Astarkhanid dynasty, which ruled the Khanate of Bukhara until the middle of the eighteenth century. From the sixteenth century there were almost continuous contacts between the Khanate and the Russian Czars. The Khanate was interested in unobstructed passage for Muslims to cross Russian-held territory to reach Istanbul via the Black Sea, on the way to Mecca for the pilgrimage.[10] The Russian Czar Peter the Great (1689–1725) and his successors showed increasing interest in economic and political penetration of Central Asia. They established diplomatic relations with the Central Asian Khanates and sent several expeditions to Central Asia. For example, a military expedition headed by Bekovich-Cherkasskii was sent to build a fortress at the mouth of the Amu Darya, intended to coerce the Khans of Khiva and Bukhara.[11]

After the reign in Bukhara of Khan Abd al-Aziz (1645–1680) many *bek* (ruler of a province or principality) became to all intents and purposes independent. The authority of the Khan weakened and a *bek* or *ataliq* ('guardian') ruled in his name. In 1740 Nadir Shah of Iran attacked and subjugated Bukhara. By the end of the eighteenth century in the Farghana Valley, traditionally a part of Bukhara, a hundred years of increased autonomy culminated in the emergence of the Khanate of Kokand.[12] In Bukhara, the *ataliq* Rahim Bi of the Manghit tribe became *Khan* in 1753. His successor Danyar Beg took the title *ataliq*. But his son Murad, also known as Mir Masum, in 1785 assumed the superior title *Emir*[13] (lit. 'Commander'), instead of *Khan*. All his successors, Haydar (r. 1800–1826), Husayn (r. 1826), Nasrullah (r. 1827–1860), Muzaffar (r. 1860–1885), Abd-al Ahad (r. 1885–1910) and Alim (r. 1910–1920), retained the title Emir. Consequently, the Khanate became known as the *Emirate of Bukhara*.

The political history of the Manghit dynasty was characterised by a struggle to centralise power in the face of the separatist tendencies of the individual principalities. In the reign of Emir Nasrullah (1827–1860), Bukhara defeated the Khanate of Kokand and also attacked Khiva, ransacking and annexing Merv. Nasrullah ruthlessly eliminated his rivals and tried to build up a professional army;[14] he succeeded in continuously increasing the power he was able to wield from his capital. The instrument of this power was a heavy and complex administration, organised at central, provincial and village level, and divided into political, financial, juridical and religious domains.[15] The taxes he raised to pay for this bureaucracy earned Nasrullah a reputation for rapacity amongst the people.[16] Meanwhile, Russian expansion to southern Central Asia began in earnest. Tashkent fell in 1865 and Irjar, Khojand and Nau (territories of the Bukharan Emirate) in 1866.[17]

Emirate of Bukhara as a Russian Protectorate

In the reign of Emir Muzaffar (1860–1885) Bukhara suffered a crushing defeat in its war with Russia (1866–1868). Samarkand was occupied by Russian forces on May 2, 1868. On June 23, a Russo-Bukharan treaty was concluded, by which the Russians were permitted to annex the regions of Dizakh, Samarkand, Katta Qurghan and the upper part of the Zarafshan valley. The Emir agreed to pay 500,000 roubles as war reparations to Russia, and surrendered the right to establish diplomatic relations with countries other than Russia; Russian subjects acquired the right to possess immovable property, such as warehouses etc., in the Emirate, and to conduct trade without interference from the local authorities.[18]

To organise its conquered territories, the Russian government established, in 1867, the Governor-Generalship of Turkistan, with Tashkent as its capital. General K. P. Von Kaufman became its first Governor-General.[19] In September 1873, a so-called friendship treaty, containing 18 clauses, was concluded between Russia and Bukhara. Clause 5 declared all the towns and villages of the Emirate open to Russian traders. The safety of caravans carrying goods to and from Russia was guaranteed by the government of Bukhara. Russian industrialists were allowed to operate freely in the towns and settlements. Clause 15 allowed the Emirate of Bukhara to have a permanent representative in Tashkent (already under Russian rule). Similarly, Clause 16 gave the Russian government the right to send a political representative to Bukhara.[20] It was in accordance with this treaty that Czar Alexander III established the office of the Russian Imperial Political Agent in Bukhara, in January 1886. The Imperial Political Agent was nominated by the Russian Foreign Ministry, and was subordinate to the Governor-General of Turkistan and the Russian Defence and Foreign Affairs Ministries.[21] The chief aim of the Political Agent was to control the activities of the Emir and his government. He was also responsible for the organisation and management of Russian settlements, and protection of the interests of Russian traders and industrialists. The establishment of the Russian Protectorate neither abolished the Emirate, nor changed its internal political system. However, it did bring substantial changes to the internal life of the country, and severely curtailed the power of the Emir.

Dissolution of the Emirate of Bukhara

Abd-al Ahad succeeded Muzaffar as Emir in 1885. During his reign (1885–1910) a reformist movement, known as the *jadid* movement, began taking root. Initially it focused on the modernisation of the system of education (for details see Chapter 3). Gradually it became more political in orientation. The movement later evolved into the Young Bukharan Party, which, with the help of the Bolshevik Red Army, was instrumental in overthrowing the Emir Alim in 1920. Subsequently, on the ruins of the Emirate, the Congress of Representatives of the Nationalities of Bukhara proclaimed the establishment of the *Bukhara Khalq Shuralar Jumhuriyati* (People's Soviet Republic of Bukhara). However, on September 19, 1924, at the Fifth All-Bukhara Congress (*Bishinchi Butun-Bukhara Qurultayi*) the title *Bukhara Khalq Shuralar Jumhuriyati* (People's Soviet Republic of Bukhara) was replaced with *Bukhara Sovet Sosyalistik Jumhuriyati* (Bukhara Soviet Socialist Republic).[22]

The Bukhara Soviet Socialist Republic survived until autumn 1924. Following the approval of the delimitation project by the Central Executive Committee of the USSR, on 27 October 1924 the Bolsheviks proclaimed the creation of new republics and autonomous regions in Central Asia. On

18 November 1924 the Central Executive Committee of Bukhara passed the decree on dissolution of the government of Bukharan Republic.[23] Bukhara was divided into three ethnically based administrative territorial units. As a result of this 'national delimitation of the Central Asia', the Uzbek Soviet Socialist Republic, along with Turkmen Republic were created by the end of 1924. Most of the former Emirate of Bukhara, apart from its Turkmen districts, was incorporated into the Uzbek SSR, which also included Samarkand, Tashkent and the Farghana Valley. The central and eastern parts of the Emirate constituted the Tajik Autonomous SSR within the Uzbek Republic. Later, this was elevated to the status of Tajik Soviet Socialist Republic.

BOUNDARIES AND PEOPLES

Boundaries

The boundaries of the Emirate of Bukhara were never fixed, but expanded or contracted according to the strength or weakness of the ruler. According to A. Burnes, writing in 1834, the Khanate was located between the parallels of 36 and 45 degrees North latitude, and the meridians of 61 and 67 degrees East longitude.[24] E. K. Meiendorf, in 1834, places it between 37 and 41 degrees North, and 61 and 66.3 degrees East.[25] N. Khanykov, in 1843, places it between 37 and 43 degrees North and 80 and 88 degrees East.[26] Hutton, in 1875, regards the last as misprints for 60 and 68 degrees.[27] According to Khanykov, in 1843, the Khanate was bounded by the Bukan mountains in the north, the Aktau, Karatau and Shahr-i-Sabz mountains in the east, and Balkh in the south-west. In the west there was no natural boundary, and 80 or 81 degrees East longitude was considered the boundary with Khiva.[28]

During the period of the Russian Protectorate, the Emirate was bounded in the north by the Aral Sea, the Syr Darya (Jaxartes), and the Khanate of Kokand. In the east it extended to the Pamir mountains. In the south the Amu Darya separated it from Afghanistan. The Khanate of Khiva formed the western boundaries of the Emirate.

Population Size

The size of the population of the Emirate deserves special attention. We encounter several estimates, varying from 2,000,000[29] to 3,600,000.[30] Meyendorff, writing in 1820, estimates the population of Bukhara to be 2,478,000.[31] Kislyakov gives a figure of 2 million or a little over.[32] Most of the archival documents, and a military engineer, Ermoliev, who lived in Bukhara and studied its socio-economic conditions for a considerable period, estimate it at 2.5 million.[33] In an archive document containing

15

statistics for the Bukharan People's Soviet Republic the population of the Emirate, at the beginning of the twentieth century, is given as 2,066,000.[34] In light of the above facts the figure of 2.5 million seems plausible.

Social Composition

The population of the Emirate was divided into *dehqan* ('farmers'), *sahranashin chorvodar* ('nomad cattle-breeders') and *shaharnashin* ('town-dwellers'). The latter comprised *kosib* ('artisans'), *tujjor* ('merchants'), *ammaldor* ('civil servants'), *sipoi* ('military'). Other important segments of the population were the *ulama* (which included functionaries such as *mudarris, mulla, ishan, akhund* etc., numbering in all 45,000), money-lenders, workers, big land owners (*bai*), and *mullabachai* ('students').[35] According to Ishanov, 65% of the population was settled, 20% were nomads and 15% semi-nomads.[36] During the period of the Protectorate, especially at the beginning of the twentieth century, the penetration of the capitalist mode of production into the Emirate led to the formation of a tiny native bourgeoisie and working class.

Ethnic Diversity

In the Emirate there were many Turkic tribes, such as the Manghit and Qipchaq, several of these tribal names were common to larger Turkic ethnic groups such as the Karakalpak, Kazakh, Kirghiz, Turkmen, Uighur and Uzbek. In addition, there were Afghans, Arabs, Indians, Iranians, Jews, Tajiks, and others, most of whom had been living together with the Turkic groups for centuries. Various authors have reported the size of these ethnic groups or their percentage in the population of the Emirate. However, these calculations seldom agree with one another.[37] The reason behind this was that, owing to the scattered nature of the population and the mixing and dispersal of the various ethnic groups, neither the government nor the intelligentsia had detailed data about these groups. Moreover, most of the people did not identify themselves primarily according to ethnic origin.[38] Most of the Bukharans knew both the Turki and Farsi (Tajiki) tongues. The European style of ethnic-linguistic consciousness was yet not introduced in Central Asia. To some extent religion, common culture, customs and economic community within the Bukharan state provided the basis for the community of Bukharan population, people called themselves Bukhari (except for foreigners like Russians) or Bukharali (Bukharan in English).[39]

The Uzbeks were scattered from one end of the territory of the Emirate to the other, however, their important areas of concentration were the valleys of the Surkhan Darya, Kashka Darya and Zarafshan Rivers, and were predominantly involved in agriculture and breeding livestock. The Tajiks lived in the eastern part of the country, in Qarategin, Darvaz, Garm,

Baljuvan, Kulyab, Kurgan-tube and the Western Pamirs. They were also involved in agriculture and raising cattle and sheep. The Turkmen lived in the regions of Chaharjui and Kerki, depending largely on livestock. The Karakalpaks and Kazakhs inhabited the regions of Kerminah and Nur-Ata. The Jews were settled in the cities and were mostly engaged in trade and crafts. There were small settlements of Arabs in the regions of Qarshi and the city of Bukhara.

In the second half of the nineteenth and at the beginning of the twentieth century, following the construction of the Trans-Caspian Railway, and the opening of navigation on the Amu Darya (November 13, 1887), the influx of Russian businessmen, traders, officials, artisans and workers accelerated. They founded Russian settlements such as *Novaya* ('New') Bukhara, also called Kagan, *Novyi* ('New') Chaharjui, Kerki, Termez, Amirabad, Faryab, Sarai etc. By the beginning of the twentieth century approximately 60,000 Russian subjects, including the Russian troops, lived in these settlements.[40] According to Soviet sources the Uzbeks constituted 51% of the total population, the Tajiks 31.5%, the Turkmens 10%, the Karakalpaks, Kazakhs, Jews, Russians, Tatars, Armenians and Persians 7.5% collectively.[41]

SECULAR AND RELIGIOUS ADMINISTRATIVE STRUCTURES

Political and Administrative Structures

Central Administration: The head of state was called *Emir al-Momineen* (lit. 'Commander of the Faithful') or Emir. Both legislative and executive powers were concentrated in his hands. The rulers of Bukhara, Nasrullah (1827–1860), Muzaffar (1860–1885), Abd-al Ahad (1885–1910) and Alim (1910–1920) all belonged to the Uzbek Manghit tribe. All high officials of the state, such as the *Qushbegi*, *Divonbegi*, *bek* etc., and the supreme commander of the army, were accountable to the Emir directly. Any offence committed by them was liable to be heard in the court of Emir. The Emir, the highest judicial authority, personally heard major criminal cases, such as adultery, theft, highway robbery etc. Moreover, the Emirs of Bukhara considered themselves to be descendants of the Prophet Muhammad. Their names therefore contained the title *sayyid*, e.g. Sayyid Abd-al Ahad. By virtue of being *sayyid* they also headed the *ulama*. Hence, both temporal and spiritual powers were united in them. They had control over every single aspect of government. Nothing could happen in the Emirate without their sanction. According to Semyonov

> even trivial daily administrative and routine domestic details were narrated to them.[42]

There was a nominal consultative body, the *Jamoa* (lit. 'Gathering' or Assembly), whose members were appointed by the Emir. The appointees mostly belonged to the landed aristocracy, high military and civil officials and *ulama*, who were vitally interested in preserving the ruling feudal order in the Emirate.[43] Khanykov confirms that the members of the body included the landed aristocracy, high officials and the *ulama*. The representatives of the landed aristocracy and high officials on the *Jamoa* were led by the *Qazi-i-Kalan* and those of the *ulama* by the *Sheikh-ul-Islam*. The *Qazi-i-Kalan* sat on the Emir's right and the *Sheikh-ul-Islam* on his left.[44] Initially, the chief function of the *Jamoa* was to advise the Emir on foreign affairs. However, its role changed substantially when the Emirate became a Protectorate of Russia, since from this period onwards such matters were effectively handed over to the Protector. The *Jamoa* thereafter functioned as a consultative body in matters of internal affairs only.[45] It is worth mentioning that it was not a permanent body with fixed members.

The highest official in the central administration, the first deputy to the Emir, was called *Vazir* ('Minister') or *Qushbegi-i-Bala*[46] (lit. 'Grand Master of the Beg'). In modern terminology *Qushbegi-i-Bala* would be equivalent to Prime Minister. Besides the management of the everyday affairs of the state, with the sanction of the Emir, his duties also included receiving the complaints and petitions of the people, and meeting the Russian Imperial Political Agents. The latter used to send twenty to forty letters daily, to which the *Qushbegi-i-Bala* was obliged to reply.[47] He was also in charge of the finance department, the state treasury and the bureaucracy.[48]

The second highest official in the Emirate was the *Zakatchi Kalan* (lit. 'Grand Collector of *zakat*'). The Bukharans called him *Qushbegi-Payan* (lit. 'junior *Qushbegi*'). He was responsible for the collection of *zakat* on livestock and all imported and exported goods. The collection of *kharaj* ('land tax') was managed by his subordinate, an official called *Divonbegi* (head of the civil bureaucracy). The central governmental apparatus of the Emirate was run by these three men. All the administrative and managerial officials, including the collectors of the *zakat*, *kharaj* and other taxes, were subordinate to them. Other officials working at central level included the *Qazi-i-Kalan* ('Chief Justice'), *Ishan Rais* (the official who enforced the Islamic code of ethics and correct weights and measures in the market), *Mirshab* (the chief of the night police) and *Mira'b* (the official in charge of the distribution of water).[49]

Provincial Administration: The Emirate of Bukhara was composed of a number of principalities (*valayat* in Tajiki, *beklik* in Uzbeki and *bekstvo* in Russian sources; henceforth, *valayat*). The number of *valayat* varied from time to time. However, at the end of the nineteenth century, twenty-eight *valayat* were counted, namely, Chaharjui, Kerminah, Ziautdin, Nur-ata, Khatirchi, Kitob, Shahr-i-Sabz, Chirakchi, Yakkabagh, Guzar, Baisun, Qarategin, Denau, Hissar, Darvaz, Baljuvan, Shugnan, Roshan, Kulyab,

Kurgan-Tyube, Kabadiyan, Sherabad, Kelif, Kerki, Burdalik, Kabaklik, Qarshi and Norazim.[50]

The ruler of a *valayat* was known as *bek* (Uzbeki) or *hakim* (Arabic/ Uzbeki) in western Bukhara, and *mir* or *shah* (Tajiki) in eastern Bukhara. (Hereafter, for the sake of simplicity, we will use *bek* to refer to this official). The *bek* were appointed by the Emir from amongst the leading Uzbek, Tajik or Turkmen landed aristocracy, on the recommendation of the *Qushbegi*. The Emir could also dismiss them. The administration of the *bek* in a *valayat* was almost a replica of the central administration, likewise comprising collectors of land revenue, *dostarkhanchi*, *mirshab*, *zakatchi* etc. The number of employees in the office of a *bek* reached 200 to 300.[51] The *mirshab*[52] was responsible for the maintenance of law and order in his area, and was considered to be a pillar of the Emirate. He was in charge of the jail (*zandan*) and the guards. The officer in charge of the police station (*dzharib*) was called *dah-boshi*, under whom worked around a hundred *shabgardam* ('policemen'). The *mira'b* controlled the distribution and use of water. The *mirzobashi* (chief secretary) and *mirza* (secretaries) etc., handled the other clerical tasks.[53]

District and Village Administration: The *valayat* was subdivided into *tumen* or *amlakadari*. The head of an *amlakadari* was called *amlakadar*. He was appointed by the *bek* from amongst the local landed families. He executed orders on behalf of the *bek*. The *amlakadar* assessed and collected revenue through his subordinates. He systematically reported all the events that occurred in the *amlakadari* to the *bek* for his opinion, received instructions and acted accordingly. In order to carry out the administrative functions of an *amlakadari*, a fairly large number of functionaries were employed in the offices of the *amlakadar*.[54] The city of Bukhara was a separate administrative unit, administered by the *Qushbegi*. Nine *amlakadari* were attached to the capital, namely Qarakul, Zindan, Pirmast, Ghijduvan, Vaghanzi, Vobkent, Shafrikan and Yartepin.

The *amlakadari* consisted of yet smaller administrative units. They were called *kent*[55] in western Bukhara and *mir khazarstvo* (in Russian sources) or *saad* in eastern Bukhara (hereafter, we will use the term *kent* when referring to this administrative unit). A *kent* consisted of several villages (*qishlaq* or *arbobstvo*, henceforth, *qishlaq*). In the Qarategin *valayat*, for example, a *kent* consisted of 6 to 10 villages.[56] The head of a *kent* was called *amin* or *mirkhazar* and the head of a *qishlaq* was the *aqsaqal* (Turki: 'white-bearded', 'village elder') or *arbob* in Tajiki (henceforth, *aqsaqal*). The *aqsaqal* were elected to their posts by the population of the village in both eastern and western Bukhara.[57] The tenure of the post was not fixed; the *aqsaqal* held office until another person was elected by the population. However, the election of the *aqsaqal* was subject to the approval of the *bek*. *Amin* and *aqsaqal* were responsible for the collection of land revenue and other taxes. *Bek* and most of the other officials did not receive a fixed salary from the state, but exacted their expenses from the *dehqan*.[58]

Armed Forces of the Emirate

Traditionally, the army was raised by the *bek*. For this purpose, *bek* were granted *tankhwa* lands (see further below), which in turn were cultivated by their fellow tribesmen. The *bek*, in exchange for *tankhwa* lands, committed themselves to place at the disposal of the Emir troops raised on their land. However, Emir Nasrullah, faced with a threat from the powerful *bek*, realised the need for a regular army that was personally loyal to him. Hence, in the 1840s a regular army was formed. It consisted of 1,000 soldiers (*sarbaz*), 11 cannons and 2 mortars.[59] The commander of the army was called *Topchi-Boshi Lashkar*. The battalion commanders (*datkho*) and squadron commanders (*toksabo*) were subordinate to him. The battalions and squadrons were subdivided into companies (*dasta*), half-companies (*nim dasta*), platoons (*rasad*) and half-platoons (*bara*). They were led by a junior lieutenant (*uzboshi*), sergeant-major (*chehraogasi*) and lance corporal (*dah-boshi*).[60]Army officers were paid a salary by the Emir, along with their *tankhwa* land. The *Topchi-Boshi* was paid 15,000 roubles, the *datkho* and *toksabo* 6,000 each, the *uzboshi* 270, the *chehraogasi* 140 and the *dah-boshi* 90 roubles per annum.

The life of a Bukharan *sarbaz* ('soldier') was very difficult. They were paid 4 roubles a month, in contemporary terms a mere pittance, and lived in army barracks (*sarbazkhona*). Most of the *sarbaz* engaged in farming or petty trade to meet their expenses. The term of service was not fixed: boys of 11 years of age served alongside elderly men of 70; the ranks were filled by illiterate, landless peasants, fugitives and newly freed serfs.[61] Although the Bukharan army achieved some victories against the neighbouring Khanates it was no match for the Russian army. Its lack of modern technology rendered it ineffective in modern warfare, as was proved beyond doubt in the war against Russia in 1866–1868. Subsequently, the Emir used the army mostly to quell internal dissent and rebellion.

In 1890 the number of the Bukharan army was increased to 13,500, comprising 13,000 infantrymen and 500 cavalrymen. Eight thousand soldiers were deployed at Bukhara, 2,000 at Shirbudun, barely five kilometres away, and 1,000 each in Shahr-i-Sabz, Kulyab and Baldzhuan *valayat*. Five hundred cavalrymen and 620 artillerymen, armed with 120 cannon, were stationed in the fort of Bukhara under the Commander-in-Chief. At the turn of the century the Bukharan army was reduced to 10,000 soldiers. In 1908, it consisted of ten battalions of infantry, i.e. 8,200 soldiers, 52 officers and 12 battalion commanders; two squadrons of cavalry, i.e. 600 soldiers, 5 officers and two squadron commanders, and 300 artillerymen.[62] The Emir spent significant resources on the army: according to the estimates of the Russian Political Agent the annual expenditure on the army was 1,308,867 roubles.[63]

System of Justice

The Emir was the highest judicial authority in the country and, as explained above, personally heard all the major criminal cases. The *Shari'a* was the supreme law of the Emirate. Most of the Bukharans belonged to Sunni Hanafi school of law. The system of justice was highly stratified. Members of the ruling Manghit tribe were considered to be superior to all others and enjoyed many privileges. High-ranking civil and military officials were not held responsible for the first nine crimes that they committed against the person or property of ordinary people.[64] However, they were accountable for their wrongdoing against the interests of the Emirate to the Emir alone.

The rest of the population was divided into various categories: *sipoi*, *ulama*, *tujjor* ('merchants') and *fuqara* ('rabble'). Legally the *sipoi* fell under the jurisdiction of the Emir, the *ulama* under the *Sheikh-ul-Islam* (head of the *sayyid* and *hadji*), while the merchants were dealt with by the *Rais Ishan* and the masses (*fuqara*) by the *qazi*. The chief of the Justice Department was the *Qazi-i-Kalan*, who was appointed by the Emir. The *Qazi-i-Kalan* had jurisdiction over the criminal and civil affairs of the Emirate pertaining to the *fuqara*.[65] Apart from his authority in the Emirate, the *Qazi-i-Kalan* also enjoyed some extra-territorial jurisdiction, particularly in matters of personal status laws. Thus, disputes between Bukharans and the Muslims of the Governorate-General of Turkistan involving inheritance, marriage, divorce etc. were adjudicated by him.[66]

Besides its judicial obligations, a significant function of the justice department was to ensure that Islamic moral standards were observed in the community. For this purpose a parallel system of supervision was established. The chief of the supervising authority in the city of Bukhara was called the *Ishan Rais*. His responsibilities also included ensuring that the correct weights and measures were used in market trading.[67]

As far as the systems of justice in the *valayat* and *amlakadari* are concerned, it is worth mentioning that criminal justice was administered by the executives of the Emirate, while all civil cases up to the value of 500 tillai (local currency, 1 gold tillai = 16 roubles) were adjudicated by the *qazi*, verbally and publicly. The *qazi askar* dealt with civil cases pertaining to the army, up to the value of 500 tillai. The *qazi* were appointed by the Emir himself from amongst the *ulama*.[68] Under the *qazi*, there were several *mufti* ('jurisconsult', one who is qualified to pronounce a *fatva*) and *mulazim* (personnel who execute justice).[69] For example, under the *qazi* of the city of Bukhara (who was normally the *Qazi-i-Kalan*), there were 12 *mufti*, collectively called *divon mufti*. The *qazi* based his judicial verdict on the *rivayat* ('religious opinion formed on the basis of the Traditions') pronounced by the *mufti*. In the *valayat* the *mufti* were appointed by the *bek* on the recommendation of the *Qazi-i-Kalan*. The officials of the judicial-supervisory system, when delivering verdicts, often tried to protect the interests of the Bukharan state.

Religion and Organisation of Religion

The religion of the overwhelming majority of the Emirate's population was Islam of the Sunni Hanafi school of law. Though the idea of priesthood is foreign to Islam, in the Emirate of Bukhara (as in many other countries of the Islamic world), an institutional structure had developed – a graded hierarchy of professional men of religion, with recognised functions and powers, somewhat reminiscent to the Christian priesthood. The origins of this religious hierarchy can be traced back to the Sultanate of the Great Seljuqs, when schools and schoolmen were organised to counter the threat of revolutionary heresy.[70] The chief Sunni religious officials included the *Qazi-i-Kalan*, *qazi*, *mufti*, *mudarris* ('teacher', one who is in charge of a *madrasa*), *domulla* ('teacher', one who is in charge of an elementary Quranic school), *rais* ('chief official of a town'), *mulla* ('a lower grade member of the religious class'), *azanchi* ('one who chants the call to obligatory prayers'), *imam* ('one who leads the prayers') and *ishan* ('Mystic', Sufi teacher) etc. The *mulla*, *mudarris*, *azanchi*, *imam* and *ishan* were subordinate to the *akhund*, who held the high clerical title of *sadr*.[71] The *akhund* also exercised control over *madrasa* ('college of religious learning') and *maktab* ('elementary Quranic school').[72] In the religious hierarchy, the *sadr* came first, and beneath him were the *alim* (learned man, religious scholar), and then the *mufti-askar*.[73] There were also *Shi'a* religious officials in the Emirate. They had their own *mulla*, *ishan*, *hadji* etc. The head of the *Shi'a* officials was called *Mujtahid*.[74]

There were many *sayyid* and *hadji* in the Emirate. The *sayyid* considered themselves to be (and were generally accepted as) descendants of the Prophet Muhammad through his daughter Fatima and son-in-law, Ali, while *hadji* (not to be confused with *haji* 'pilgrim') were considered descendants of the first Arab conquerors of Central Asia.[75] Semyonov traces the origin of *hadji* to the word *hodja*. Bukharans gave the name *hodja* ('master' or 'owner') to the Arab conquerors who settled in Bukhara in the seventh century. The Bukharans had been forced at the time to share their houses with them.[76] The head of the *sayyid* and the *hadji* was called *Shaikh-ul-Islam*.[77]

The Emir, as a *sayyid*, was chief of this large and complex religio-clerical structure. He appointed people of his own choice to all the clerical posts mentioned above.[78] These officials, drawn almost always from the social class of *sayyid* and *hadji*, along with the *mulla*, played a very significant role in the affairs of Emirate. Together they formed a powerful religious institution, whose function was to be the guardian of the faith and the law. It had a vested interest in the defence of tradition and religious conservatism. Its members were the ideological defenders of the Emir's regime, declaring it to be a divine and ideal system. In the name of Allah they called upon the people to obey the Emir, depicting the Emir's person as holy and his authority inviolable. According to Semyonov, the *ulama* were a cohesive, conservative institution opposed to any new thought, so powerful that even the Emir had to consider their opinion before taking any important decision.[79]

ECONOMY

In the nineteenth century agriculture was the backbone of the economy of the Bukharan Emirate, involving some 85% of the population.[80] This was mostly irrigated agriculture, though some seasonal (*bogar*)[81] farming was practised in the mountains and foothills of eastern Bukhara. The nomadic and semi-nomadic populations were also involved in agriculture, though this was confined to the land adjacent to their winter camps and was very limited in scale.[82]

Agriculture and Animal Breeding

The main crops were wheat, barley, rice, maize, cotton, sesame, lucerne, hemp, millet, flax, clover and several different types of lentils.[83] The *dehqan* were engaged in production of vegetable crops, cattle-breeding, sheep-rearing, including *karakul* ('wool') making. The climate is favourable for horticulture, and gardening was popular almost everywhere in the Emirate, both in the villages (*qishlaq*) and in the cities. Mazov states, 'almost in every household there was a fruit garden'.[84] The people of the Emirate grew pumpkins, melons and water-melons as well as some fruits which were famous for their high quality in Bukhara, e.g. apricots, apples, pears, peaches, figs, quinces and several sorts of grapes. Some original strains of grapes were cultivated in the mountainous *amlakadari* (districts) of the Kashka Darya and Surkhan Darya oases.

In the regions where cotton and grain were cultivated, animal breeding was of secondary importance. It was mainly practised by the nomadic and semi-nomadic populations in the drier and hillier areas such as Surkhan Darya, Denau, Urchin, Baisun, Hissar, Kulyab and Sherabad *valayat*.[85] In Kulyab *valayat*, for example, 405,000 head of sheep, goats, cattle, horses, donkeys and camels were counted in 1909.[86] Eastern Bukhara provided cattle as beasts of burden and for meat and dairy to the western part of the Emirate and to the Samarkand *oblast* ('region') of Turkistan.[87] The population of eastern Bukhara largely bred the Tibetan goat. The wool of these goats was long and soft and cloth and ropes were made from it; more than 479,600 head were counted in 1914.[88] According to Gulishambarov there were over 20 million livestock in the Emirate in 1913, i.e. 10 million sheep, 6.5 million goats, 1.7 million horned cattle, 1 million donkeys, 500,000 camels and 400,000 horses.[89] However, he does not mention his source. In one of the archival documents the number of livestock in the Emirate is estimated to have been much less: something over 6,310,000 head in 1914, including 2,185,000 in eastern Bukhara.[90]

Radobylskii writes that many *dehqan* did not own a pair of oxen, but instead ploughed the land on a cooperative basis (*sharakat*). Poor *dehqan* joined together to form a *kosh* ('pair of oxen') and ploughed their land by turns. Sometimes, instead of two oxen, a pair was formed of an ox and a horse.[91] Landless *dehqan*, small landholders, and *dehqan* who lacked working cattle and other implements of agriculture, offered their labour to the *bai* ('big landowners') and government officials. Their poverty forced them to become *chairikar* ('share-croppers'). The tenants of *vaqf* lands paid from 1/10 to 4/10 of their yield to the *vaqf*.[92] Moreover, the lands of big landowners and officials, such as *bek*, *amlakadar* etc., were cultivated through *hashar* (unpaid labour by *dehqan*).[93]

The Russian agronomist Liko writes that the division of the yield between the owner of the land and the share-cropper depended upon which of them provided the five elements necessary for the process of agricultural production, namely, land, irrigation water, seeds, working cattle and labour. He identified the following kinds of tenancy:

1 *Dehqan* leased the land and paid 1/4 to 1/2 of the yield to the owner.
2 *Dehqan* leased the land, working cattle and implements and paid 2/5 to 3/4 of the yield to the owner.
3 *Dehqan* leased the land, working cattle, implements and seeds and paid 1/2 to 4/5 of the yield to the owner.
4 *Dehqan* leased the land, working cattle, fertilisers, seeds, *kharcha* ('pocket money') and clothes. He was a real *bewatan* ('landless farm worker'), in Russian *batrak* ('pauper'), and for his labour the landlord paid him 1/4 to 1/6 of the yield.[94]

Owing to the pauperisation of the *dehqan* and the introduction of money-commodity relationships, the process of buying and selling land accelerated.[95] Consequently, the gap between *bai* and *bewatan* widened. This process of emerging class differentiation in the *qishlaq* of Bukhara at the end of the nineteenth century is substantiated by documentary evidence.

In the year 1314 AH (1896–1897), Kazakbei Hodjibei Ogli sold to Abdulqahar Abdulfattah 1.25 *tanab* of *amlak* land for 20 *tillai*.[96] The land was situated in the Qaum-i Abu-Muslim *amlakadari*. The same year, this Abdulqahar Abdulfattah Ogli bought, in the same *amlakadari*, from Ghaibnazar Abdulkarim Ogli, 0.75 *tanab* of *amlak* land for 200 tenga (1 silver tenga = 76 copecks).[97] Also in that same year, he bought, again in the same *amlakadari*, 1.5 *tanab* of *amlak* land for 400 tenga from Babahodji Mirza Hodja.[98] This Abdulqahar again bought land in the year 1316 AH (1898–1899).[99]

This process of formation of big landlords on the one hand and pauperisation of *dehqan* on the other was a widespread phenomenon all over the Emirate. By the year 1905, 25% of the agrarian population was landless.[100] The *vasiqa* documents ('land transfer deeds') in the archives of the *Qushbegi* of the Bukharan Emirate reveal that buying and selling of land in the Emirate occurred on a massive scale after the year 1905.[101] Even Czarist officials and functionaries serving in the Emirate and Turkistan *Krai* (territory) bought land from the *dehqan* in the Emirate.[102]

Land Tenure

In theory, the system of land ownership in the Khanate was defined by the *Shari'a* (the divinely ordained pattern of human conduct): land belonged to Allah, but His Vicegerent on earth, the Caliph (here the Emir) could dispose of it. State land was called *amlak*. Since the time of the Arab conquest, the *mulk* ('private') land which belonged to the settled and nomadic populations of Central Asia had been counted the property of Allah and His Vicegerent. However, the right of the *dehqan* to use the land was preserved. They had to pay *kharaj* ('land tax') to the state. The annual rate of *kharaj* was one tenga (equivalent to 15 copecks) per *tanab* in cash or 1.5 *charek* (1 *charek* = 5 lb, or 2.048 kg) in agricultural produce. Such lands were normally termed *mulk-i-kharaj*.

The Emir could also sell land to private individuals. In this way state lands (*amlak*) turned into private (*mulk*) lands. If the owner of *mulk* land surrendered 2/3 of the land he bought from the state, the rest (1/3) was cleared of all forms of taxes. Such lands were termed *mulk-hurr-khalis* ('tax free lands'). Since ordinary *dehqan* could rarely acquire such properties, they tended to remain under the control of the big landowners. For example, in 1920, in the Zarafshan valley alone, 3,700 desiatinas of irrigated land belonged to big landowners.[103]

Mavat lands ('dead' lands, uncultivated for whatever reason) were considered the property of the state, i.e. *amlak*. The Emir could bestow state land on civil and military personnel (*ammaldor, sipoi*), when it became known as *tankhva*, and the recipient person *tankhvador*. Normally state lands were given to state functionaries as *tankhva* on the condition that they paid taxes and provided one horseman to the Emir's troops in return for every *tanab* (a *tanab* varied from area to area: generally, 1 *tanab* = 3,600 square steps, or 2,730 sq. m.) of irrigated land. On the death of the *tankhvador* the land returned to the state.

Vaqf lands were properties whose revenues were spent on a charitable institution such as a *madrasa*, mosque or *khanqah* ('monastery'). Such lands were either gifts from the sovereign or individuals. *Vaqf* lands were exempt from taxes. Normally *vaqf* lands were controlled by the *ulama*.

In historical literature opinions regarding land-holding vary. For example, Meyendorff divides the land into five categories, (i) state land (*amlak*), (ii) *kharaj* land, (iii) land granted for military service (*tankhva*), (iv) private lands (*mulk*) and (v) *vaqf* land.[104] Khanykov, however, arbitrarily divides the total cultivable land in the Emirate into three categories: *kharaj* lands, *mulk* lands, and *amlak* lands.[105] Kouznietsov also divides the land of the Emirate into three categories but his categories are different from those of Khanykov: *kharaj* or *amlak* lands, *mulk* lands, and *vaqf* lands.[106] Alexander Lehmann, a contemporary of Khanykov, describes the division of land in the Emirate as *mulk* lands, *mulk-i-kharaj* lands, *amlak* lands, *vaqf* lands, *dakhiach* and *tankhva* lands.[107] By dividing the land into six categories Lehmann confuses the issue. He probably misunderstood the distinction between *mulk* and *mulk-hurr-khalis* lands.

In archival documents several authors refer to four categories of land holdings: *zamin amlak* ('State's', 'Emir's' or 'ruler's lands'), *mulk kharaj* ('tax-paying lands belonging to private individuals'), *mulk-hurr-khalis* ('tax-free lands belonging to private individuals'),[108] *mulk vaqf* ('lands belonging to charitable institutions').[109]

The following documents also indicate the division of the Emirate's land into four categories:

1 On December 8, 1894 the Russian Political Agent in Bukhara, Lessar, described for Governor-General Vrevskoi the following four categories of land holding:[110] *mulk* lands, *dakhiach* lands, *mulk-i-kharaj* and *vaqf* lands. Here *mulk* lands means *mulk-hurr-khalis* and *dakhiach* lands seem to be *amlak* lands.

2 Captain Dzhidzhikhia, who lived in the Emirate for a long period and was the author of several works on Bukhara, wrote to the Chief of Staff of the 1st Turkistan Military Corps (Report No. 41), 'In Bukhara the ownership of the land is of four types, *amlak* lands, *mulk* lands, which are subdivided into *mulk-hurr-khalis* and *mulk-i-kharaj*, and *vaqf* lands.'[111]

3 Mirza Nasrullah, Qushbegi (Prime Minister) of Bukhara, answering a query of the Russian Political Agent, wrote on December 6, 1912 that in Bukhara there existed four categories of land: *mulk-hurr-khalis*, *mulk-i-kharaj*, *amlak* and *vaqf* lands.[112]

4 The inspector of cotton markets in the Emirate, Khalmukhammedov, wrote to the Russian Political Agent in 1904 that Bukharan land was divided into four categories: *mulk-hurr-khalis*, *mulk-i-kharaj*, *dakhiach* and *amlak*; he classifies *vaqf* lands as *dakhiach*.[113] Another document, *Voprosy Zemlyapolzovaniya v Bukhare*, dated 1923, also divides Bukharan land into the above-mentioned four categories.[114]

The total area suitable for cultivation in the Emirate during the period of the Protectorate was 2,250,000 desiatinas (1 desiatina = approx. 2.7 acres).[115] However, even during the First World War only 1,800,000 desiatinas of land were under cultivation.[116] Out of that, 10.2% of the land was *mulk-hurr-khalis*, 15.2% *mulk-i-kharaj*, 24.6% *vaqf* and 50% *amlak*.[117] The pre-eminence of state ownership over private ownership of land is evident. The most fertile lands were owned by the Emir, his officials, the *ulama* and the big landowners. In eastern Bukhara alone, the Emir owned more than a thousand desiatinas of land.[118] The *dehqan* constituted more than 85% of the population but did not possess more than 15.2% of the land.

Irrigation

In the Emirate, 57.5% of arable land was irrigated and 42.5% un-irrigated.[119] Most of the un-irrigated land was in Shahr-i-Sabz and Kitob *valayat* and in the centre and south of present-day Tajikistan. In the Pamirs only 320 hectares were cultivated. The grain production was sufficient to last until spring, after which the Pamiris had to eat mulberries and grass.

The chief source of water for the Emirate was the Amu Darya, which flowed for 440 km across the Emirate's territory. Owing to topographical problems the water of the Amu Darya was not used much for irrigation purposes. However, the waters of other rivers, such as the Surkhan Darya, Kashka Darya and the Zarafshan were used. Artificial irrigation was and still is absolutely essential in this region. The construction of a large-scale irrigation system required substantial resources of money and men, also a major organisational structure. Irrigation works were therefore carried out by the state. This in turn facilitated the centralisation of power.[120]

During the period of the Protectorate, a significant role was played by the Russian government and businessmen in organising irrigation works. They invested part of their capital in such projects. Towards the end of the nineteenth century irrigation works were accomplished on the River Zarafshan, which flowed across more than 214 versts of Bukharan territory. In July 1892, Gelman, a Russian communications engineer, was appointed technical head of the construction of irrigation canals, under the direction of the Bukharan government. The Governor-General of Turkistan, with the approval of the Czar, instructed him to manage only such projects in the Emirate as affected the interests of the Turkistan Territory.[121] All construction projects relating to irrigation, construction and maintenance of roads and passes were considered to be included in this category. Gelman was also entrusted with the supervision of the equitable distribution of the water of the Zarafshan within the boundaries of the Emirate. More than half his salary (7,500 roubles per annum) was paid by the Bukharan government, the rest (6,000 roubles) by the Russian government.[122]

The task of widening the old irrigation canals and constructing new ones was accomplished under the leadership of Gelman, along with two other Russian engineers who also helped to provide Bukharan *dehqan* with water from the Zarafshan. Such schemes led to a substantial development in cotton-growing and boosted agriculture as a whole. The Bukharan government spent 12,600 roubles annually on these officials.[123]

The Czarist government instructed them to fulfil the following additional tasks:

(a) To study the natural, historical and economic conditions of the country.
(b) To collect all sorts of data which could assist in the correct planning of the development of agriculture and the clarification of the relative importance of its different branches.
(c) To render all kinds of help to cotton-growing, horticulture, grape cultivation and wool-making.
(d) To take measures to increase the area of fodder cultivation and the spread of useful fodder plants.
(e) To improve the field plant culture and spread valuable new sorts of crops.
(f) To improve cattle breeding.
(g) To establish experimental institutions and model farms.
(h) To establish stores for agricultural machinery, instruments and mineral fertilisers.[124]

It is evident from the above that the Russians were interested in boosting productivity in the Emirate. According to Massalskii, in 1892 there were 25 *ariq* ('canal') on the right bank of the river Zarafshan and 18 on the left.[125] In 1899, according to Sitnyakovskii, there were 32 *ariq* on the right bank and 20 on the left of the Zarafshan.[126] In seven years nine new *ariq* had been drawn from the river. According to archival documents, and confirmed by Olufsen, the irrigation work continued in eastern as well as western Bukhara in the early twentieth century.[127] Khoroshkin writes that 'the common feature of the *ariq* of the Zarafshan region was that they were all drawn from the Zarafshan River and terminated in the fields without any back-flow to the River'.[128] Despite such a developed irrigation system the people of the Emirate suffered from a shortage of water.[129]

In the Zarafshan valley shortages were frequent, firstly, because of an extension of the total area under cultivation, both in the Bukharan and the Russian parts of the Zarafshan valley (a result of the intensified trade in agricultural products, especially of cotton, after the construction of the Trans-Caspian Railway line), secondly, because a large share of the Zarafshan river water was being used in the Russian-controlled area of Samarkand region.

A special Joint Commission was constituted to resolve the question of the distribution of the Zarafshan river water between the Emirate and the Russian- controlled areas. In 1902, representatives of the Governor-General of Turkistan and the Emir of Bukhara reached an agreement. Bukhara's share in the water of the river Zarafshan was fixed at 230 million cubic sadzhen (1 sadzhen = 1.83 metres) out of a total 803 million cubic sadzhens.[130]

However, since the Russians controlled the water of the river Zarafshan they could easily manipulate the supply to the Emirate. For example, according to Russian officials, in the early 1880s, for 15–20 days there was no water at all, not even to irrigate a garden owned by the Emir Muzaffar himself.[131] Donish, mentioning the shortage of irrigation water in Bukhara, wrote that *dehqan* for several days or even weeks did not receive water from the Zarafshan. He advocated the digging of a canal from the Amu-Darya to meet the shortages.[132]

Crafts and Industry

During the nineteenth century silk-weaving and paper-making were at a very developed stage in Bukhara. Mazov states that there were 100,000 cloth-making (wooden) hand-looms in the Emirate.[133] According to the Bukharan elders, in the city of Bukhara and its adjacent suburbs there were 12,000 hand-looms. Gafurov writes that there were nine large weaving workshops in the city alone, each containing fifty to sixty looms.[134]

In Bukhara, as in some other cities of the Emirate, artisans were concentrated according to their profession into separate quarters (*mohallah*) of the city. Twenty-three quarters of the capital were named after the trades of the people who resided there,[135] such as blacksmiths, fitters, smelters, coppersmiths and jewellers. For example, the jewellers and coppersmiths lived in the centre of the city. Tanners lived in four quarters: shoe-making was a well-developed industry.[136]

The second most important city in the Emirate was Qarshi, where the textile industry was highly developed. There were 25 large textile firms, as well as coppersmiths, blacksmiths, fitters, turners, potters and shoe-makers. Cottage industries were also active in Shahr-i-Sabz, whose tanners were especially praised. Artisans such as saddlers, soap-boilers, potters, black-smiths, knife-grinders, candle-makers, bakers, confectioners, stone-masons and carpenters constituted a significant layer of the population; the textile industry, however, was less developed in Shahr-i-Sabz.[137]

In the final decades of the nineteenth century, Russian capitalists started investing their capital in cotton-ginning and cottonseed-oil factories; these were constructed mostly in the so-called Russian settlements, such as *Novaya* Bukhara (Kagan), Chaharjui, Termez and Kerki, though some factories were also built in the cities of (old) Bukhara, Kermin, Zerabulak, Ghijduvan and Ziautdin. According to data collected by the Russian Political Agent, there were 28 trade-industrial units in Termez by 1916.[138] At the beginning of the twentieth century there were 35 cotton-ginning factories in the Emirate. A full list[139] of the factories and their locations is given below:

1	*Novaya* Bukhara:	12 cotton-ginning factories and a cottonseed-oil factory
2	Chaharjui:	3 cotton-ginning factories, 1 cottonseed-oil factory, 1 wool-cleaning factory and 1 brewery
3	Station of Karakul:	1 cotton-ginning factory
4	Station of Kizl-Tepe:	2 cotton-ginning factories
5	Old Bukhara:	1 cotton-ginning factory
6	Kerminah:	3 cotton-ginning factories
7	Ziautdin:	2 cotton-ginning factories
8	Kerki:	4 cotton-ginning factories
9	Termez:	3 cotton-ginning factories and 1 cottonseed-oil factory
10	Ghijduvan:	1 cotton-ginning factory
11	Zerbulak:	2 cotton-ginning factories
12	Dzhilikul:	1 cotton-ginning factory

Some of these factories were owned by Bukharans, e.g. a cotton-ginning factory in Chaharjui was constructed by the government of Bukhara. Moreover, there were ten brick-making factories at the station of Karakul and some lime water factories were situated in Kerminah. A printing press and a power station, to provide electricity to the capital, were constructed by the Russians in Old Bukhara.[140] A few tobacco and match factories, and three breweries, owned mostly by Russians, also functioned in the Emirate.[141]

There were deposits of gold, copper, iron, sulphur, mercury, coal, oil, marble, alabaster and other useful minerals in the Emirate. Significant deposits of gold were located in the Baljuan, Darvaz and Qarategin *valayat* and near *Novaya* Bukhara,[142] but throughout the period of the Protectorate no serious development of the mining industry took place. However, in an effort to monopolise gold-mining for Russian businessmen, the Governor-General of Turkistan, Baron Vrevskii, on February 24, 1896, issued a decree about the gold industry in the Emirate, whereby Russian citizens were allowed to search, explore and extract gold from deposits, strata and conglomerates situated in unoccupied *amlak* lands.[143] The concessionaires had to pay the Bukharan treasury 2 roubles per desiatina for the right to exploit the land. In the case of private lands, the gold seekers had to enter into an agreement with the owner. The extraction of gold within the boundaries of the Emirate by foreign firms, and Russian firms connected with foreign capital, was prohibited. The Bukharan government had a right to appoint its representative to observe the actual work. All gold extracted by Russian concessionaires had to be deposited with the Bukharan government. The government, in return for the gold, issued credit bonds at the rate of the St. Petersburg stock exchange.[144] The said decree, after approval by the Czar, served as a basis for the acquisition of land from the Bukharans for gold exploration. The fact that the decree was issued by the Russian authorities is significant, because it indicates that the Bukharan Emir had lost the right to use the natural resources of his country.

Taxation

During the period of the Protectorate, as in the past, broadly speaking, two kinds of rents were levied: the first were taxes, the second was *begar* ('unwaged labour'), called in Russian sources *barshina* ('corvée'). Source material shows that the peasantry paid 40 different basic and 10 supplementary taxes to the state, civil and religious officials.[145] For a list of these taxes see Appendix Three.

The list cited in the Appendix is far from complete. Bukharan officials considered several other taxes as basic taxes too. There were also secondary taxes such as *hukmana* – a tax paid to the *qazi* to pronounce a judgement; *khatmona* – a tax on the circumcision of a male child; *taloqona* – a tax on the dissolution of a marriage; *shodeona* – a tax on child birth; *nikohona* – a tax on marriage; *jul* or *obrok* (in Russian) – a discretionary tax, e.g. if the Emir travelled to Petersburg, Crimea or the Caucasus, people might have to pay a tax to meet his expenses. 'The people of the Emirate were strangled by these taxes. If a child was born to a *dehqan* he had to pay a tax. If he bought a cow, a goat or a sheep he had to pay a tax. Only the air in Bukhara was tax-free', write Gafurov and Prokhorov.[146]

The Emir and his officials grossly abused their powers when collecting taxes. Several instances of the sale or bondage of the daughter or son of a *dehqan*, who was unable to pay his taxes or loans, have been recorded. The non-payment of taxes by the *dehqan* led to the sale of his property. If he had a daughter, she was forced to marry and the bride money went to the state treasury as payment for the arrears. If the defaulter had a son, he was sold as a *bacha* (into bondage).[147] In January 1914 a Russian veterinary doctor witnessed the sale of the daughter of a *dehqan* to pay his debts.

> One Uzbek defaulter [he reports] on the demand of an official of the *bek*, sold his daughter for 400 roubles.[148]

If the debtor had no children to sell, he was forced to become a serf and to serve for a long period. Aini wrote at length about these abuses.[149]

The other category of rent, known as *begar* or *hashar* or *barshina* (Russian), usually took the form of unwaged labour by the *dehqan* for the *bek*, *amlakadar*, *mirshab*, *qazi* or other officials. *Dehqan* were forced to work in their fields during the periods of sowing, weeding and harvesting. Reaping and thrashing grain in the fields of the officials and clergy took a substantial amount of peasants' time. *Dehqan* often had to work in the fields of the officials when their own crop required harvesting urgently. Moreover, *dehqan* looked after the livestock of their officials. They were mobilised to construct dirt roads and official buildings.

> As a whole, the *barshina* rent took away from the *dehqan* 3/4 of his working time,

writes Gafurov.[150]

The situation of the masses in the Emirate worsened to such an extent that in 1891 the inhabitants of Shahr-i-Sabz and Kitob complained to the Governor-General of Turkistan against the oppression of the Emir Abd-al Ahad. Citing examples of the cruelty and greed of the Emir, the inhabitants wrote about the acts of robbery committed by the troops accompanying the Emir during the Shahr-i-Sabz expedition.[151] They mentioned that the Emir's people took away their daughters and sons by force and disgraced them.

> We until now, [the complaint proceeds] patiently bore all the offences, oppressions and injustices committed by the Emir, who often visits our province these days. He causes us all possible oppression, offences and insults to such an extent that we have developed an aversion to him.[152] At last, not finding protection anywhere [concludes the complaint] we hope to find it with the Government of the Russian Emperor. We request the Russian consul to protect us, liberate us from the tyrannical Emir, his violence and oppression.[153]

The complaint was forwarded to the Russian Foreign Ministry and was reported to the Czar. The Czar directed the Foreign Ministry to advise the Emir, through the political agent in Bukhara, to restrict violence and arbitrary rule.[154] The Emir did not pay any attention to the Czar, neither did the latter follow it up in any other way at that time.

Income of the Emirate

The chief source of state income in the Emirate was the collection of taxes such as *zakat*, *kharaj* and *aminona*. The rest of the taxes collected from the population were mostly consumed by the local administration and a very insignificant amount reached the state treasury.[155] It is extremely difficult to estimate the exact annual amount of *zakat*, *kharaj* and *aminona* that were collected and deposited in the treasury, owing to the absence of relevant historical data. However, in archival documents there are estimates, collected by the Russian Political Agent for the year 1912, according to which 4,366,733 roubles of *kharaj* were deposited in the treasury of the Emirate.[156] The amount actually collected, however, was considerably higher. Samsanov, the Governor-General of Turkistan, reported to the Russian Defence Ministry in 1909 that the *kharaj* deposited in the Bukharan treasury was 1.5 to 2 times less than what was actually collected.[157]

In the early twentieth century, the amount levied as *zakat* on exported and imported goods was 2 to 3 million roubles per annum.[158] However, in 1912 the collectors of *zakat* deposited in the Bukharan treasury only 825,000 roubles.[159] A significant part (more than 60 to 70%) of *zakat* (and other taxes) was consumed by the collectors. The annual collection of *aminona* is estimated at 1.5 million roubles.[160] More than 400,000 roubles per annum were collected as *aminona* on the sale of cotton, wool and karakul.[161] However, according to the figures given by the Imperial Political Agent, 75% of *aminona* was consumed by the collectors and only 375,000 roubles were deposited in the treasury of the Emirate.[162] Aini estimates the annual income of the Bukharan treasury as 30 million roubles.[163] Logofet gives an estimated figure of 18 million roubles.[164] Data collected by the Russian Imperial Political Agent suggests a figure of 14.5 to 15.5 million roubles.[165] These figures do not include another important source of income for the Bukharan treasury, *toksan-tartuk*. This was the presents sent annually to the Emir by local officials such as the *bek*. One unit of *toksan-tartuk* consisted of nine attired horses, nine bales of clothes – each bale containing nine *khalat* ('robe')-, nine carpets and nine flat-weave rugs. Some *bek* sent 21 *toksan-tartuk* for a single reception.[166]

Expenditure of the Emirate

The Bukharan treasury did spend some of its income on social welfare, although some historians categorically deny this. For example, Logofet writes that the Emir's government did not spend 'even a copeck' on the welfare of the people and the country.[167] We know that the Bukharan government spent 500,000 roubles on the construction of a railway line in 1901.[168] The government also used to spend more than 400,000 roubles per annum on the maintenance of Russian specialists, such as agronomists, foresters and doctors, who worked in the Emirate. Telegraph and post offices, hospitals and veterinary centres were built at state expense. In 1910, the Emir sanctioned 26,595 roubles, in 1912, 300,000 roubles and in 1913, 320,000 roubles to destroy locusts.[169] From 1912 to 1917 the Emir spent 109,000 roubles per annum on health care and education. The annual expenditure on the army was 1,500,000 roubles.[170] Around 600,000 to 700,000 roubles were granted annually to the *ulama*.[171] From 1914 the state began paying a salary to some of the *bek* and *amlakadar*.[172] Aini gives an estimated figure of 2,200,000 roubles for overall annual expenditure.[173] The Imperial Political Agent suggests a figure of 11.5 to 11.6 million roubles.[174] It seems that during the period of the Protectorate the Emir of Bukhara, under the influence of the Russian Imperial and Turkistan colonial governments, and public opinion, started spending some money in the social sector.

INTELLECTUAL ENVIRONMENT IN THE EMIRATE

Information about the intellectual life of mid-nineteenth-century Bukhara is scanty. This is largely because relatively little indigenous literature was produced. This, in turn, was the result of several factors: the low level of literacy among the population (less than 5%); the absence of a supportive environment to reinforce the expansion and diffusion of education in general; and the attitude of the *ulama* towards the written word.

Bukhara at this period was still a largely oral society. Interaction of social agents was predominantly on a direct, face-to-face basis. Thus writing was of limited use, and tended to be regarded as a specialised technical skill. The ability to read and to write (and the two were considered different skills, separately acquired) was considered necessary for only a few spheres of activities. Most areas of life did not require the use of the written word.[175] Literary texts were often transmitted orally, as were culture and *adab* (proper conduct).[176] Even in trade, as late as the 1870s, large-scale transactions were carried out orally, with the personal guarantee of special intermediaries (*qasid*) taking the place of written documents.[177] Hence, reading and writing in Bukhara were the concern of a select few. The acquisition of these skills required long years of study in a *madrasa*. No printing press existed in Bukhara until the early twentieth century (the first printing press was established in 1901 in Kagan, a Russian settlement).

It is worth noting that when Ahmad Donish (for details see Chapter Two) wrote books, the conservative *ulama* of the day remarked that, 'The time for writing books has passed. One should be holy and specially gifted to write a book'.[178] The attitude of the conservative *ulama* may be summed up as follows. Free will and the rational use of intelligence had a very subordinate place in their intellectual scheme of values. The main path to good life lay in submission to God and in prayer. A good (obedient) person could expect reward in the after-life. Most of the *ulama* would only accept as legitimate their own interpretation of the *Shari'a*, and *rivayat* (customary laws). However, their understanding of these laws was often outmoded and contrary to the spirit of Islam. *Taqlid* ('blind acceptance') of the teachings of a senior *alim* or authority was the order of the day. Persecution of those who did not conform totally to the majority's system of values and beliefs was not uncommon, in spite of the Quranic precepts such as:

> There is no compulsion in religion. The right direction is henceforth distinct from error....[179]

Religious minorities such as the Shi'a Muslims and Jews were sometimes the targets of violent attacks.

The chief literary output of the day took the form of anthologies (*divan*) of poetry. Since such works appeared in manuscript form, they reached relatively few people. Other literary activities, carried out by the *ulama*, included the keeping of records, the making of testaments, the settling of inheritances, and similar tasks. Newspapers and journals in Turki and Farsi began to penetrate into Bukhara from neighbouring Turkistan, other Muslim regions of Russia and the rest of the world at the turn of the century. The first Bukharan newspaper appeared in 1912 and was shut down by the authorities in 1913. (For details of foreign and local publications see Chapter Three, especially pp. 93–96).

The intellectual climate of Bukhara was dominated by religious traditions, especially Sunni Muslim doctrine and practices. There had been some *Shi'a* influences during periods of strong Iranian political presence in Central Asia. However, the numerical majority of the Sunni peoples meant that their interpretation of Islam prevailed. The educational curricula, organisation and practices articulated this religious orientation both at lower and higher school level. The *maktab* and the *madrasa* were the main channels for transmission of religion and culture, also for training the future religious and civil officials. Moreover, the *ulama*, the dominant intellectual class in society, were directly associated with the *madrasa* either as teachers *(mudarris)* and controllers, or had qualified from those institutions to become religious or civil functionaries *(qazi, mufti, domulla, rais,* etc.) of the Emirate. As regards the views of the *ulama* on particular issues, only a summary can be found in books written by the reformist *(jadid)* intellectuals at a later period. These are mostly critical of the positions taken by the *ulama*.[180] Some additional information on the intellectual climate is provided by the Central Asian writers and by certain foreign travellers, similarly by a few European and Russian history writers at a later date. An adequate understanding of the intellectual environment of Bukhara requires an examination of its system of education.

One of the best known Tajik writers, Sadradin Aini (1876–1954), who himself studied in a *maktab* in the village of Sectare and later attended *madrasa* in Bukhara, has described in detail, in his numerous works, the intellectual environment and system of education in Bukhara of his time.[181] Recollections of his school days can be found in *Maktab-i Kuhnah* ('old school').[182] Another source of information is Abdal Rauf Fitrat (1886–1938), who in such works as *Munazara, Bayant-i-Sayyah-i-Hindi,* and *Rahbar-i-Najat,* gave a critical evaluation of the educational and intellectual environment of Bukhara of the early twentieth century. Other useful foreign sources include travelogues, historical treatises and reports by people who visited Bukhara.[183] For a slightly earlier period, the famous Russian traveller, N. Khanykov has provided us with a comprehensive account of the content of the syllabus taught in Bukharan schools in the mid-nineteenth century.[184]

From these works it is clear that there was a fairly dense network of educational establishments in Bukhara.[185] Around the mid-nineteenth century the number of *madrasa* in the Emirate of Bukhara was estimated to be 180 with some 15,000 students; there were also around 1,800 primary mosque schools (*maktab*), which taught another 150,000 pupils.[186]

Some scholars, basing themselves on this numerical information, and after examining the account given by reformist thinkers have erroneously concluded that, during the mid-nineteenth century, the intellectual, educational and cultural level of the population was very high.[187] However, V. P. Nalivkin, a Russian ethnographer, wrote in 1891 that

> ... together with a large number of schools there is a good deal of illiteracy among the population. ... [188]

Many foreign observers and scholars were in general agreement that the level of literacy was very low in Bukhara and that approximately 1% of the population was literate throughout Central Asia. Moreover, foreign visitors also confirmed that the intellectual life in Bukhara was marked by dogmatism and religious fanaticism, and education given in schools was based on theology.

For example, according to the famous traveller Arminius Vambery,

> Bokhara considers itself the great pillar of Islamism, and the only pure fountain of the Mohammedan religion.[189]

For him, the chief characteristic of Bukharan Islam, was, no doubt, 'the wild fanatic obstinacy' with which Muslims clung to every single point of the Quran and the traditions, looking with terror and aversion upon any innovation; directing all their efforts to the preservation of the religion at that precise standard which marked its existence in the days of the Prophet and the first four Caliphs.[190] Vambery further noted that,

> Fanaticism, the chief cause of hypocrisy and impiety, has disfigured every religion,

but in Bukhara he says, it appeared in 'glaring colours', and wore a disgusting aspect

> Here, religion, in order to improve the mind, deals chiefly with the body; here, in order to exercise moral influence, the devotee is occupied with physical trifling, and, neglecting the inner man, as may be supposed, every one strives for outward appearance and effect. In Bukhara the principle reigns paramount: 'Man must make a figure, – no one cares for what he thinks.' A man may be the greatest miscreant, the most reprobate of human creatures; but let him fulfil the outward duties of religion and he escapes all punishment in this as well as in next world.[191]

An example of this principle of outward formulas reduced to practice, is that of the laws of cleanliness, which in Central Asia were observed with 'strict and scrupulous exactness', although he explains, the most disgusting filthiness is to be met with.[192]

The English scholars Skrine and Ross observed in the nineteenth century that, in *madrasa* of Bukhara,

> the curriculum embraced theology, Arabic, law and 'worldly wisdom'. Students who are conscious of a vocation for priesthood are subjected to a probation severer than which is prescribed to the candidates for admission to La Trappe or Chartreuse. They must obey all the precepts of Mohammed's code, and painfully practice to pronounce the shibboleth La Allaha ill Allah, thousands of times without drawing breath. Thus they attain to the coveted degree of Ishan, are qualified to instruct others, and receive the blindest devotion from the lower orders. No training can be conceived which is more calculated to inspire self-conceit and fanaticism. Now the priesthood of Bokhara and other cities of Central Asia have all been subjected to these sinister influences at a period of their lives, when the plastic mind receives impressions which can never be effaced; and the schools and colleges are officered exclusively from the sacerdotal caste. Before the advent of the Russians to power, the mullas directed the whole mechanism of government. The most cruel and the treacherous of the old Amirs respected their lives and liberties and shaped his conduct on their counsels.[193]

Eugene Schuyler, an American who visited Turkistan in 1870s, wrote that

> When Islam arrived on the civilised soil of Europe and Asia, it yielded enough to outside influences to permit of an extraordinary development of learning and civilisation, where art, science, and philosophy all found their votaries. Since that time it has been expelled in great part from Europe; waves of barbarism have passed from Asia, which effectually destroyed civilisation and enlightenment there, and threw nations into a state of torpor and stagnation from which they have never recovered. This, however, was not the effect of Mohammedanism, though that religion has had its part in keeping up this state of things. Relieved of external influences, fanaticism and ignorance had full sway. Yet the present state of Mussuluman countries seems hardly worse than that of Europe in the dark ages preceding the Reformation, if we take into account the difference of races and national character. Unfortunately, the contact of Christian civilisation with Mohammedan nations has, thus far, only served to develope faults and vices under a gloss of civilisation. Reform and progress, to be stable, must come from within.

He anticipated another 'great revival' of Islam.[194]

System of Education

The educational system of Bukhara, in the period under discussion, was formed by two type of schools: *maktab* (elementary school or mosque school) and *madrasa* (secondary level school and/or university level).

The number of primary schools had been 1,800. There were more than 300 *maktab* in the city of Bukhara alone.[195] In the Emirate as a whole there were around 200 *madrasa*, which were almost always financed by *vaqf* ('charitable endowments', such as land, shops or caravanserai) incomes. At the beginning of the present century in the city of Bukhara alone, there were 185 *madrasa* but only 22 provided instructions, the rest provided only accommodation.[196] Fitrat has listed 33 institutions of higher learning in Bukhara.[197] There were also vocational schools training people in memorising the Quran (*qorikhana*) and schools at which pupils learnt by heart legends about the prophets and other religious texts (*daloilkhana*).

Clerical control of learning in Bukhara was an unchallenged principle until the early twentieth century. The *ulama* prided themselves in retaining a traditional religious orthodoxy which had not only the blessing of time but also the aura of Divine Will.[198] Power to appoint teaching staff was vested in local political rulers who exercised this right when they appointed *mudarris*. In case of suspect qualification of a teacher, a judgement from *qazi* court settled the matter. Educational administration thus served as an important point of confluence between secular rule and religious authority.

Primary Education: Elementary schools were as a rule attached to mosques and were known as *maktab* or *maktabkhana*. *Maktab* in Arabic literally means a place where writing is taught, yet in Bukhara writing was not included among the subjects taught in this type of schools. The basic aim of these schools was to teach boys to memorise the basic articles of the Quran and give them instruction in religious duties. Each elementary school for boys was conducted by a single teacher called *domulla* or *maktabdar*. They were often graduates of *madrasa*, but most of them had significant gaps in their general knowledge and had no knowledge of the art of teaching. No formal salary was granted to the teachers. They were supported by the community and pupils gave them presents every time a book was finished or when pupils began learning a new book. Sometimes a fee of 1–3 *tenga* per annum was paid by the pupil. School for girls was conducted by a woman called *atunbibi* or *bibikhalifa*, who in most cases was the wife of the local *mulla*.

It was the father's duty to bring his son to the *maktab* and deliver the child to the teacher. The remark made by the father on this occasion: 'The flesh is yours, the bones are mine', expressed the basic relationship among parent, teacher and child. The parental authority was thus transferred directly to the teacher.[199] According to Olufsen, if the boys failed to appear at *maktab* by age seven, they were 'fetched and their parents scolded or fined'.[200] Corporal punishment was common in such schools and was thought of by teachers as a means of inculcating correct behaviour and habits, by which discipline could be maintained in the school. Aini illustrates such punishments in detail.[201] The period of attendance was not precisely defined and varied between four to ten years. Children over ten often left school because they had to help parents with their work.

In *maktab* study began from the age of six. Each class had from ten to forty pupils. Each pupil learned his lesson individually. A senior pupil (*khalifa*) chosen from among the more advanced pupils assisted the teacher in his work. Pupils began their study with learning the Arabic alphabet, followed by practise of vowel points and reading combination of letters. The purpose of teaching these combination of letters had little to do with learning or even memorisation, rather it was to facilitate the correct pronunciation of the Arabic words contained in the Quran.[202] The first book they learned in *maktab* was called *Haftyak* (lit. 'One Seventh' [of the Quran]), an abridgement of the most important passages of the Quran. The *Haftyak* was studied for 2–3 years in a language (Arabic) entirely unknown to the pupils. No effort to understand the meanings was undertaken, consequently, pupils were forced to learn it by rote.

Another book taught in the *maktab* was *Chaharkitab* (lit. 'Four Books')[203] comprising: (i) *Nam-i-Haq* ('True Message') a tract in verse by Sharifuddin al-Bukhari, dealing with rules of fulfilment of ritual obligations of ritual purity, fasting and prayers; (ii) *Char Fasl* ('Four Chapters') that provided a statement in prose of the bases of belief, the Five Pillars of Islam and ritual purity; (iii) *Muhimmat-ul Muslimin* (lit. 'Munitions of Muslims') by an anonymous author, that provided information on four subjects important to all Muslims: the unity of God (*tauhid*), fasting, prayers and ritual purity; (iv) selections from *Pandnama* ('Book of Advice') of Fariduddin Attar, a major work in *adab* tradition.[204] Other books taught in the *maktab* included: *Farz-i-ain* ('Exact Obligation'); a collection of writings of the Muslim saint Ahmad Yasavi; two volumes written by Sufi Allahyar (d. 1723) including *Maslak-i-Muttaqin* ('The Path of Believers'); and *Raunaq-ul-Islam* ('Light of Islam'), written in Turki, in 1464 by Vepai.[205] The poetry of Fuzuli (1498–1556) and Ali Sher Navai (1441–1501) was also taught where Turki speaking pupils outnumbered Tajiki speakers.

In spite of attending *maktab* for four to ten years, many pupils were unable to read anything written in their own language because none of the vowel points to which the pupil was accustomed were ever placed on letters making a word in any other document except the Quran. In the languages, written in the Arabic alphabet, the pronunciation of a word had to be guessed from the message of the sentence of which it was a part. Anything memorised by the child in Arabic was nonsense to him. Thus, pupils forgot most of what they had memorised, except a few passages of the Quran which were required for the performance of the daily prayers and other religious and traditional activities. Soon after graduation the pupils who finished the *maktab* were almost as illiterate as those who did not go to school at all.

Higher Education: After completing attendance at *maktab*, boys from well-to-do families, especially sons of *ulama* and wealthy merchants, and the talented youth from country districts, who desired higher education, went to study at *madrasa* in urban centres. Students studied the following books during the first three years of their study at *madrasa*:

(i) The study began with *Bidan* (know!) – a customary name of an anonymous treatise on Arabic grammar, widely used in Central Asia as a textbook. This book explained fundamentals of Arabic grammar in Tajiki with examples in Arabic.[206]

(ii) Students also studied *Nisab-ul-Sibian* ('Course for Youth'), an arrangement of Arabic words and their equivalent in Tajiki in poetry form.[207] This book was compiled in 1221 by Abu-Nasri Farahi and was also used in Iran and India.

(iii) Students also read *Avval-i-Ilm* ('Beginning of knowledge') – a book written in Tajiki that covered the most essential religious rules in a question-answer form.

(iv) *Al-Muizzi*, an anonymous treatise on Arabic morphology attributed to Izzuddin Zanjani (1257) and *Avomil al-In'a* ('Necessary Factors'), written by Abdulqahar Jurjani (d. 1080), that dealt with Arabic syntax were used to learn Arabic etymology and syntax. Students memorised Arabic idioms and learnt their meanings in Tajiki.

(v) This was followed by a partial reading of *Qafia fi-n-nahv* ('Rhyme in Grammar') – one of the most widely read textbooks on Arabic grammar, written by Ibn al-Hajib (d. 1249). The book discussed Arabic syntax in some detail.[208] The study of these books was considered sufficient to become a *mulla*. Sometimes students took up to ten years to complete this stage.[209]

The next stage of advanced learning began with the reading of *Sharh-i-Mulla* ('Explanation of *mulla*'), a commentary written by Abdurahman Jami (d. 1492) on *Qafia fi-n-nahv*. This stage took five years and included the study of Najamuddin Qazvini's (d. 1276) book on logic, *Arrisalat ash-Shamsia fi-l-Qavaid al-Mantiqia* (Treatise on rules of Logic), commonly known as *Shamsia*. Students spent another year in reading a commentary by Qutbiddin Razi (d. 1365) on *Shamsia*, known as *Hoshia-a-Qutbi* ('Notes of Qutbi'). Simultaneously, students studied *Aqaid-i-Nasafi* ('Beliefs of Nasafi'), a theological compilation by Najmuddin Abu Hafs Nasafi (1068–1148). Later a commentary on *Aqaid-i-Nasafi* by S'adaddin Taftazani (d. 1361) was studied for four years. *Tahzib ul-Mantiq va-l-Kalam* ('Refinement of Logic and *Kalam*'), a compilation of logic and theology written by Taftazani was studied for two years and then *Hikmat-ul-Ain* ('Exact Wisdom') written by Najamuddin Qazvini, dealing with natural history and metaphysics, was studied for two more years. For another two years students learned *Mulla Jalal* – a commentary written by Jalal-ud-Din

Dawwani (d. 1502) on a theological treatise called *Aqaid ul-Adudiyat* ('Beliefs of Adud') by Adud ad-Din al-Iji (d. 1326). Later students learned *Hadith* ('Sayings of the Prophet Muhammad').[210]

Khanykov pointed out that,

> And thus we see that the cycle of the sciences cultivated in Bokhara is not inconsiderable, since it comprehends 137 books; but the uniformity is also very great; besides which, we must observe, that it scarcely at all corrects the evils, or supplies the wants of the primary education of the Bokharians. For the mind, which in the first period of its cultivation, is bound in the chains as it were, by learning by heart without understanding anything, is subsequently exercised on points of theology alone.[211]

As is evident from the above, the curriculum comprised books of theology, mostly commentaries, written at least three centuries before. Some textbooks which were used during the nineteenth or early twentieth centuries in Bukhara were first authorised during the twelfth century or earlier. Very few texts were less than three centuries old. The curriculum of the nineteenth century concerned itself almost entirely with theological subjects.[212] Mathematics was taught solely in connection with the study of the law of inheritance. After acquainting students with the four functions of arithmetic, they proceeded to geometry, for it was important for measuring and dividing up plots of land. Algebra was not taught.[213] Regarding historical and geographical knowledge, the *mudarris* taught that since its creation the world had been inhibited by seven races: Chinese, Turks, Europeans, Arabs, Persians, Hindus and Negroes; that there were seven zones in the earth with seven seas, seven heavens holding seven planetary systems. The earth, they taught, is composed of four elements, i.e., water, fire, soil, and wind, which shape and govern earthly happenings. Medical teaching was equally limited. The learned scholars identified three main bodily organs: the head, chest and stomach. Blood circulation was not even considered.[214]

The main thrust of the curriculum was religious teaching. This emphasised salvation through predestination – God save them whom He will.[215] However, even books of theology (mostly commentaries and glosses produced over centuries), were not studied by the students in full. Instead, they concentrated on the marginal notes written by other commentators on the books.[216]

> Nothing is better calculated to give strength to fanaticism, than an education of this kind, which, instead of being founded on common sense, is based on limited ingenuity, exerting itself to confound an opponent with words, and not with thoughts,

concluded Khanykov.[217]

State of Education System: Education had declined to such an extent in the late nineteenth and early twentieth centuries that, despite a very heavy emphasis on the learning of Arabic language and theology,

> there was hardly a well-educated person in town who could read and explain appropriately a single page of *tafsir* of the Quran or Tradition, or could read two or three simple Arabic poems,

remarked Fitrat.[218] The *ulama*, finding books written in Arabic difficult, used to turn to the books of the *Shari'a* in Persian. After twenty years of learning and twenty years of teaching they could become *mufti*. They considered that religious matters depended upon their opinions and aims, so they interpreted the verses of the Quran according to their wishes and freely re-invented the Traditions. They attained high positions in Bukhara but had no conception of modern sciences.[219] The knowledge they were able to deliver, in the field of jurisprudence, was that:

> during the [ritual] ablution, 'those who blow their nose with the left hand or do not wash their foot from the right side will suffer Hell-fire for 70,000 years'; 'those who fail even once to greet an *alim* will become infidels'; 'the sins of those who pass along a street which has been touched by the feet of an *alim* even once will be forgiven, and they will go to heaven'....

In the field of religious belief:

> in the fourth heaven, there lives an angel who has 70,000 heads, every head has 70,000 tongues and every tongue can speak in 70,000 languages....[220]

It has been claimed that Muslim education in general articulated most prominently the following values:[221]

- supernatural (but unknowable) cause and effect
- tradition for tradition's sake
- elder, paternalistic authority not subject to challenge
- submissiveness, humility before those in authority and who are learned
- pride and dignity in identifying with Islam
- material and financial reward for correct behaviour and success; physical punishment and shame for incorrect behaviour and failure
- inferiority of the female sex
- non-pragmatic outlook; primacy of religious and social relations over practical interests
- ignorance of the natural world
- superstition as an accepted means to knowledge
- freedom to attend the schools, according to one's desires for religious knowledge.

By and large, these features were closely reflected in the practices and intellectual ideas that were taught in Bukhara at that time. God's Will and design for man was regarded as the basis of the faith. The Divine Will was also held responsible for natural phenomena, such as floods, fires, earthquakes, and rainfall. Free inquiry as a means of finding alternatives and choosing of a different future was suppressed at the individual and societal level.

Despite all the shortcomings in the education system, however, a number of outstanding thinkers and writers did appear in Bukhara. These included the following: the poet, diplomat and court astrologer Ahmad Makhdum Donish (see Chapter Two); the satirical poet Abd al-Qadir Savdo (1823–1873); the court secretary, historian and poet, Mirza Abdal Azim Sami (1835–1907); the court poet (whose work shows him to have been a bitter critic of Bukharan morals and treatment of women) Shamsuddin Makhdum Shahin (1859–1894); the poet, historian and renowned government official, Sharif Jan Makhdum Sadr Zia (1865–1931); the poet and government official renowned for his honesty, Mirza Hayit Sahba (d. 1918); the future president of the reformist movement, Abdal Vahid Burhanov (1877–1934); also Sadradin Aini (1876–1954) and Abdal Rauf Fitrat (see Chapter Four).

Although figures such as these emerged from the institutions described above, they were more the exception than the rule. Not only did they engross themselves in the magnificent old literature taught in the *madrasa*, but also independently mastered and analysed the history of Islam, learned geography, took an interest in astronomy and astrology, and the natural sciences. They also interested themselves in practical matters, such as techniques of irrigating arid land. Several of them had travelled abroad and thus widened their horizon. These talented Bukharans composed and performed music, wrote poetry, practised calligraphy, disputed religious questions with learned theologians, and discussed scientific causes of natural phenomena and disasters. In their literary and conversation meetings held in Donish's and Sadr Zia's homes arguments ranged beyond literature and art to politics, religion and social issues.[222] This small group of scholars represented the first stirrings of a rationalistic and reformist trend of Islam in Bukhara. The *jadid* movement grew out of this environment, in opposition to the prevailing attitudes in Bukharan society at large. (See Chapter Three).

RUSSIAN CONTACTS

Construction of the Railway Line

A new era in Russia's relations with Bukhara began after the Imperial government's decision to build a Central Asian railroad. The idea to construct a Trans-Caspian railway line was initiated by Czarist military strategists in Turkistan as part of their plan to connect the Turkmen towns of Ahal and Merv with Russia. The suggestion was put forward by Kaufman, the Governor-General of Turkistan, to the authorities in

St. Petersburg in the 1870s.[223] Various routes suggested by different officials were considered. Finally, after a clash between Russian and Afghan troops at Penjdeh on March 18/30, 1885, which brought Russia and Britain to the verge of war in Central Asia, Russia decided to extend the Trans-Caspian railway eastwards from Kizl-Arvat.[224] This would strengthen Russia's military position in Central Asia and provide the long-sought rail link between Russia and Turkistan.

Following this decision, construction work was started; by 1885 the track had reached Ashkabad. On June 25, 1885, the Russian authorities concluded a treaty with the Emir of Bukhara to allow the passage of the railway across the territory of the Emirate. According to the terms of the treaty, the Emir took responsibility for providing *amlak* lands, without compensation, for the construction of the line and other relevant facilities, e.g. railway stations, depots and warehouses.[225] Private lands would have to be bought at fair market prices by the Russians with the help of the Emir. Thus, the main construction costs were borne by the colonisers, but the Emir partially supplied the land. The Bukharan government also promised to render help in provision of labour and construction materials.[226] The track reached Merv in 1886. At the end of the same year it reached Chaharjui and the Amu Darya, and in 1888, Samarkand. A railway station was constructed at Kagan or New (*Novaya*) Bukhara. This settlement was 11 versts and 400 *sadzhen* away from old Bukhara.[227] New Bukhara and old Bukhara were connected in 1901, for which line, an extension of the main track, the Emir paid 500,000 roubles.[228] In 1913 the Kagan-Qarshi-Kerki-Kelif-Termez and Qarshi-Guzar-Kitob railway lines were constructed. The main aim was military, i.e. to reach the Afghan border. The total cost was paid by the Russians, while the Emir provided some of the land.[229]

The railway line connected the southern and northern regions of Bukhara with the central part, i.e. the Zarafshan Valley. This facilitated the import of goods to the Emirate and the export of local products. Before the construction of the railway line, trade had been conducted by caravans which travelled from Bukhara to Orenburg, Samarkand and Tashkent, and from Bukhara through Balkh to Kabul and Herat and on to Kandahar and Mashhad. All the trade of the Emirate was concentrated in the hands of the merchants of the city of Bukhara. However, the situation changed after the railway connected Bukhara with Moscow and Nizhnii Novgorod via Tashkent and Orenburg. The freight charge by caravan from Bukhara to Orenburg was 3 roubles per pud; the charge by rail from Bukhara to Moscow and Nizhnii Novgorod was only 70 copecks per pud.[230] Hence, the old caravan merchants were replaced by new traders, especially in cotton and *karakul*, such as *trazudar* (lit. 'weighers', meaning commission agents), *ijaridar* ('leading cotton or *karakul* broker') and *pakhtakash* ('small buyers'). Goods transporting firms, trade counters, postal and telegraph offices and printing press also appeared (printing press was established at Kagan in 1901).

The railway line also had great cultural impact, since it ended Bukhara's physical isolation, brought an influx of outsiders and enabled European civilisation to enter what was still virtually a medieval state. Railway stations, with their neat, painted buildings, uniformed staff and European-type Russian settlements *Novaya* ('New') Bukhara (Kagan), *Novyi* ('New') Chaharjui, Kerki, Termez, Amirabad, Faryab, Sarai, etc., emerged in the Emirate. These little islands of Western civilisation were equipped with nineteenth-century Russian technological achievements, such as electrical lighting, postal-telegraph office, movie houses, industrial enterprises, schools, hospitals, churches, etc. As Count Pahlen put it, the trend of local life was geared to Europeanisation.

> The railway engine pulling into a station symbolised victory over the desert. Cleanly-dressed Russian railway porters wearing the trade mark of their calling, a white apron, greeted the weary traveller at the station and conducted him to a comfortable cab, generally drawn by two horses. He was then driven to the European quarter at a spanking trot along straight, wide avenues lined by a double row of trees, through which he glimpsed the irrigation canals, running parallel to the street; passed one-storied flat-roofed houses and was at last brought to a spacious hotel with spotless rooms, bathrooms and modern furnishings.[231]

Russian Impact on Bukharan Agriculture

The process of specialisation in the agriculture of Bukhara, to produce raw materials for Russian industry, started as a result of the intensive penetration of Russian capital into the Emirate. This penetration intensified in the 1880s, after the construction of the Trans-Caspian railway line. This line, in Lenin's words, 'began to open up Central Asia for the [Russian] capitalists'.[232] The launching of the Amu Darya fleet on November 13, 1887, connecting Chaharjui with Kerki and Termez, also played a significant role in bringing Russian capital to these cities and surrounding areas. Earlier, in 1887, diplomatic negotiations to open a branch of the Russian State Bank in the Emirate were initiated between the governments of Russia and Bukhara. These were successfully concluded in 1894 and towards the end of the same year the first branch was opened in the Emirate.[233]

Meanwhile, Russian firms started financing cotton-growing *dehqan*. The joint stock company Poznanski and Co., began distributing money in advance of the cotton crop in the Emirate in 1889.[234] The following year, Russian firms extended their financing of *dehqan* to *karakul* and wool. During the 1890s, agricultural financing (*bunak*, as the Bukharans called it) spread extensively. By 1899 several million tengas were credited towards the next crop of cotton.[235]

Russian manufacturing companies situated in Bukhara could borrow from the branch of the Russian State Bank, and other private banks lent up to 40 million roubles per annum.[236] The firms in turn extended this money in the form of loan to the *trazudar* and *ijaridar*, at a yearly interest rate of 12%, compounded. The Russian firms never purchased cotton without the involvement of local middlemen.[237] The *trazudar* and *ijaridar* distributed *bunak* among the smaller *pakhtakash*, who purchased cotton from the *dehqan* for the parent firm(s), and proceeded to tie the *dehqan* down with usurious loans. *bunak* was often granted in the spring. After pledging land or property as security, a *dehqan* received a loan, which could be granted in the form of goods, e.g. tea, soap or kerosene oil. Loan agreements had to be attested by the *qazi*. According to the established norm in the Emirate, the *dehqan* had to sell his cotton to the agent from whom he had borrowed.

Various Russian firms and individuals were competing with each other to grant more loans and purchase the maximum amount of cotton.[238] Sometimes the competition became fierce and the Russian Political Agent in Bukhara had to intervene as arbitrator. Questions relating to the distribution of *bunak* provoked some heated meetings between the representatives of the Political Agent and the Bukharan ruler in the 1890s.

In 1897 the chief *Zakatchi* of the Emirate, Astanakul bek, suggested to the Russian Political Agent, Ignatiev, that he forbid Russian buyers of cotton from granting *bunak* to poor *dehqan*.[239] The same suggestion was forwarded several times to the Czarist government during 1897–98. However, the granting of *bunak* continued.[240] In 1899, at the insistence of the Emir Abd-al Ahad, Ignatiev called several meetings of Russian firms and private individuals involved in granting *bunak*. The meetings were held on several occasions, including January 19, March 5 and March 26.[241] During these discussions the Russians initially refused to stop the distribution of *bunak*, but finally agreed to the suggestion of the Bukharan government. New rules for the buying and selling of cotton were formulated. One of the 15 clauses states that: 'According to the Emir's desire, from August 1, 1899, by the agreement between the Bukharan government and the Imperial Political Agent, the practice of the distribution of so-called *bunak* loans for the future crop of cotton to *trazudar* and *pakhtakash* is completely abolished.'[242] The remainder of the clauses enumerate the markets for the buying and selling of cotton, the maximum number of *trazudar* and *ijaridar* in a cotton market, duties of the cotton inspectors and so on.[243]

However, despite this agreement the distribution of *bunak* continued. The *dehqan* often desperately needed money, and the Russian businessmen needed cotton. So, with the help of brokers, they entered into deals and the covert distribution of *bunak* continued. At the beginning of the twentieth century the practice was still prevalent on quite a wide scale.[244]

The credit extended by the Russian buyers enhanced the specialisation of Bukharan agriculture and bettered the material position of the *dehqan* to a certain extent. It rendered great help to the *dehqan* in constructing new irrigation canals and widening the existing ones. During the 1880s, the *dehqan* in Bukhara cultivated low-quality local cotton called *ghuza*. The Czarist government wanted to spread the cultivation of American varieties of cotton in the Emirate. Therefore, Mazov, a cotton trader from Orenburg, arranged land on lease from the government of Bukhara on the right bank of the Amu Darya, near the Farab railway station of the Trans-Caspian line, and sowed American cotton there on 30 desiatinas. The same year the joint stock company Kudrin and Co. sowed American cotton on 40 desiatinas of land situated 35 versts from Chaharjui. Owing to the flooding of the Amu Darya that year, both cotton crops were ruined after the appearance of the shoots,[245] but the initiative paid off and some *dehqan* cultivated American cotton the following year. Dobson confirms the cultivation of American cotton in 1889 in the Zarafshan Valley.[246] However, though American cotton was better in quality and fetched a better price than the local variety, it was slow in replacing local cotton. The following impediments are cited by Yuferov:

1 American cotton was more labour-intensive, since it had to be harvested several times over (depending upon the flowering of the cotton buds), while local cotton was collected in one go.[247]
2 The traditional method of calculating the cotton yield: it was estimated, like other crops, in terms of roots, i.e., by the number of plants rather than the number of buds. The buds of the American cotton flowered at different times and were larger in size, hence, before permission to collect the crop was granted by the Emir's officials, at least half the cotton was dispersed by the wind.[248]
3 American varieties needed more water than the local cotton and Bukhara suffered from a shortage of water.
4 The use of primitive technology in Bukharan agriculture.
5 The complicated tax system.

To accelerate the cultivation of American cotton in the Emirate of Bukhara, in 1911, a Russian businessman took *amlak* land on lease in Kurgan Tube and Kabadian *valayat* and sowed American cotton on 2,000 desiatinas. This greatly influenced the *dehqan* and in 1912–13 almost everyone was growing American cotton there.[249] During the First World War, owing to the increased demand for Bukharan cotton in Russia, many measures were taken to boost cotton production in Bukhara. For example, in the Farghana valley American cotton seeds were distributed amongst the *dehqan* at a fixed price. In eastern Bukhara in 1915, the production of cotton reached

100,000 *batman* (1 batman = 8 puds or 131.104 kg) of which 90% was American cotton.[250]

By 1913 the total area under cotton cultivation, according to data collected by the Russian Political Agent, had risen to 62,000 desiatinas.[251] Gulishambarov gives a figure of 75,000 desiatinas.[252] We do not possess direct figures for cotton cultivation in the Emirate before it became a Protectorate of Russia, but in 1880–81 410,000 puds[253] of cotton was exported from the Emirate to Russia. In 1913, the figure was 2,624,000 puds;[254] the increase is roughly six-fold.

In the light of the above it is evident that Russian businessmen, and of course the government, introduced important and fundamental changes into Bukharan agriculture. Total area under cash crops cultivation, especially cotton, increased, eventually subsistence farming and grain production decreased, money-commodity relationship strengthened and agrarian capitalism facilitated.

Russo-Bukharan Trade

Trade contacts between Russia and Bukhara had already existed for centuries. In the early twentieth century a significant increase in trade took place between these states. In the 1880s, Russian industrial goods visibly replaced western European goods in the markets of Bukhara. In 1891–94 a series of meetings was held in St. Petersburg to discuss the question of the inclusion of Bukhara and Khiva within the Russian Customs and Tariff system.[255] Negotiations on this point were also held with the Emir.[256] From 1 January 1895, the customs independence of the Emirate vanished. The Emirate was included in Russian Customs jurisdiction and the import of western European industrial goods was totally forbidden.[257] Later, at the insistence of the Russian government, currency reforms were introduced, making the Russian currency valid in the Emirate. As a result, Russo-Bukharan trade increased still further.

In Russo-Bukharan trade relations the question of the collection of *zakat* and *aminona* had a special significance. *Zakat* and *aminona* were collected on every commodity sold in the Emirate, including Russian goods. *Zakat*, as the Bukharan *Qushbegi-i-Bala* informed the Russian Political Agent, 'is one of the fundamental dogmas of Islam. It is obligatory for every Muslim to pay 2.5% *zakat* on the proceeds of sale of goods to purify his wealth'.[258]

The question of the abolition of *zakat* arose because of instances of illegal extortion of *zakat* and *aminona* by Bukharan collectors from Russians. The collectors charged up to 5% and even 7.5% *zakat* instead of 2.5%.[259] Sometimes Russian traders refused to pay *zakat*, especially when it was levied on cash. In the 1880s some Russian traders urged the Czarist government to abolish the collection of *zakat* in the Emirate. For example, Konyukhov Lukin, the registrar of the trade-industrial firm N. Kudrin and

Co., requested the Russian Foreign Ministry on December 2, 1886, to act to abolish the collection of *zakat*.[260] However, the Czarist government refused all such proposals, considering that abolition of *zakat* would lead to increases in other taxes.

In 1915 the Emirate of Bukhara exported 2,624,000 puds of cotton to Russia. According to the figures of the Russo-Chinese Bank, 1,800,000 and 2,000,000 *karakul* skins were exported to Russia in 1909 and 1912 respectively.[261] The export of wool to Russia increased 35-fold. Around 50,000 carpets, 25,000 puds of raw silk and silk cocoons and 250,000 puds of dry currants were exported to Russia annually. After 1895 the Emirate imported iron and iron products worth 1,294,000 roubles, crockery worth 1,039,000 roubles, various industrial products worth 15,974,000 roubles, and grain and sugar worth 9,140,000 roubles from Russia. By the beginning of the twentieth century 96.5% of Bukhara's total imports came from, and 88% of the total exports went to, Russia. In 1907 goods worth 27 million roubles, in 1908 worth 29 million roubles, and in 1909 worth 30 million roubles, were exported from the Emirate to Russia, Turkistan *Krai* and other countries.[262] During the same period Bukharan imports amounted to 21 million roubles in 1907, 23.5 million in 1908, and 25 million in 1909. In 1913 Bukhara imported from Russia 264,000 puds of finished goods worth a total of 15,974,000 roubles, 235,000 puds of iron and iron products worth 12,940,000 roubles, and 45,000 puds of crockery, worth 1,039,000 roubles. Together they constituted 96.5% of Bukharan's total imports.[263] The total turnover of Bukharan foreign trade before the First World War reached 75 million roubles.[264]

This indicates that the Bukharan economy had been thoroughly integrated with Russia and had become subservient to the Russian economy. Bukhara served as a market for Russian finished goods and industrial products and at the same time provided cheap raw material, especially cotton, to Russian industry. Apart from industrial goods Bukhara had to import grain from Russia.

Russian Financial and Technical Services

The following Russian banks opened branches in Bukhara in the last two decades of the nineteenth century: Russian Bank for Foreign Trade, *Russko-Aziatskii* Bank, *Moskovskii Uchyotnyi* Bank, *Azovsko-Donskii Kommercheskii* Bank, *Sibirskii Torgovoi* Bank,[265] *Soedinyonnyi* Bank[266] and *Volzhsko-Kamskii Kommercheskii* Bank. Some of these banks had connections with foreign capital, for example, *Russko-Aziatskii* and *Soedinyonnyi* depended upon French finance, while the Russian Foreign Trade Bank and *Sibirskii Torgovoi* Bank depended upon German capital.[267]

In the Emirate there were also Russian manufacturing firms, under the titles of *obshchestvo* ('society', 'company') and *tovarishchestvo* ('partnership') as well as Russian counters (offices) for transporting goods. They organised the transportation of Bukharan agricultural products within the Emirate, to Russia and to the Turkistan Governorate-General. Some of the biggest transportation counters were situated at New Chaharjui and Termez.[268] Some of the biggest Russian manufacturing companies and associations active in the Emirate included the *Aktsioniarnoe Obshchestvo Khlopkochistitelnogo i Masloboinogo Zavoda* ('Joint Stock Company of Cotton-Ginning and Cottonseed-Oil Factory') at *Novaya* Bukhara, the Eastern Bukharan Association for Cotton Purchase, the Central Asian Trade and Industrial Association N. Kudrin and Co., the Joint Stock Company Louis Zalm,[269] the Brothers Kraft Trading House, the Joint Stock Company Cotton, the Association of Yaroslavl's Grand Manufacturers, the Trading House Shtekher and Tsimer, the Trading Houses Badior, Adam Osser, Levin, Flaxman, Polyak Shapir and others.[270] Some of these companies were joint ventures, as for example, the Joint Stock Company Russo-Bukharan Trade and Industry, which had a capital of 2,250,000 roubles. Half the capital was invested by the Bukharan government and the other half by Evan Stikhev and Co.[271]

CONCLUSIONS

To summarise the main points made in this chapter, in the second half of the nineteenth century, after becoming a Russian Protectorate, Bukhara opened up to the capitalist economy. As a result of the introduction of a money-based commodity economy, the buying and selling of land accelerated. The pauperisation of the *dehqan* led to the availability of cheap farm labour. The extension of *bunak* by Russian banks encouraged cash crops and specialised farming, i.e. agrarian capitalism. The construction of the Trans-Caspian Railway accelerated this process. Russian settlements, banks and finance companies, trade counters, goods transporting firms, outlets for pesticide, seeds and fertilisers, postal and telegraph offices and printing press appeared. Moreover, the merchants of the city of Bukhara lost their privileged position as caravan traders. Beneficiaries of the growing cotton and *karakul* trade, new merchants and middlemen such as *trazudar, ijaridar* and *pakhtakash* emerged.

The introduction of a cash economy resulted into the creation of an economic surplus that could be reinvested in a number of ways. The economy began to diversify, jobs in the service sector began to appear, and provided an economic base for activities that had hitherto not been possible. A space arose in Bukharan society for those not attached to existing structures of authority and influence. The emergence of a new merchant class was not the only consequence of this diversification of economy; it also provided the necessary material conditions in which booksellers, publishers, translators, and professional school teachers could survive. A hitherto traditional, immobile and isolated society slowly and imperceptibly changed under the Russian influence. These various developments brought society face to face with the new world. Without this transformation of the economy the emergence of the reformists as a social category would have been impossible.

The challenges and the opportunities of this new world could not be met by the old practices, especially the old system of education, values and political structure. However, the orthodox *ulama*, the traditional custodians of the faith and society, in the name of religion, clung to the old practices and opposed any change. Not only were the *ulama* opposed to reforms because they had stakes in the old system, but also because of their (lack) of education they could not perceive that there existed a problem. Some middlemen and merchants and a few intellectuals having an experience of both the worlds realised the gravity of the situation and advocated changes in the field of education, culture and political structure. The Emir of Bukhara occupied a position in the middle initially, but sided with the clergy when it mattered. Leading thinkers and men of action tried their best to find a way out of this situation. Reform proposals (educational, cultural, political and economic) were formulated and some even presented to the Emir. We shall examine these developments in the next chapters.

Chapter Two

Ahmad Makhdoom Donish

SOURCES

Czarist and Soviet, Russian and Central Asian, scholars unanimously consider Ahmad Donish to be the most brilliant and progressive thinker of nineteenth-century Bukhara. There is also general agreement that he was the precursor of the enlightenment movement in Central Asia. During his life-time, however, his work had limited circulation.

1 Rasul Hadi-Zade, an eminent Tajik Soviet orientalist, in his book *Istochniki k Izucheniyu Tadzhikskoi Literatury Vtoroi Poloviny XIX Veka* ('Sources for the Study of Tajik Literature of the Second Half of the 19th Century'), written in 1956, claims that some of Donish's work was included in manuscripts and published anthologies (*tazkira*) of the pre-Soviet period, but that the progressive elements in his thinking were under-represented by compilers such as Afzal, Abidi and Muhtaram, who were themselves of a conservative leaning. They portray Donish as a quiet, modest poet, loyal to the Emirate. Those who held less conformist political views, such as Hashmat, Shar'i and Sadr Zia, however, depict Donish as an innovative thinker.[1]

2 In pre-Revolutionary Russian literature we find a few pages about Donish, written by the Russian traveller L. F. Kostenko, in his work *Puteshestvie v Bukharu Russkoi Missii v 1870 Godu* ('The Journey of the Russian Mission to Bukhara in 1870'), published in 1871.[2] He writes that Donish, or Mir Ahmad as he is sometimes called,[3] was of humble origins but nonetheless notable amongst the Bukharans for his brilliance. He confirms that Donish was Secretary to the Bukharan embassy during the parleys with the Russian mission in 1870, and that he had visited St. Petersburg.[4] Donish is also mentioned in two brief articles in the Russian newspapers *Golos* ('The Voice') and *Novoe Vremya* ('The New Times'), which covered the visit of Bukharan emissaries to St. Petersburg in 1874.[5]

3 The systematic study and analysis of the life and works of Ahmad Donish began after the 1917 Russian Revolution. One of the most important contributions is the work by Sadradin Aini[6] (1878–1954). Aini's

commentaries on Donish are important for three reasons. Firstly, because he knew Donish personally, and had direct experience of the educational, social, cultural and political milieu in which he lived and worked. Secondly, Donish shaped his political outlook, since it was under his influence that Aini became a *jadid* activist.[7] Thirdly, Aini, one of the very few *jadid* to survive the purges of the 1930s, was a leading light of the Soviet establishment. Thus, his views not only have the immediacy of his own experience, but are a clear reflection of the regime's view of Donish. Aini mentions Donish for the first time in his work *Tarikh-i Emiran-i Manghitia Bukhara* ('History of the Manghit Emirs of Bukhara'), which was published in 1920 in the journal *Shu'ala-i Inqilab*[8] ('Flame of Revolution'), and subsequently appeared as a book in 1923.[9] Here Donish is described as a highly educated intellectual who condemned, overtly and covertly, the tyranny of the Bukharan Emirs and the reactionary Muslim *ulama*, and who was tolerated at court by the Emir Muzaffar only because of his skill as an astronomer/astrologer. He commanded considerable respect among the ruling circles in Russia and, according to Aini, the Emir was aware that the Russians might react negatively if he was to dismiss Donish. The Bukharan *ulama* despised Donish and spread evil rumours about him. Aini suggested that his readers acquaint themselves with Donish's *Navadir-ul-Voqai* ('Rare Events'), which contained most of his important ideas.[10]

In a later work, *Bukhara Inqilabi Tarikhi Uchun Materiallar* ('Materials on the History of the Bukharan Revolution'), published in 1926, Aini compared Donish with 'the rising morning star in the murky night of Bukhara.[11] In *Namuna Adabiat-i Tajiki* ('Patterns of Tajik Literature'), published in 1926, Aini provides the first, albeit short, biography of Donish, and stresses the importance of his fearless and open criticism of the regime of the Bukharan Emir and the shortcomings of the *ulama*. He does not elaborate upon Donish's political views. However, he comments upon the admirable simplicity of Donish's language and his criticism of Bedil's (d. 1721) difficult and pretentious language. Aini informs his readers that Donish was not only a writer of prose but also a poet, although few of his poems have survived.[12] In *Vospominaniya* ('Reminiscences'), Aini writes about his meetings with Donish and describes his life in considerable detail.[13] He also gives a survey of the contents of his principal work, *Navadir-ul-Voqai*, and argues that Donish's ideas were progressive for his time.[14]

4 A second stage in the assessment of Donish's work was initiated by the eminent Russian orientalist Evgenii Edvardovich Bertels (1890–1957), a graduate of the Faculty of Oriental Languages at St. Petersburg University (1920). The chief aim of his 21-page article, written in 1933 and published in 1936,[15] was, he says, to describe the technical aspects of the manuscripts of Donish's works.[16] Nevertheless, he makes some brief but important observations on the development of *jadid* literature. He notes that the works created by the Central Asian urban bourgeoisie in the middle of

the nineteenth century marked a significant move forward, leading, in the twentieth century, to the emergence of the so-called *jadid* school; it is therefore important, he argues, to begin the study of *Jadidism* from this period.[17] At the same time, Bertels alludes to Donish as the 'father' of modern Tajik literature, identifying him as a major influence on subsequent Tajik literature, even of the Soviet period. His article is concerned with Donish's works *Navadir-ul-Voqai* and *Traktat «Risolaji tarjumaji ahvoli amironi Bukhoroji Sharif»* (*Zhizneopisaniya emirov svyashennoi Bukhary*) ('A Treatise on the History of the Emirs of Bukhara the Noble').[18] Bertels describes one of the sections of Donish's *Navadir-ul-Voqai*, namely, *Risala Dar Nazm-i Tamaddun vo Ta'vun* ('Treatise on Patterns of Civilisation and Cooperation'), as a political treatise in which Donish's ideas on the state and reform are expounded in an orderly manner. As Bertels points out, this chapter is of great importance for the history of *Jadidism* in Central Asia because it encapsulates the chief goals of the *jadid*.[19]

5 Satim Ulugh-Zade (b.1911) wrote a pamphlet entitled *Ahmad Donish*, which was published in 1946.[20] Using Donish's *Navadir-ul-Voqai* and *Risala ya Mukhtasari az Tarikh-i Sultanat-i Khonadon-i Manghitia* as source material, Ulugh-Zade provides a biographical account of Donish's life. He also discusses the war of 1866–1868 between Russia and Bukhara, drawing on Donish's account of those events. Ulugh-Zade emphasises the fact that Donish's world-view was significantly influenced by Russian culture, especially after his visits to St. Petersburg. Like Aini, he points out that Donish could not at first imagine the Emirate of Bukhara without an enlightened king, but later accepted the inevitability of the destruction of the Emir's power.[21] Although Ulugh-Zade considered Donish to be the greatest thinker of nineteenth-century Bukhara, unlike Bertels, he did not consider him to be seminal for the development of the *jadid*. Ulugh-Zade argued that the *jadid* never entertained the overthrow of the Emir. Rather, they advocated a partial reform of the system, thereby serving the interests of the national bourgeoisie.[22]

6 Another view of Donish's life and works is provided by Babadzhan Gafurovich Gafurov (b. 1908), First Secretary of the Tajik Communist Party (1946–56) and a noted Soviet orientalist and historian. In *Istoriya Tadzhikskogo Naroda* ('History of the Tajik People'), published in 1949, he argues that Donish advocated the establishment of an enlightened monarchy, and, further, that he sympathised with the ideas of utopian Socialism.[23]

7 The Soviet orientalist Abdulghani Mirzoev, after careful examination of the original manuscript of *Navadir-ul-Voqai* (written in Donish's own hand),[24] fixed the date of completion of *Risala Dar Nazm-i Tamaddun vo Ta'vun* as 1875, and thus suggests that Donish wrote this treatise on reform after his three visits to Russia, and incorporated in it both his European and Bukharan experiences.[25]

8 Hadi-Zade, in *Istochniki k Izucheniyu Tadzhikskoi Literatury Vtoroi Poloviny XIX Veka*, studied Donish's political views on the basis of *Risala Dar Nazm-i Tamaddun vo Ta'vun*, and, like Mirzoev and other Soviet scholars, concluded that Donish's reform project was influenced by the European, especially Russian, model of state structure. In his view, Donish instigated an ideological revolution amongst the forward-looking people of Bukhara.[26] This view is also held by Ibrahim Mominov in his doctoral dissertation, *Iz Istorii Obshchestvennoi i Filosofskoi Mysli Uzbekistana Kontsa XIX i Nachala XX Vekov* ('From the History of the Social and Philosophical Thought of Uzbekistan at the End of the Nineteenth and Beginning of the Twentieth Century'), presented in 1949, at the Institute of Philosophy, USSR Academy of Sciences, Moscow. He maintains that Donish and his followers created political awareness amongst the forward-looking people of Uzbekistan.[27]

9 In the introduction to her Russian translation of Donish's work *Risala Ya Mukhtasari az Tarikh-i Sultanat-i Khanadan-i Manghitia*, under the title *Traktat Akhmada Donisha, 'Istoriya Mangitskoi Dinastii'*,[28] I. A. Nadzhafova argued that initially Donish's ideas were aimed at transforming the Emirate from feudal despotism to enlightened constitutional monarchy. However, Donish understood in the second phase of his creative work that reforms were not possible, and advocated the destruction of the Manghit dynasty.[29]

10 Z. Radzhabov, another well-known Soviet orientalist, has written on Donish in two major books. In the first, *Iz Istorii Obshchestvenno-Politicheskoi Mysli Tadzhikskogo Naroda vo Vtoroi Polovine XIX i v Nachale XX Vekov* ('From the History of the Socio-Political Thought of the Tajik People in the Second Half of the 19th and at the Beginning of the 20th Century'), published in 1957, he devotes a full chapter (52 pages) to Donish, in which he argues that Donish called upon his people to learn from the Russians, but at the same time to resist the colonial policies of the Czars; thus, Donish wanted to use the enemy's own science and technology against them.[30] Donish did not realise, however, that this would mean direct participation in the revolutionary struggle and the forming of an alliance with the revolutionary Russian people. According to Radzhabov, this discrepancy led Donish's followers in two diametrically opposed directions. One group worked primarily for social and educational reforms, but opposed revolution, while the other was in favour of revolution.[31] Radzhabov, like Ulugh-Zade, does not accept that Donish was a *jadid*, since the *jadid* worked for partial reforms,[32] while Donish, he believed, advocated radical change.

Radzhabov's second work, *O Politicheskom Traktate Akhmada Donisha*[33] ('About Ahmad Donish's Treatise on Politics'), published in 1976, comprises 125 pages and deals exclusively with Donish's work *Risala Dar Nazm-i Tamaddun vo Ta'vun*. Here Radzhabov attempts to analyse

Donish's political thought. He traces Donish's evolution from an 'enlightener', wanting limited reform, to his call for the overthrow of the Emir.[34] Radzhabov's work, though interesting, suffers from a number of shortcomings, the most serious being the weakness of the translations from Tajiki into Russian. For example, Radzhabov translates the tenth point of Donish's section on the armed forces of the Emir thus:

> The enemy should be beaten to the end without giving him the opportunity to rest. One should not dismiss the army soon after the war because the enemy, after gathering strength, can attack again.[35]

A more accurate reading would be:

> Small victory is enough, one should not follow the enemy to the end. Many victories have been turned into defeats by doing that. One should be vigilant and should not dismiss the army soon after the victory because the enemy may gather strength and attack again.[36]

As is evident from this example, which is by no means unique, the meaning is drastically altered in translation. Radzhabov also tends to interpret Donish's views in terms of the prevailing Communist ideology. Most significantly, he fails completely to take into account the antecedents of Donish's thought, especially the links with well-known earlier Muslim thinkers such as, for example, Abu Hamid Muhammad al-Ghazali (1058/9–1111).

Besides the works described above, Bagauddinov, Braginskii, Mirzo-Zade and many others wrote about Donish but, by and large, they express similar views.

BIOGRAPHICAL SKETCH

Ahmad Donish was born in Bukhara in 1827, the son of a poor *mulla*. His father, Nasir, originally a *dehqan*, came from the village of Sogd in the Pirmast *amlakadari*. Nasir began his studies in a local school and later joined a *madrasa* in Bukhara. After completing the *madrasa*, he decided to stay in the city and became the *imam* of a mosque in one of the *mohalla* ('quarter') of the city. He constructed a house in the *Kucha-i-Sangin* ('Stone Street'), where Ahmad Donish was born.[37]

Donish's mother was a literate woman, known to have been a poetess, who opened a girls' school in her house. Donish got his primary education from his mother. He learned to read and write at home and, even as a child, attempted to write poems. He was also very fond of drawing and used to draw geometrical figures on the walls.[38]

His father wanted Donish to become a *qari* ('one who recites the Quran'), and sent him to the *maktab* ('elementary Quranic School') at the age of nine. Learning the Quran by heart involves frequent recitation of the verses, and Donish suffered from a congenital stammer, making it very difficult for him to recite. He gradually came to dislike his father's wishes:

> I did not like the continuous repetition of the same verses and could not develop a desire to learn them by heart. I felt that it was a sheer waste of labour. I observed that a *qari* could only teach children, and thought, why am I compelled to become that? The end result was a bunch of noisy children and a teacher who beats them every so often,[39]

wrote Donish.

The famous orientalist Arminius Vambery, who visited Bukhara in the second half of the nineteenth century, describes a similar school in these words,

> The greatest interest attaches to the primary school posted in the very centre of the bazaar, and often in the immediate neighbourhood of between ten and fifteen coppersmiths' workshops. The sight of this public school, in which a Mollah, surrounded by several rows of children, gives his lessons in reading, in spite of the noise, is really comical. That, in a place where sturdy arms are brandishing hammers, hardly a single word is audible, we may readily suppose. Teachers and pupils are as red in the face as turkey-cocks from crying out, and yet nothing but the wild movement of the jaw and the swelling of the veins indicate that they are studying.[40]

Donish began playing truant from school and spent most of his time in the main squares of the city: *Registan* ('Desert') and *Labe-Hauz-i-Divonbegi* ('Bank of the Pond of Divonbegi'). There he listened to the stories narrated by street story-tellers. He was fascinated by stories about the Prophets and saints and about rulers' battles for power. Whenever Donish disappeared from his school or home, his father always found him in gatherings where history was being narrated. Donish remained at the *maktab* for three years. He wrote later,

> I was extremely unhappy when I was learning the Quran by heart: having hardly mastered a verse, I had to move on to another. At times I would write the text on a piece of paper and cheat the teacher.[41]

However, with great difficulty, in three years, he managed to memorise the Quran. But

> I forgot every thing soon. During the second reading of the Quran, I faced the same difficulties. I was sick of all that, became lazy, dull and lost every trace of my intellectual faculties. In the end my memory actually weakened,[42]

Donish explained.

Not finding his education at the *maktab* fruitful, Donish entered the *madrasa* on his father's advice. The official curriculum at the *madrasa* included: the Arabic language, its morphology and syntax; logic; rhetoric;

Muslim interpretation of the natural sciences; rules of ablution, fasting, burial and pilgrimage to Mecca; procedure of buying and selling; rules for owning and freeing slaves; rules of marriage and divorce, and other practices established by the *Shari'a*, necessary for religious or state activities.[43] His years of education at the *madrasa*, although fraught with serious economic difficulties, played a significant role in Donish's intellectual development. The peaceful atmosphere of his cell at the *madrasa* gave him ample opportunity to study history, literature, astronomy/astrology, geometry, fine arts and music on his own. He learned the art of calligraphy independently, without any guidance, and invented certain new methods and rules.[44] In order to meet his expenses at the *madrasa* he worked as a scribe and wrote other people's *divon* ('collection of poems') and illustrated them. He also painted landscapes and animal figures in the classical miniature style.[45]

The Emir's chief architect noticed Donish's work and was impressed by the talent of the young artist. He recommended Donish to the Emir for service at court. The Emir called Donish to the court and ordered him to rewrite, in simple hand-writing, books of medicine and history. For every rewritten manuscript Donish received 10 *dirhams* ('silver coins'). In the early 1850s, when Donish was almost 25, his mentor, the chief architect, died. Donish was then promoted by the Emir to the vacant post, for a fixed salary of 1,000 *dirhams* per annum.

> From dawn to dusk the Emir compelled me to sit in the palace and consulted me on questions formerly answered by my deceased predecessor. Moreover, architects and artists worked on my orders,[46]

wrote Donish.

His work at the court of the Emir gave him ample opportunity to observe closely the ways of the Emir, his Ministers and other high-ranking civil and military officers. While working as an architect and calligrapher at the court, Donish continued his studies in astronomy, history and other natural and social sciences. Aini confirms that he could foretell the exact time of lunar and solar eclipses.[47] Donish's talents earned him great respect at court. He was called Ahmad *Kalla* (Ahmad 'the head'), both because of his vast knowledge in various fields, and because he physically had a big head.

In 1857, during the reign of Emir Nasrullah, the government of Bukhara sent an official delegation to St. Petersburg. Its main purpose was to offer condolences to the Russian government on the death of Czar Nicholas I, and to congratulate the new Emperor Alexander II on his accession to the Russian throne. Another purpose of the delegation was to begin negotiations to strengthen and expand trade links between the two countries. Donish was appointed as Secretary to the delegation. The Emir personally charged him to

study the local [Russian] internal state structure, the position and standing of
the Russian government, and report back to the Emir.[48]

Until that time the Bukharan government's only sources of information
about Russia were Bukharan traders and travellers. Donish reached St.
Petersburg on January 9, 1857 and stayed there until January 12, 1858.
Besides taking part in official negotiations and meetings with ministers and
other officials of the Russian government, Donish was able to visit some
important places, such as the Technological Institute, the Emperor
Alexander's manufactory, St. Isaac's Cathedral, the porcelain factory, the
Imperial Botanical Gardens, the Museum of the Imperial Academy of
Sciences, the Pulkovskii Astronomical Observatory, the Mint, and *Tsarskoe
Selo*.[49] He was impressed by the level of scientific, technological and
cultural achievements in Russia.

Muzaffar, Nasrullah's son, succeeded him as Emir in 1860, after a brief
power struggle, despite the fact that Emir Nasrullah had nominated his
grandson as his successor. After taking control, Emir Muzaffar drove out all
the ministers and officials of his father's time because he suspected them of
supporting his rival.[50] The atmosphere of endless intrigues, slanders and
calumny compelled many to resign from court service, and most were
reduced to a state of poverty. Donish somehow survived, remaining in court
service, though without a specific post.

By this time Donish had gained recognition as a scientist and artist in the
most enlightened and civilised circles. He tried to influence the Emir to
bring about reforms, primarily in the field of science and education. In a
qasida ('song of praise') devoted to Emir Muzaffar, he wrote that if the head
of a state wishes the prosperity of his country, he should seek out eminent
and educated scientists, writers, doctors, artists and should not be
surrounded by bloodthirsty scoundrels and tyrants.[51] The Emir paid little
attention to Donish's advice.

After the war of 1866–1868 and the conclusion of a peace treaty with
Russia, Emir Muzaffar sent a mission to St. Petersburg, in which Donish
again participated. The aim of the mission was to convey the Emir and his
government's feelings of loyalty and friendliness to the Russian Emperor
Alexander II, and also to request the Czar to return some of the land that
had been annexed after the war (including Samarkand). The mission reached
St. Petersburg on November 2 or 3, 1869 and remained there until
December 10, 1869.[52] On his second visit to St. Petersburg Donish observed
the political, economic and cultural life of Russia in greater detail. He visited
the Agricultural, Geological and Transport Museums, the Observatory,
the Paper Mill, the State Bank Treasury, the Glass and China Factory, the
Shipyard, the Kronstadt fort, etc. He also watched operas and ballets and
attended the unveiling of the memorial to Catherine II. He became a firm
friend of Qazimbek, a dragoman of the Russian Foreign Ministry, whom

Donish considered a well-educated and civilised person. Qazimbek generously helped Donish to understand the general features of Russian society and the customs and ways of life of the Russian people. In official meetings and receptions Donish was given special attention and respect by the Russian ruling circles because he was the most educated and erudite member of the mission. On his return from St. Petersburg, Donish's stature at court grew further and in 1871–72 Emir Muzaffar awarded him the senior religious title, *Uraq* ('a clerical title granted to the *sayyid*, the descendants of the Prophet)'. The Emir also offered him a high administrative post in the central state apparatus. Recognising the fact that without fundamental restructuring of the system of government, he could not improve the general situation of the country, Donish declined the offer.[53]

In 1873 the Emir again sent a delegation to St. Petersburg, this time in connection with the Czar Alexander II's victorious Khivan campaign and the wedding ceremony of his daughter. The head of the delegation was Abdulqadir Dodokho; Donish was his first deputy. The delegation reached St. Petersburg on January 6, 1874 and stayed there for a month and a half. During this trip Donish had the opportunity to meet the Russian Emperor personally. On one such occasion, the Czar said,

> You are praised as a well educated man, having visited this area twice or thrice.[54]

As a mark of respect the Emperor presented Donish with a microscope, a compass, a pair of binoculars and a globe.[55]

Two brief articles in the Russian newspapers *Golos* ('The Voice') and *Novoe Vremya* ('The New Times'), which covered the Bukharan emissaries' visit to St. Petersburg in 1874, also mention Donish. The former reported that 'There are two secretaries to the Bukharan delegation, Mirza Ahmad Uraq and Mirza Abdul-Wahab. Mirza Ahmad (i.e. Donish) is conspicuous, owing to his education and enlightened views of life. Having visited St. Petersburg earlier, in 1869, he has written his memoirs about Russia, in which he describes his impressions of the European way of life and civilisation in a sound and interesting way. This Mirza Ahmad Uraq is a writer and poet, and at the same time an astrologer, who foretells the future'.[56]

The newspaper *Novoe Vremya* reported that 'Mirza Mir Ahmad, who holds the title of *Uraq*, is the second highest officer of the embassy. He visited St. Petersburg for the first time in 1857, in the retinue of Mulla Dzhan, who, on behalf of the Emir Nasrullah, congratulated His Highness, the Emperor Alexander II on his accession to the throne. He visited Russia for the second time in the retinue of Tura Dzhan, son of the present Emir. This wise man, who fully justifies the trust the Emir reposes in him, has come to convey the Emir's feelings of loyalty and gratitude to the Russian government for granting him patronage'.[57]

On his return the Emir once again offered Donish a responsible position in the state apparatus. Donish told the Emir that he must introduce reforms if he wanted him to accept any post in the administration.[58]

In the late 1870s, the Emir appointed Donish as a *qazi*, initially of Guzar and later of Narpai. The main purpose of the appointment was to keep Donish out of the capital because the Emir was fearful of his growing popularity among the intelligentsia. In the 1880s, after the death of Emir Muzaffar, Donish returned to Bukhara and became the head of the Jafar Khoja library. There he continued his creative work. When his enemies, especially the *ulama*, realised that he was no longer the Emir's favourite, they tried to declare him a heretic.[59] The progressive intelligentsia of the time came to his rescue and gave him moral support. Poets, musicians and scientists gathered constantly at Donish's house for literary and musical functions. Very often questions of the social structure of Bukhara were discussed at these gatherings. Sometimes Donish gave accounts of his visits to Russia. People such as the poet-musician *mulla* Karamat Dilkash, musicians and tambura players such as Muhammad Saleh and *mulla* Sikandar, singers such as qari Kamal and Mirza Zuha, the flute player Tursunkhadzha, the calligrapher *mulla* Abdullo, and the poets Shamsudin Shaheen and Muztarib attended these gatherings. In the last years of his life Donish fell ill and was bed-ridden. He died in Bukhara in March 1897.

DONISH'S WORKS

Donish was a prolific writer. He wrote in Farsi. Much of his work has been lost because he used to give away his writings to his friends. Although he wrote a number of books, the two most important surviving manuscripts are *Navadir-ul-Voqai* ('Rare Events') and *Risala ya Mukhtasari az Tarikh-i Sultanat-i Khanadan-i Manghitia* ('A Short Treatise on the History of the House of the Manghit Emirs').[60] The most significant part of *Navadir-ul-Voqai* is *Risala Dar Nazm-i Tamaddun vo Ta'vun* ('Treatise on Patterns of Civilisation and Cooperation'). This work, along with *Risala ya Mukhtasari az Tarikh-i Sultanat-i Khanadan-i Manghitia*, give a fairly clear picture of Donish's political philosophy and his social thought. *Navadir-ul-Voqai* was written in 1875,[61] and *Risala ya Mukhtasari az Tarikh-i Sultanat-i Khanadan-i Manghitia* was written at the end of Donish's life, around 1895–97.

Another important manuscript, *Majmua-i Hikoyat-i Ahmad Kalla* ('Collected Works of Ahmad Kalla' [i.e. Donish]) was written in 1877. According to Mominov 'the book narrates important historical events of Central Asia, pertaining especially to the nature of Ulugh beg's rule and the sayings of the famous poet Jami. The book also contains Donish's critical views of *Kalam* ['scholastic theology']'.[62]

Donish's work *In Risalaist Islah Mioni Shi'a vo Sunni* ('Direction Regarding Peace Between Shi'as and Sunnis'), written in 1894, deals with the history of Central Asia, especially the struggle between Shi'as and Sunnis. Mominov states, 'this work analyses the religious teachings and the search for a path towards truth. It studies 'true' religion and the story of how every Muslim, Christian or Jew considers his religion to be true. It also deals with the appearance and nature of the sects and gives suggestions on how to regulate religious differences and the struggle between the sects. He analyses the philosophical thought of Rumi, Ghazali, Bedil and other thinkers. Judging by this work Donish seems to be a free thinker'.[63] Radzhabov calls this work *Namus al-Azam* ('Fundamental Law').[64]

Most of Donish's astronomical opinions are contained in his diaries *Dafter-i Taqvim* ('Table of Periodicity'). Mominov states that Donish was critical of the geocentric world view and substituted the heliocentric cosmology.[65]

Primary Sources

1 *Navadi-ul-Voqai* ('Rare Events'): The present study is based on the sections of *Navadir-ul-Voqai*, a collection of 23 separate works. Together they deal with a wide range of subjects, from a reform project for Bukhara to advice on family and social matters. Eight copies of the manuscript are known. Two are in the Firdausi Tajik State Library, Dushanbe; one is in each of the libraries of the Tajik State University and the Institute of Language and Literature of the Academy of Sciences of Tajikistan, Dushanbe; three copies are in the Institute of Oriental Studies, Academy of Sciences of Uzbekistan, Tashkent; and one is in the Institute of Oriental Studies, Academy of Sciences of Russia, St. Petersburg branch. This last copy is in Donish's own hand. The work has not as yet been published in full. However, in 1957 extracts from Donish's own copy of *Navadir-ul-Voqai* were published in Tajikistan.[66] Later these extracts were translated into Russian and published in 1960 under the title *Puteshestvie iz Bukhary v Peterburg* ('Journey from Bukhara to Petersburg'). In 1964 it was translated into Uzbeki by the Academy of Sciences of Uzbekistan, in cooperation with the Institute of Philosophy and Law, Tashkent. In 1976 the first section of the manuscript, *Risala Dar Nazm-i Tamaddun vo Ta'vun*, was published in the original Persian in Dushanbe.[67] The copy used in the present work is a microfilm copy of the manuscript of *Navadir-ul-Voqai* in the Institute of Language and Literature, Academy of Sciences of Tajikistan, Dushanbe, inventory No. 1635. Written on low quality paper, approximately 210×250mm, it comprises 700 pages. The handwriting is fairly legible, and *Nasta'liq* script has been used.

Risala Dar Nazm-i Tamaddun vo Ta'vun ('Treatise on Patterns of Civilisation and Cooperation', hereafter, *Risala*): The particular focus of this study, consists of 108 pages (6–113) of the manuscript of *Navadir-ul-Voqai*.

It is divided into a preface (*muqaddama*), three chapters (*fasl*) and a conclusion (*khatama*).[68] The chapters are as follows:

Chapter 1 On the Virtue of Rulership, the State and the Ruler's Attitude towards God.[69]
Chapter 2 On the Attitude of Rulers towards the Army and Retinue.[70]
Chapter 3 On the Ways of Exercising Rule and Understanding the Needs of Subjects.[71]

The *Risala* is addressed to the Emir Muzaffar, and contains a reform project for Bukhara based on the Uzbek and European systems of government.[72] The *Risala* is similar in style to the books of advice for rulers that constituted a popular genre of classical Arabic and Persian literature. These works are often witty, but the confusion between ethico-religious and practical criteria, and the quest for rhetorical effect, often prevent a rational consideration of the subject matter. They do not usually provide a systematic treatment of the problems of government, state or society. Exceptions are the works by Abu Yusuf Mawardi (d. 798), whose approach was strictly rational within the limits of his doctrinal postulates, and Abu Nasr Farabi (d. 950), who attempted to reconcile Platonic theories with Islamic concepts.[73] Such authors of books of advice, however, do not touch upon constitutional law and political theory, and simply take for granted the existence of an Islamic state in whatever form they can themselves conceive it. Some of the best known and most interesting books of advice were written in Persian, during the Seljuq period, for example, the *Qabusnama*, composed in 1082 by Kai Kaus ibn Iskandar;[74] the *Siyasatnama* of Nizam al-Mulk (1018–1092),[75] and the *Kitab Nasihat Al-Muluk* of Abu Hamid Muhammad al-Ghazali (1058/9–1111).[76]

Donish followed the pattern of these earlier compositions, using edifying anecdotes and aphorisms to illustrate his precepts. What is exceptional about his work is that it communicates fresh and sensible ideas that reflect the actual problems of Bukhara. His reactionary contemporaries rejected this approach because, they said,

> The time for writing books has passed. One should be holy and specially gifted to write a book.[77]

Donish, however, notes with sorrow that not only were his contemporaries ignorant of the fact that hundreds of books were being published in Iran, Turkey and European countries, but most of them could not even imagine the existence of other countries.[78]

2 *Risala ya Mukhtasari az Tarikh-i Sultanat-i Khanadan-i Manghitia* ('A Short Treatise on the History of the House of the Manghit Emirs'): The work now usually known by this title was first cited by Professor E. Bertels in his article 'Rukopisi Proizvedenii Akhmada Kalla' (*Trudy Tadzhikistanskoi*

Bazy Akademii Nauk SSR. Vol. 3, Moscow 1936). He used a single copy of the work, given to him by Fitrat in 1933.[79] This manuscript is entitled «*Risolaji tarjumaji ahvoli amironi Bukhoroji Sharif*», which Bertels translated as *Zhizneopisaniya emirov svyashennoi Bukhary.* However, Bertels believed that this title was given to the work by scribes after Donish's death, and preferred himself to call it *Risola* or *Traktat.*[80]

By 1960, five copies of the work had been discovered in various *fondy* ('archives') of Central Asian libraries.[81] The treatise was first published in Stalinabad under the title of *Tarikhcha* ('Short History') in Tajiki in 1959.[82] The following year it received a scholarly edition, edited by Abdulghani Mirzaef, who collated all five manuscripts and published it in Stalinabad in the original *Nasta'liq* script.[83] He preferred to give it the title *Risala ya Mukhtasari az Tarikhi Sultanati Khanadani Manghitia* ['A Short Treatise on the History of the House of the Manghit Emirs'].

A Russian translation of the same work by M. N. Osmanov, entitled 'Istoricheskii Traktat', was published in 1960 under the editorship of Kh. S. Aini and R. Hadi-Zade.[84] Another Russian translation of the same work by I. A. Nadzhafova, under the title *Traktat Akhmada Donisha, 'Istoriya Mangitskoi Dinastii'*, was published in Dushanbe in 1967.[85]

In Mirzaef's edition, the *Risala ya Mukhtasari az Tarikh-i Sultanat-i Khanadan-i Manghitia* (hereafter, *Risala Mukhtasari*) consists of 170 pages (3–173).[86] The work begins with extensive discourse on the rhythm of the historical process and then briefly discusses the reign of the Manghit Emirs. We can roughly divide the work into two parts: (i) the historical account of the reign of Emir Danyal (1758–1785), Shah Murad (1785–1800), Hayder (1800–1826) and Nasrullah (1827–1860), of which Donish could have only an indirect knowledge, based on oral reports and existing written material; (ii) the eye-witness account of the reign of Emir Muzaffar (1860–1885) and Abd-al Ahad (1885–1910).

In the *Risala Mukhtasari*, discussing the rhythm of the historical process, Donish concludes that the world cannot continuously prosper, for, if there is eternal prosperity, people will multiply at an exorbitant rate, leading to catastrophic epidemics.[87] Therefore, there are periods of 'rise' (prosperity) followed by periods of 'fall' (decay). Periods of prosperity, for Donish, are associated with life, water and justice, and periods of decay with death, lack of water and tyranny.[88]

In Islam there is a widely held belief that every century or millennium, a *mujaddad* ('renewer') appears in every community (not limited to Muslim societies) to create equilibrium. Donish believed that if the *mujaddad* appears for a millennium, the first five hundred years are a period of rise and the following five hundred years are a period of decay. If the *mujaddad* appears for a century, the community prospers for the first fifty-year period and then decays for fifty years.[89] Donish considered Tamerlane (1336–98) the *mujaddad* for the eighth Islamic century, and Sultan Mirza Hussain

Bayqara (1469–1506), Emir Abdullah Khan II (1557–98), Subhan Quli Khan (1680–1702) and Emir Shah Murad (1785–1800) *mujaddad* for their respective centuries.[90]

Donish praises Emir Shah Murad (1785–1800), known in Bukhara as Emir Masum, for his just rule[91] but criticises his predecessor Danyal (1758–1785) and Emir Murad's successors for misrule and tyranny. Donish's interpretation of his own time is that it is a period of decline.[92] He openly criticises Emir Muzaffar and Emir Abd-al Ahad for vice, greed, despotism and incompetent government.

Donish's account of the reign of Emir Muzaffar and Abd-al Ahad carries particular weight because he was a first hand observer of those events, and even an active participant. He reports facts, critically evaluates them and adds his own interpretation and suggestions.

MAIN THESES OF DONISH'S WORK

Donish believed, in accordance with traditional Muslim concepts, that man is in essence a combination (*murakkab*) of *aql-i-sharifa* ('noble intellect' or 'reason') and *nafs-i-kasif* ('lower self'). Faith and infidelity are part of man's essence: sometimes faith and at other times infidelity dominates him. The domination of reason leads towards intellectual thinking and draws his attention to the spiritual and temporal worlds. The domination of his lower self leads man's attention towards sensory objects and lower spirits.[93] Donish thought that man is free to choose and to take different paths because the purpose of his creation is not known. However, he favoured a middle path and considered *aql* ('reason') and the *Shari'a* to be the best guide to the middle path. One should not follow that which is not permitted by *aql* and the *Shari'a*.[94]

Although Donish does directly state this, it should be borne in mind that in the earliest period after the Prophet of Islam, Muslims had regarded reason and tradition as complementary, and reason and revelation, or reason and *Shari'a*, were not seen as distinct. Later, in the eighth and ninth centuries, an opposition between reason and *Shari'a* was introduced by Muslim rationalists called Mu'tazila, who declared both theology and basic moral principles to be fit objects for human reason to investigate.[95] In reaction to this almost unbridled freedom of human reason, the orthodox, in complete disregard of the attitude of early Islam, totally rejected human reason, citing the Power and Will of God as the only factors governing human life and action.[96] Donish wanted to restore reason to its original role, not distinct from *Shari'a*.

Donish took a firm and progressive philosophical position on the issue of divine destination and freedom of will, maintaining that man possessed free will.[97] This stance encouraged freedom of thought and action. Early Muslims, too, had regarded man as responsible for his actions and strongly rejected deterministic interpretations of Islam. However, during the Middle Ages, the balance of forces on the question of free will changed, and subsequently remained overwhelmingly in favour of determinism. Muslim philosophers in general advocated a pure rational determinism; Sufism, on the basis of these philosophical teachings and the theological doctrine of the Unity of God, preached monistic determinism; and *Kalam* taught a complete theistic determinism. Politically, this attitude had sustained, and had been sustained by, despotism.[98] Against this background, the importance of Donish's ideas of human freedom of thought and action, and their progressive nature, can readily be understood.

Donish also advocated the independent reading (translation) of the basic texts of Islam and only then for a comparison to be made with the translation of earlier authorities.[99] This implies that he was against *taqlid* and tended to support *ijtihad*.

What a 'Just' Ruler Ought to be

After long consideration of the deplorable situation of Bukhara, Donish identified the chief cause of its decline as the rulers' violation of the *Shari'a*. He believed that

> to rule a country is a great job. It is like deputising for God. He [the ruler] should be Godlike in all his *awamir o nawahi* ('do's and don'ts'). This means fulfilling one's duty to God. The essence of ruling is knowledge and the performance of [good] deeds.[100]

> Like a passenger, man has been sent to this world for a limited period; his beginning is the lap of his mother, his end the grave. The material world should not become an aim in itself. The ruler should engage himself in worldly things only to fulfil essential needs. Whoever strives for more than the bare minimum, it will become deadly poison to him. Nothing is dearer to God than just rule. A day's rule by a just *sultan* ('ruler') is worth more than sixty years of prayers.[101]

Donish knew from experience the arbitrary nature of the rule of the Bukharan Emirs, their greed for excessive wealth, their disregard for the welfare of the people. He wrote,

> To govern a country is a delicate issue, it is a science, one should be very careful about it. Rulers should take pride in justice and fairness. If he [the ruler] wants to serve God, he should be kind and serve the people.[102]

The *Risala* revolves around the idea of a 'just' ruler. It encapsulates ten principles cited below as a basis for good governance. Donish conveys these ideas in succinct phrases, illustrating them by reference to verses from the Quran, sayings from the Traditions, and examples from the lives of the four rightly guided Caliphs and other great Muslim rulers. Donish does not give any titles to his precepts. For the sake of clarity we have given titles in accordance with the content.

1 Fairness:

In every situation that arises the ruler should imagine that he is the subject and the other person is the ruler; anything that he would not sanction for himself, he should not sanction for others. To do so would be to make fraudulent use of the authority entrusted to him.[103]

To illustrate this precept Donish recounts that

On the day of Badr[104] the Prophet Muhammad was sitting in the shade when Gabriel[105] came down and said: '[O Prophet of God], you are in the shade and your companions are in the sun. How is this?' Subsequently God's Prophet declared: 'If any person wishes to be saved from Hell and enter Heaven, when death finds him he must remember the words [There is no god but God]; and he must never sanction for any Muslim that which he would not sanction for himself'.[106]

Donish added that

once, the Caliph Mamun had been out riding with Yahya, the Chief Justice of Baghdad. On the way out, Mamun rode in the shade and Yahya in the sun. On the way back home, Mamun rode in the sun and Yahya in the shade. The judge offered to change sides with Mamun because it was shady on his side. Mamun declined the offer, saying, 'on the way out, you rode in the sun and I in the shade. It would not be fair to accept your offer.' The judge said, 'we are always under the shade of the Caliph, riding in the sun for a while would not harm us.' 'You are modest', Mamun replied, 'but I would not violate the principle of justice'.[107]

2 Efficiency:

[The ruler] should not keep petitioners waiting at his court. As long as the Muslims have grievances, he need not occupy his time with supererogatory religious observances; redressing the grievances of petitioners is more meritorious than any work of supererogation.[108]

The illustration that Donish provides here is that

one day, Umar ibn Abd al-Aziz had been attending to the people's affairs. He continued until the time of the noon prayer, and afterwards went home and rested for one hour. His son asked him, 'how can you be sure that death will not come at this very hour, when somebody may still be waiting at the court for redress of a grievance and you will have failed in your duty towards him?' 'You are right', he answered; and he rose and went out.[109]

The Bukharan Emir's own behaviour was very different, as the following passage from Donish shows:

> After morning prayers, before 10 o'clock, many people gather in the Emir's palace, those who come with presents or those who are summoned from the provinces. Most of them come without taking a bath, fearful of being late. The Emir receives the gathering in a disorderly way and calls for reports to be sent to the palace. He examines the reports and if he does not understand them he refers them to the clerks. They explain the matter to him, and if a decision is pronounced by the Emir they write it down; alternatively the matter remains unattended.[110]

A specific example is provided by the case of the local police chief of Ghijduan, who reported the burglary of a house and the murder of two or three persons. A complaint was lodged by the owner of the house against the accused. The police asked for instructions, unable to investigate the case as they had no authority to arrest the thieves.

> If those criminals go to the desert it will be very difficult to arrest them. If the Emir is awake, the matter can be decided before the sun rises. If he is asleep, the decision may be taken after the evening prayer, or even the next day. In short, the investigation of a murder or theft will start only after two or three days. By that time the criminals may have reached Khwarezm.[111]

Donish recommended a system of regular audiences for the redress of grievances and for keeping a check upon officials.

3 Lack of Ostentation:

> [The ruler] should follow the rightly guided caliphs in matters of eating and dress. He should not make a habit of indulging sumptuously in eating and wearing finery; for without contentment, justice will not be possible.[112]

Donish cites as an illustration the story concerning Umar ibn al-Khattab,

> who asked Suleyman, God be pleased with him, 'Have you heard anything about my way of life that might be objectionable?' 'I have heard', he replied, 'that you have been putting two loaves on the tray for your meals, that you possess two shirts, one for night-time and one for day-time'. 'Is there anything else?' asked Umar. 'No', he replied. 'By God', said Umar, 'both these two things shall cease'.[113]

Donish added that

> the day Ali became Caliph he went to the bazaar and bought a shirt. Its sleeves and skirt were long. He cut them with a knife. He was asked why did he do that? 'It is closer to purity and modesty', he replied, 'that suits more the way of the believers'.[114]

Donish advised rulers not to indulge their passions, and warned against worldly evils such as the love of wealth and power for their own sake. Since no distinction was made in the Emirate of Bukhara between the state treasury and the Emir's personal purse, the Emir could spend unlimited resources from the state treasury on his personal well-being.[115]

4 Gentility:

'[The ruler] should make the utmost effort to behave gently and avoid governing harshly. He should not feel burdened while listening to long petitions, and should not shy away from talking to the elderly and orphans'.[116] The Prophet said that rulers who treat their subjects gently will themselves be treated gently at the Resurrection, and prayed: 'O Lord God, treat gently those rulers who treat their subjects gently and treat harshly those who treat their subjects harshly'. He also stated: 'To be entrusted with authority and given command is a fine thing for one who exercises it rightly, but an evil thing for those who exercise it wrongly.'[117]

Donish illustrates this point further by reporting some anecdotes such as:

Hisham ibn Abdal Malik, who was one of the Caliphs, asked Abu Hazim, [who was a saint and ascetic among the *ulama*], 'What policy would lead to salvation in this [royal] task?' He replied, 'Whenever you receive a *dirham*, receive it from somewhere that is lawful, and spend it somewhere that is lawful.' 'And who is capable of doing this?' asked the Caliph. Abu Hazim replied, 'One who refuses to endure Hell and prefers the repose of Paradise'.[118]

Donish wanted the ruler to be kind, gentle and accessible to the common people. In Bukhara, however, it was forbidden to utter aloud the name of the Emir; his subjects did not even dare to look directly at his face. Semyonov reports that

As the Emir's carriage reached the waiting crowd, the people prostrated themselves so that they could not see the face of their ruler.[119]

(For further illustration of this precept given by Donish see Appendix One, a).

5 Consistency:

[The ruler] should not give satisfaction to any person, if to please him a contravention of the *Shari'a* is required. He should be steady and firm in his decisions. Inevitably one party will not be pleased with the ruler's decision; a just ruler cannot satisfy all the people. If the ruler's judgement is impartial and selfless, he should not fear the anger of the people.[120]

69

Donish illustrates this precept by citing that

'Umar ibn al-Khattab used to say, 'Every day when I rise, half of mankind is displeased with me, and it will be impossible to please both the contestants who are to come before me. But a man would be exceedingly ignorant if, for the sake of satisfying human creatures, he failed to satisfy the True God'.[121]

The Emir and his officials publicly declared themselves to be adherents of the *Shari'a*, but, as Donish knew, they frequently violated it. When the Bukharan judges imprisoned offenders the rich and influential could buy their freedom while the poor had to serve long sentences for minor offences. Donish cites many violations of the *Shari'a*, such as, for example, the levying of the *aminona* tax. The laws of the *Shari'a* were used to oppress the people, and to justify the Emir's actions. Donish did not oppose the *Shari'a*, rather, he believed that if the ruler followed the 'real' *Shari'a*, the situation would improve. He did not, however, elaborate his understanding of the 'real' *Shari'a*.[122] Distressed by the crimes that were being committed by the rulers under the guise of the *Shari'a*, he tried to persuade the Emir to introduce written statutes.[123] If the subjects were satisfied with their ruler, he said, God would be satisfied with him, and vice versa.

6 Compassion:

[The ruler] should not frighten the people by his haughtiness and pride. He should endeavour to be the darling of the people through his kindness and generosity. He should keep the troops and the subjects pleased.[124]

Donish points out that according to the Traditions,

the best rulers were those who loved their subjects and were loved by them. The worst rulers were the ones who hated their subjects and in turn were hated by them. If the rulers cursed the people, the people would curse them too. A ruler should not let himself be so deluded by the praise he gets from any who approach him as to believe that all his subjects are pleased with him. On the contrary, such praise is entirely due to fear. He must therefore appoint trustworthy persons to carry out espionage (*tajassus*) and inquire about his standing among the people, so that he may be able to learn of his own shortcomings.[125]

7 Restraint:

[The Ruler] should be aware of the danger of the power and authority entrusted to him. He should understand that in authority there is a great blessing, since he who exercises it righteously obtains unsurpassed happiness, and a good name in this world and the world hereafter. But if any [ruler] fails to do so, he incurs the wrath [of God and the people] and earns an eternal bad name.[126]

The dangers of misuse of authority are attested, according to Donish, by this story told by Ibn Abbas:

> One day God's Prophet came and took hold of the ring of the door of the *Ka'bah*. Inside the edifice of the *Ka'bah* was a group of Quraysh. He told them that the *imams* and *sultans* would be drawn from the Quraysh as long as they should do three things: if asked for mercy, to show it; if asked for judgement, to render it justly; and if their word were given, to keep it. Should any one of them not do these things, the curse of God, God's angels and all God's slaves would rain down upon him, and neither his obligatory nor supererogatory acts of worship would be acceptable to God on High. The Prophet once said: There are three persons on whom God will not look at the Day of Resurrection: the *sultan* who is an oppressor, the old man (*pir*) who is an adulterer, and the dervish who is a boaster.[127]

Donish illustrates this point by many other sayings, including the following:

> The Prophet said that no slave of God [i.e. human being] who has been entrusted with subjects by the Lord can cheat them and neglect their advice without being debarred from Paradise by God. Other sayings of God's Prophet are these: 'If any man is granted authority over the Muslims and does not look upon them as he would look upon the members of his own household, tell him that he will get his place in Hell.' 'Two persons in my community will be denied my intercession: the tyrant *sultan* and the innovator who practices such exaggeration in religion that it goes beyond the limit'. 'The harshest torment at the Day of Resurrection will be for the unjust *sultan*'.[128]

(For further illustration of this precept given by Donish see Appendix 1, b).

8 Discernment:

> The ruler should always be thirsting to meet devout *ulama* and seek their advice; and he should avoid meeting *ulama* with worldly ambitions who might inveigle, flatter and seek to please him in order to gain undue privileges by stealth and deceit.[129]

Donish's illustrations of this precept include such anecdotes as the following:

> Once, Shaqiq al-Balkhi, God have mercy on him, came into the presence of Harun al-Rashid, who said, 'you are Shaqiq, the ascetic.' 'I am Shaqiq', he replied, 'but not an ascetic.' Harun asked him for a word of advice. 'God on high', he replied, 'has seated you in the place where the Truthful [i.e. Abu Bakr Siddiq] sat, and demands from you the same truthfulness as from him. He has set you in the place of the Discerning [i.e. Umar] and demands from you the same discernment between right and wrong as from him. He has put you in the position of the Two Lights [i.e. Uthman], and demands from you

71

the same modesty and generosity as from him. He has placed you in the station of Ali ibn Abi Talib, and demands from you knowledge and justice such as were his.' Harun told him to continue. 'Yes, willingly', he replied; 'God on High owns a house called Hell, and He has made you the janitor of that house. He has given you three things: the public treasury, the sword and the whip. He has told you to keep your people out of Hell with these three things. When an indigent person comes to you, do not deny him access to the public funds; put the oppressors to death with the sword; and when a person disobeys God's commands, chastise him with the whip. Unless you do these things, you will be foremost among the denizens of Hell, and other rulers will replace you.' Harun told him to continue further. 'You are a fountain', he replied, and the subordinate officials are like streams. If the fountain is clear, there can be no damage from silt in the channels; if the fountain is turbid, there will be no hope [of maintaining] the channels.[130]

The holder of authority should keep these anecdotes before his eyes and accept these counsels, which have been given to others before him. From every *alim* whom he meets, he should seek counsel; and every *alim* who meets kings should give this sort of advice, without suppressing the Word of Truth and without flattering their conceit so as to share their tyranny.[131]

(For further illustration of this precept given by Donish see Appendix 1, c).

9 Justice:

[The ruler] should not be negligent of the corruption and oppression of his officials; he should not impose upon the people wolf-natured oppressors as government officials. If any official is found guilty of corruption and oppression, he should be made accountable and dealt with sternly, so that other officials learn a lesson. He must not be content only with personally refraining from injustice, but must discipline his subordinates, slave-troops[132] and servants and never tolerate unjust conduct by them. For he will be interrogated not only about his own unjust deeds but also about those of his subordinates.[133]

Donish illustrates these precepts with sayings such as:

Umar sent a letter to Abu Musa al-Ash'ari [the governor of Basrah], a letter in which he wrote: 'The happiest master of subjects is one whose subjects are happy with him, and the unhappiest is one whose subjects are unhappy with him. Beware of being extravagant, lest your officials come to regard you as such; for you will then be like a sheep which sees a green pasture and feeds copiously until it grows so fat that its fatness is the cause of its destruction, namely of its being killed and eaten.'[134]

(For further illustration of this precept given by Donish see Appendix 1, d).

10 Dispassionate:

[The ruler] should not be dominated by pride and anger, but should be gentle and modest (though not to the extent that incompetent people may congregate around him), or because of pride and anger he will not be able to meet anybody. If pride dominates the king, that arouses anger, and anger will impel him to revenge. Anger obscures and erodes the intellect ... it will be necessary for the ruler in all his affairs to bend his inclinations in the direction of forgiveness; as prophets and holy men (*avlia*) did, if he is determined to rule with pride and anger he will be unwise, ruled by passions like a wild beast.[135]

Donish illustrates the precept by citing the following stories:

Abu Ja'far [al-Mansur] ordered the execution of a man who had committed treason. Mubarak ibn Fazalah, who was present, said: 'O Prince of believers, listen first to one of the sayings of God's Prophet': Hasan al-Basri quotes God's Prophet as having stated that on the Day of Resurrection, when God's creatures are being assembled on the plain, a herald will cry out: 'Let any person who is entitled to favour from God on High stand up. None will stand up except those who have pardoned others.' After hearing this the Caliph pardoned and released the man. Most holders of authority become so angry when a person speaks abusively of them that they proceed to shed his blood. On such occasions the ruler should recall what Jesus said to Yahya: 'If someone talks about you and tells the truth, thank God, and if he tells a lie, thank God all the more; for God will have added [a credit item] to your ledger with no exertion on your part'.[136]

(For further illustration of this precept given by Donish see Appendix 1, e).

Reading *Risala Dar Nazm-i Tamaddun vo Ta'vun*, one is impressed by Donish's subtlety and sagacity. One of the conditions he sets for a just ruler is that he should be loved by his subjects (precept 6). In the case of Emir Muzaffar, to whom these words were chiefly addressed, the situation was quite the reverse. By advancing the idea of a just and popular ruler, Donish was also providing a critique of the Emir.

To sum up, the spirit of these precepts and the subsequent exemplification provided by Donish is essentially revivalist. In proposing his model of government, Donish constantly drew on the teachings of the Prophet Muhammad, his four rightly guided Caliphs, and other eminent and prudent Muslim rulers. He presents his model of government as close to the system which existed in the *khilafat-i rashida* ('rightly guided Caliphate').

Donish's ten principles are set forth in Chapter 1 of the *Risala*. They, and the subsequent examples used to illustrate them, have much in common with those recommended by Ghazali (1058–9–1111) in his book *Nasihat al-Muluk* ('Counsel for Kings').[137] Donish did in fact frequently quote from the works of Ghazali, though without acknowledgement. What is new in

Donish's work is that he adds certain specific conditions. Thus, for example,

> If the ruler does not provide irrigation water to the farmers in time and cannot keep the roads secure from robbers, he has no right to collect *zakat* or *ushr*. If the army cannot defend the people, its maintenance on *zakat* and *ushr* money is not lawful.[138]

Here the contrast with Ghazali is evident, since for Ghazali

> rulership is a gift bestowed, i.e. predestined, by God, and the ruler will be accountable for it to God on judgement day. This implies that the ruler does not owe his power, and is accordingly not accountable for it, to fellow men (be they subjects, troops, *ulama*, or indeed Caliphs).[139]

Donish, however, thought the relationship between ruler and ruled formed a social contract. Thus, as is clear in the example cited above, he considers that the ruler loses the right to collect revenue and other taxes if he is unable to provide irrigation water and security to his subjects. This indicates that Donish accepts the monarchy but demands of it a degree of accountability. His intent, here, is clearly reformist.

Donish was aware of contemporary European concepts of the equality of citizens before the law. As he wrote in 'Dar Vasoyoi Farzondon va Bayoni Haqiqati Kasabhao Peshahao',[140]

> Greek and European thinkers, after a historical analysis of the causes of social upheavals and revolutions in their countries, concluded that they happened because the rulers rewarded one group of people, while they persecuted another by arrests and confiscation of property and wealth. Consequently, the rulers lost the confidence of their subjects, and instead of showing loyalty, the subjects revolted against the rulers. These thinkers, after deliberation, decided that all human beings have an equal right to share peace, work and wealth, pleasure and pain, because they are descendants of one father. Nobody has a right to privilege and special treatment, especially those who do not deserve it. Claims to surplus wealth and high position in society should be justified by a person's knowledge and capabilities. The state itself should be viewed as a living organism of which everyone should demand his rights. The level of rewards and punishments should be strictly fixed and its record be kept in special buildings. Appropriate rewards for merit and punishment for every offence should be stipulated to avoid arbitrariness. The king, like all other people, should receive a salary from the state and not interefere in judicial affairs.[141]

ON STATE STRUCTURE

In his thinking on the state Donish gave paramount importance to the people. They were the wealth creators, who made possible the existence of a state structure, and an army to maintain the stability and independence of a country.[142] In his view, a state was like a city where people could not live unless the following five conditions were fulfilled:

1 There must be a strong and just king. If the ruler is either weak or an oppressor, the neighbouring states may invade.
2 The officials must be just and pious. The villages will be barren and deserted if the officials are oppressive, even though the ruler himself may be just. Oppression by the officials is the same, in effect, as oppression by the king.
3 There must be trained and experienced doctors. Without them, people will fall victim to the ills of war and epidemics. This will in turn lead to disorder and isolation (foreign visitors would be discouraged by the fear of death and disease).
4 People must be kind and friendly. They should create congenial conditions for foreign visitors, since such contacts are beneficial for society.
5 There must be enough river and spring water for irrigation. Without water, agriculture cannot develop, and this in turn will have a disastrous effect on the food supply.[143]

In his writings Donish frequently stressed the importance of having an honest and wise ruler to run the state, but he also emphasised the need for honest and wise officials to run the state apparatus. Donish believed that the Bukharan administration and the Emir's court were dominated by flatterers, time-servers, and ignorant and corrupt people. Caring only about personal advancement, they ignored the interests and prosperity of the country. Donish described them as liars of a high order who deceived the ruler at every step. Such people spread calumnies against those who were honest and conscientious in order to deny them posts at court and access to the ruler. This was the primary reason for the chaotic state of governance.[144] Since the Emir did not trust anybody, nothing could be decided without his consent. The whole burden of government rested on the Emir. The situation was exacerbated by the inclusion in the government machinery of people without merit who could not maintain order in the state's affairs because of their stupidity and lack of wise leadership. Donish believed that men of reason are sagacious, modest and accurate in performing their duties, and act responsibly and selflessly. They do not persecute the people, and accumulate wealth not for themselves but for the people and the country. Had the Emir valued rational abilities and merit, men of reason would not have shunned him, would not have avoided discourse with him. Rather men of knowledge and craft would have gathered around the Emir's court. Their collective talents and skill might have enriched the country and the treasury and the Emirate could have been transformed into a strong and modern country.[145]

The despotic nature of the Bukharan state[146] and the problems of government were, according to Donish, a legacy of Genghis Khan's invasion. Partly this was a broad current in Muslim thought, which attributed the ills of society to the customs introduced by those of Genghis's followers and descendants who converted to Islam. Specifically, the nomadic system of clans, in which property and titles were held in the family, was considered to be un-Islamic, and the custom which persisted in Central Asia until the rise of the Manghit dynasty that the Khan must be a descendant of Genghis seemed to contravene the Islamic principle of equality before God. The Manghit Emir maintained this policy of nepotism. High administrative posts in Bukhara were distributed amongst the close relatives of the Emir and the landed aristocracy, irrespective of their talents and knowledge. For example, the Emir Nasrullah himself had been the *bek* of Qarshi during the reign of his father Emir Hayder. Another of Hayder's sons, Umar Khan, was *bek* of Kerminah. Yet another son, Mir Hussain, was *bek* of Samarkand. Emir Muzaffar's sons were appointed as *bek* in quite a few *valayat*.[147] The title of *bek* was often passed on from father to son.[148] The *bek* enjoyed almost absolute power in their *valayat*.[149] They in turn appointed their own relatives to high posts in the territory under their control. Thus, in twenty-three *amlakadari* of the Hissar *valayat*, the *amlakadar* were relatives of the *bek*.[150]

Donish wanted the ruler to take personal responsibility for appointments to such posts. He should appraise people himself, selecting those with the qualities that were essential for the state, without fearing that they would disagree with him about how to rule the country.[151]

> An eloquent and astute person should be appointed as an Ambassador; a courageous and fearless person should be appointed as an army commander to repulse the enemy and conquer their forts; the humorous and witty should be appointed as companions to the ruler; just, honest, and impartial people should be appointed as *qazi*, *vazir*, *bek* etc. If the ruler does not take into account the above-mentioned qualities in choosing his officials, state affairs will remain chaotic.[152]

Since order, or the lack of it, in state affairs, primarily depended upon the activities of senior officials Donish suggested that the Emir should personally select the key officers of state, having consulted the people. Specifically, these should be two intelligent *vazir*, one to govern affairs pertaining to the income of the country, the other to oversee expenditure. They should have more authority than other government officials. A Commander-in-Chief should also be appointed to head the army and to deal with all its affairs, and a *rais* to run the administration and oversee matters concerning *qazi*, *mufti* and *mudarris'* etc. They should have less authority than the *vazir*. They should be able to act independently, without the sanction of the Emir, except where the treasury was involved. These four posts were considered instrumental by Donish. Moreover, he argued that the ruler should appoint a *musheer* ('advisor') to liaise between the Emir and the court officials. His authority would be less than that of the other four posts. His duties would include informing the Emir when the chief officials sought his approval for an action, presenting the officials' reports to the Emir, and in turn informing the officials [*vazir*, etc.] about the Emir's decisions. The *vazir*, the Commander-in-Chief, the *rais* and the *ulama* would inform the ruler through the *musheer* daily or twice a week about the work they had accomplished. In this way the Emir would remain in touch with the situation. If the Emir approved a decision taken by an official, he would mark it in the register. If he did not agree, or had doubts about a decision, he could overrule it or seek an explanation from the official concerned. If such a system were followed, it would be easier to govern the country. The ruler would have peace and more time for his work.[153] Donish thought that this division of power into various hands would help to bring order to the affairs of state. He was in favour of substantial independence for the highest officials, of a genuine devolution of power, though within strictly specified limits.

Consultation is a traditional feature of Muslim political systems. Drawing upon this, Donish put forward the idea to

> form a consultative house (*mashavarat khana*), composed of intelligent and sagacious people, and considered such institutions absolutely essential for ruling a state in his times.[154]

The members of the house were to be knowledgeable and intelligent people, drawn from all segments of the population; the state was to pay them a salary. They were to give opinions on matters of public and national importance. The Emir would then implement, if he approved, any decision enjoying a consensus in the consultative house. Donish believed that consultation helped to avoid mistakes. The house was to hold its deliberations away from the presence of the ruler, because some members, owing to shyness or fear of the ruler, might decide the matter according to his wishes. The ruler was not to insist upon his opinion and was to listen to the counsel of the members.[155] This proposal, had it been implemented, would have served to limit the absolute power of the Emir.

Donish suggested to the Emir that he take into account the knowledge and experience of candidates for all posts. He recommended that the appointment to a post and the salary should be made subject to passing an appropriate examination.[156] In his opinion the place of the individual in government and society should be determined by his labour, knowledge and experience. 'Their salary should be fixed according to their knowledge. For those who are not competent should not receive privileges.'[157]

On the question of education, Donish's view was that the teaching in the *madrasa* of Bukhara bore no relation to the civil needs of society; it was alienated from the practicalities of life.[158] He pointed this out by suggesting that the *rais* appointed to head the civil servants should be well versed in both religious and worldly sciences as well as poetry and aesthetics. If such a person was not available, two persons should be appointed to fulfil this task: one to deal with matters pertaining to the *Shari'a*, and the other to deal with matters of judicial concern, inheritance, mathematics, geometry, calligraphy, etc.[159] The British officer Alexander Burnes, who visited Bukhara in the nineteenth century wrote,

> the students are entirely occupied with theology, which has superseded all other points: they are quite ignorant even of the historical annals of their country.[160]

Vambery notes that

> with the exception of a few books of logic and philosophy, all the teaching revolves around the Quran and religious casuistry. There are people interested in poetry and history, but such activities must remain secret, because indulgence in those activities is considered to be a sin.[161]

Krestovskii writes that 'strict scholastic method' was used in the Bukharan *madrasa*.[162] Donish advocated the teaching of natural sciences, believing them essential for the preparation of enlightened officials for the state apparatus.[163]

Donish also advocated the observance of modern international codes of diplomatic conduct, with which he had come into contact during his visits to Russia. An enlightened ruler, he argued, should respect the ambassadors of other states. He should address their rulers with respect, even if he hates them and is hostile to them. This method could lead to better relations with other powers. The ruler should not suspect diplomats of espionage; they are representatives of their countries and must be treated with respect. Donish knew that the Emir's officials were ignorant of the most elementary rules of diplomatic conduct. During his visits to Russia, the Bukharan emissaries knew nothing of Russia, its society, or its people and could not talk to them tactfully.[164] He recommended that the Emir appoint astute, penetrating and enlightened people as ambassadors to foreign countries, who should be aware of the religion and laws of those countries.[165]

The need for a strong and just king is a constantly recurring theme in Donish's works since he believed that the prosperity of a country and its people depended upon him.

> The Royal throne is founded on justice. The army, the subjects, water and gold are the pillars of the throne. If any one of these pillars is damaged the whole foundation may crumble.[166]

Donish stresses the importance of the population, since it is they who are the source of a country's income, while the army is an object of expenditure.

If there is no income, the question of expenditure does not arise. Rather, a state cannot exist without its subjects and the subjects cannot remain together without a kind and compassionate ruler. Hence the ruler should be a kind and saint-like protector of the country.[167] Donish considered the ruler as the patron of his subjects.[168] The ruler himself, and the officials appointed by him, should be honest, intelligent, just and astute, men with foresight and of good repute. They should keep their word strictly and should not be lax in the conduct of their duty. When trying a case, the ruler should defend the interests of the weak and dispossessed.

> The just and wise ruler should defend the rights of the oppressed and annihilate the oppressors

stresses Donish.[169]

The ruler should take into account the needs of the people. For example, he should appoint a just *rais*, one who will not promote enmity and division among the people; a *mushrif*, who will collect tax in accordance with the law; police officers, who will secure the roads from thieves and robbers; an *amin*, who will protect people from false weights and measures at the market and ensure stable prices; a *mira'b*, who will ensure a timely supply of water for the people's land and cattle. It is the duty of the enlightened ruler to find such people and entrust them with governing. They should be paid a salary from the state treasury so that they will no longer have to seek pretexts for extracting bribes.[170] Thieves, wrote Donish, are of two kinds: armed bandits who commit robbery on the roads, and *amin* in the market, who rob the people while weighing their products. The just ruler should deal sternly with both of them, since the primary responsibility of a ruler is to defend the rights and property of his subjects from corrupt officials. The illegal misappropriation of private property by officials should be declared an act of plunder. Donish further suggests to the Emir that he assemble a group of honest people who could inform him of the real situation in the country.[171]

The barbaric punishments that were administered in Bukhara disgusted Donish.

> The people should not be maliciously convicted; beating, killing and crushing people is barbaric,[172]

he wrote. He distinguished between accidental or inadvertent crimes and conscious or planned crimes, and recommended that a lenient view be taken of the former, while the latter should be dealt with sternly. The ruler should look into prisoners' complaints and petitions. Innocent prisoners should be freed and minor offenders pardoned.[173] In Bukhara people were severely punished even for minor breaches of the Muslim code of ethics. For example, sleeping during prayer time, smoking in public and flying pigeons on a Friday all had fixed punishments.[174] Donish argues that in the interest of the people, the ruler should ensure prudence and justice by all means.[175]

Donish frequently stresses the need for the ruler to concern himself with the social and material welfare of his subjects.[176] He should be well-informed about the situation of the poor and should take steps to prevent their situation from deteriorating. Likewise, Donish suggests, he should be aware of the position of orphans and widows. The ruler should ensure the safety of the roads, constructing security posts at dangerous points, building *karavan sarai* ('inns') and keeping the roads in a good state of repair.[177]

The ruler should travel about the country to raise the morale of the people and alleviate their problems. Such journeys should be performed at regular intervals: once or twice a year, or, if the country is very large, once every three years. The Emir's retinue on such expeditions should be strictly limited, so as to reduce the huge cost of royal progresses; moreover the Emir's troops should not carry arms, since this would frighten people. Only cowards require arms, wrote Donish.[178] He knew from personal experience the distress that such expeditions could occasion.[179]

Donish considered the development of trade to be an essential indicator of a flourishing economy, and a renewed society. He realised that traders required a safe environment and advocated the appointment of a just *rais* to check the excesses of corrupt officials.[180]

Donish also appreciated the need to encourage scientists, craftsmen and artists by creating a congenial atmosphere in which they could develop their talents. He wanted the ruler to hold meetings with scientists, poets and historians to discuss the situation of the country with them.[181]

The essence of Donish's ideas on the relationship between the ruler and his subjects is very much within the Muslim political tradition, namely, that state affairs should not be run thoughtlessly and imprudently, and that exploitation and oppression of the poor are dangerous. He was well aware of the anger of the population towards the Emir, and warned him:

> Ants, when united, can defeat a cruel lion, and many flies together can defeat an elephant.[182]

Here it seems ants and flies stand for the ordinary people and the lion and elephant stand for the ruler.

He also put it less ambiguously:

> Kings are rulers of their subjects. If they annoy, oppress and create dissatisfaction among the subjects, they invite trouble and enmity to their rule. For only an unwise ruler would tear his own body with his own teeth. The ruler should not permit oppression of his subjects, or the people will curse him.[183]

Donish's opposition to the babaric and cruel punishments to which prisoners were subjected in Bukhara, his advocacy for better treatment of diplomats, and proposals for the social uplift of the poor and the underprivileged point towards a type of humanitarianism in his thought. This concern for man for his own sake may be regarded as influenced by the West, but the inspiration provided by the egalitarian spirit of Islam should not be underestimated.

Social Welfare

The third chapter of the *Risala* contains a number of suggestions for policies which the Emir could pursue to improve conditions in Bukhara. Among them are the following:

1 'The ruler should stipulate that the *qazi* does not penalise the [poor] debtor, especially if in reality the debtor is not in a position to pay back the [rich] lender. Let the [poor] debtor repay the loan according to his means. If he cannot, then the ruler should lend him [the poor debtor] that amount from the state treasury for a fixed term.'[184]

2 The ruler should form a treasury of surplus resources and appoint an *amin* as its chief. To develop trade and crafts, traders and artisans could be lent money from this treasury, for a fixed term, on interest.[185]

3 The ruler should claim rent for gardens and lands according to the lease-holder's actual income over the current year, rather than the amount stipulated in the agreement.[186]

4 Work should be made obligatory for all able-bodied and healthy citizens. Idlers should be forced to work for the prosperity of the country: roads, bridges and large buildings could be constructed by them, and they should be paid. 'If they remain idle they may become unruly and turn into thieves.'[187]

5 For the well-being and stability of the nation, the ruler should maintain physically disabled and unhealthy people at state expense. They should be given training in crafts, such as art, music, calligraphy, bookbinding, basket-weaving, etc.[188]

6 The duty of the ruler is not to rob the public but to ensure that they are properly fed and clothed. To generate resources, Donish strongly advocated the development of a mining industry in the Emirate. In a section of *Navadir-ul-Voqai*, which is presented as a dialogue with the ruler of Peshawar, Donish tells us that the Emir of Bukhara maintained his army on the confiscated property of his subjects. The Emirs could not conceive of any other source of income. They did not think of exploiting the treasures buried in the earth. The Bukharan rulers oppressed the public to collect gold, but due to their ignorance and backwardness, did not explore the areas where gold could be found, though the mountains of Badakhshan contained gold, silver, ruby, lapis lazuli and other precious stones. Donish suggested to Emir Abd-al Ahad that he request

the Russian Government to render help in the exploration of mineral resources in the Emirate. Donish hoped that if the state treasury could earn income from the exploitation of minerals, taxes on the peasantry could be minimised.[189]

7 Donish often points to the problem of water for irrigation. The shortage of water was one of the basic causes of poor agriculture in Bukhara. Donish suggests that a canal be built from the Amu Darya to irrigate the lands of the Emirate: the route he proposed ran through the regions of Kerki and Kelif to Qarshi, Bukhara and Miankal in the Zarafshan valley. To meet the expenses of constructing the canal he proposed levying an emergency tax (*Jul*), of two *tenga* per *tanab*, throughout the Emirate.[190]

Finally, Donish was concerned about the security of the country. He advocated the modernisation of the army and requested the Russian mission to render help in training the Bukharan army.[191] He wrote

> The Emir's troops are of two kinds: the people of the sword, and the people of the pen. The duty of the people of the pen should be the assessment of war booty and the analysis of controversies. The people of the sword should be engaged in repulsing the enemy and eliminating discord.[192]

Donish suggested that the Emir should first apportion a fixed amount from the treasury to support the poor, orphans, the population at large and the state officials, and then, with the rest of his income, should form an army.[193] Moreover, war should be avoided whenever a dispute could be solved by peaceful means, since, Donish believed, war was contrary to human nature, and its consequences harmful for the people and the country. If war became inevitable, it should be fought wisely and in an organised and strategic way. The army should have capable and experienced commanders, since short-sighted, weak and cowardly men could not provide leadership. The ruler should encourage his men. If young officers improved their knowledge and passed their examinations, they should be promoted. Elderly soldiers should be retired. The Commander-in-Chief himself should be courageous, wise and experienced. Donish also made the following practical suggestions:

(i) To deceive the enemy, the ruler should begin his march in another direction, but at the same time prepare for war with the real enemy.

(ii) Before a war begins, the ruler should prepare the necessary armaments, supply the army with its needs, award medals to the troops, and promise rewards in the future.

(iii) Fodder should be provided.

(iv) The ruler should not divert his attention from his troops for a single moment.

(v) The vanguard should be courageous and experienced and should have passed examinations in the art of war.

(vi) The ruler should receive information about the position of the enemy daily and should not let the enemy know about his position.

(vii) During war the option of peace with the enemy should not be ruled out, even if the enemy is a smaller or less populous country, because these factors cannot guarantee victory.

(viii) Discipline is the key to victory.

(ix) An attack should not be started if the wind is blowing in the wrong direction or if it hails. Even the position of the stars should be taken into account.

(x) 'Small victory is enough, one should not follow the enemy to the end. Many victories have been turned into defeats by doing that. One should be vigilant and should not dismiss the army soon after the victory because the enemy may gather strength and attack again.'[194]

CONCLUSIONS

Emir Muzaffar, to whom the project of reform outlined in the *Risala* was addressed, categorically rejected it. As Donish wrote in his preface to *Navadir-ul-Voqai*,

> I wrote the *Risala* taking into account both the Uzbek and the European systems of government. If my treatise was accepted, I was prepared to serve in the court for four to six hours a day and to fulfil any tedious and painstaking work assigned to me. If the Emir did not agree to it, I asked him to release me from court service. 'Let us forgive the horse's offence if he cannot manage the burden meant for an elephant.' I finished the *Risala* but nobody asked about it or felt the need for reform.[195]

According to Donish,

> the Emir scoffed at me in a private meeting [with a close courtier], saying, 'I sent a person to Russia with the embassy, and in the end he began pestering me with advice.[196] I will not send him again'.[197]

Donish finally came to believe that there could be no reform in Bukhara while the rule of the Emir continued. In *Risala Mukhtasari*, which was one of his last works, written probably in 1895–97, Donish blames the Emirs for the decline of Bukhara. He describes Emir Nasrullah as a powerful, ruthless and far-sighted ruler, who crushed every challenge to his rule from provincial rulers.

> Following the path of his father, he promoted religion and the *ulama* and fully implemented the *Shari'a*. He provided an opportunity for his *ahl-i ehtasab* ('supervisors') to forbid drinking of wine, singing and music in public.[198]

According to Donish, Emir Nasrullah did not consult wise men except in times of dire need.

> The Emir had a natural tendency to enjoy the company of young boys, and access to high goverment posts was made easier for this class of people. A large number of beautiful boys travelled with him during royal travels.[199]

Donish accused the Emir of (involvement in) sodomy. In support of his accusation, he cited Raza Quli Khan's continuation of Mirkhond's *Rozat-ul-Safa*, which stated that Emir Nasrullah had declared sodomy *halal* ('lawful') following a *fatva* by Makhdoom mufti Namangani.[200] Donish also criticises the Emir's officials and soldiers for oppressing the people by confiscating property and raising taxes. The *ulama*, fearing the Emir, issued '*fatvaha-i mulaim*' ('soft edicts'), permitting sinful behaviour, and nobody dared to point out to the Emir the real commandments of the *Shari'a*.[201]

Nasrullah's death was followed by a brief power struggle, because he had nominated his grandson to Bukharan throne, instead of his son Muzaffar. In 1860 Muzaffar emerged victorious in this power struggle. Soon after assumption of power he destroyed those who sided with his opponent. He dismissed all high officials who served in the reign of his father and confiscated their property. Donish complains that Muzaffar filled the most important governmental posts by formerly disgraced court dignitaries who had been exiled to Kerminah by the previous Emir and returned to Bukhara when Muzaffar became Emir.[202] These official treated people harshly, oppressed them, and sucked blood of the subjects.

In the first two to three years of his reign Muzaffar attacked Hissar and Kokand and conquered some territory. According to Donish his victories over small neighbours went to his head and Muzaffar became arrogant. He did not recognise anybody, except himself, in the world and began tampering with the *Shari'a* to suit his desires. For example those who stole a small coin were sentenced to death and others who committed murder were not even prosecuted. He imprisoned people for insignificant offences, the minimum period of imprisonment was three to seven years. When prisons filled of offenders, the inmates were brought out in flock and executed.[203] This state of affairs continued till *Mawra Al-Nahr* was conquered by the Russians.

After the death of Emir Muzaffar in 1885, matters became still worse, Donish wrote. In his analysis, poverty, exploitation and oppression increased still further, and 'corruption and debauchery flourished.'[204] Donish believed that all the important government posts were now held by incompetents and people of low character. For example, matters concerning science were looked after by the *Qazi-i Kalan*, and powers to appoint and transfer military commanders were entrusted to Durbin Bai [*Qushbegi Safya*], who had been a senior slave of the Emir's father; one of the ministers, Shah Mirza Inak, a slave of the Emir's, was illiterate.

Russian officials, to defend their interests, increased their interference in Bukharan affairs, and nobody dared to object.[205]

The Emir did not consult with anybody, and did not take the advice of wise people.[206]

The *Risala Mukhtasari* also contains some predictions about Bukhara's future, which Donish presents as the result of his astrological divinations. He says that

all wealth and property which has been collected into the treasury of the state and by the propertied classes through coercion and oppression, will become provisions for unbelievers and spoils for sinners. In the end the heads of the rulers (*umara*) will hang on death ropes [meaning they will be hanged], and the Emirs and high ranking officials, too, will find themselves in an extremely unfortunate position of eternal indigence.[207]

Donish further predicted that the rule of the Manghit tribe in *Mawra Al-Nahr* would end, and astonishing changes and great conflicts would take place. He foretold the weakening of the true faith and of Muslim nations, and the spread of falsehood and unbelief through the world in general, and especially in *Mawra Al-Nahr*. Donish anticipated great disturbances within a period of 36 years. To him, the signs of the decay of the government and the true Islamic faith were obvious: the presence of foolish Emirs, ignorant scholars and negligent military commanders were sufficient evidence to prove it and no further proof was required.[208] If they continued to ignore the *Shari'a*, the effect would happen twice as quickly. What else could be expected if the rulers ignored and tampered with the limits set by God?[209] As the Quran warns,

Have they not observed what is before them and what is behind them of the sky and the earth? If We will, We can make the earth swallow them, or cause obliteration from the sky to fall on them. Lo! herein surely is a portent for every slave who turneth (to Allah) repentant.[210]

'These managers, whom we call His Highness and Mr. *vazir*', maintained Donish, 'These are as the cattle-nay, but they are worse'.[211] He argued, 'If the *Shari'a* were followed, they would be removed from power many times every hour. Nobody would obey them or fulfil their orders, and no one would become a rebel or a trouble-maker by disobeying them. For, 'rule based on justice is the vicegerency [of Allah]. Rule based on tyranny is the [vicegerency] of the devil, yes he would be accursed!' Surprisingly, these words are engraved on the seals of these despicable [people]. And they themselves put these seals on their directives and orders hundreds of times a day, but they do not try to understand the meaning of these words.'[212]

Thus, having believed for many years in the possibility of reform, and having, in good faith, worked on practical and theoretical proposals to accomplish it, Donish finally came to the conclusion that only the complete destruction of the system could open the way to progress.

Donish's political and philosophical thought may have been innovative within the Bukharan context of those days. However, it was not unique within the Muslim world of that period. On the contrary, it reflected very closely elsewhere in the Muslim world, as will be discussed in Chapter Three. It also had some similarities to the ideas put forward later by the Communists. This will be discussed in the Conclusions to this work.

Chapter Three

Muslim Reformism in Bukhara: *Jadidism*

In the early twentieth century a movement to establish schools using more modern methods of instruction (*usul-i-jadid*, from Arabic, 'new method') began taking root in Bukhara. Adherents of this movement aimed at reforming the educational system in order to equip Muslims with modern knowledge and skills and enable them to catch up with Western progress. Later, they began to demand political and administrative reform, though still from an overwhelmingly Muslim perspective. Subsequently, the followers of this movement were known as *jadid* and their ideology as *Jadidism*.

As pointed out in the previous chapters, religion played a fundamental role in Bukhara in the late nineteenth and early twentieth centuries. Islam provided the reference point for all the forces that were trying either to reform or immobilise the country. *Jadidism*, which took root in Bukhara in the first two decades of the present century, became a comprehensive movement for the modernisation of Muslim society in Bukhara. *Jadid* did not envisage the adoption of alien cultural and political practices out of reverence inspired by the fact of Western domination, rather, they advocated an intensive reform achieved through reviving old institutions or creating new ones. Although this reform was conceived in response to the challenges of the West, responsibility for the reform was to lie with the Muslim community. *Jadid* were able to articulate a comprehensive argument for incorporating new cultural, technological and political practices in the language of Islamic tradition. They strove to prove that not only was reform permissible from an Islamic point of view, it was also necessary, indeed incumbent, upon Bukharans as Muslims. In advocating reform, *jadid* made use of the modern means of communication (printed word in the form of newspapers and books) and the new form of sociability that had appeared in Bukhara after it became a Russian Protectorate.

An adequate appreciation of the history of the reformist movement in Bukhara requires an understanding of the inner structure of Islam, its general development, and the mode and roots of reform in the faith. These will be briefly outlined in this section; we shall then discuss the origin and development of the reformist movement in Bukhara.

REFORMISM IN ISLAM: GENERAL BACKGROUND

The central inspiration of Islam is Allah, the One True God, and his revelations to the Prophet Muhammad. This final, complete and perfect revelation of God's Will for all of humanity is recorded in the Quran. Islam means submission to this Divine Will. A Muslim, then, is one who submits to the Will of God as revealed in the Quran. The greater part of the Quran consists of broad, general moral directives – what Muslims ought to do. The Quran envisions a society based on the unity and equality of believers before God, a society in which moral and social justice will abolish oppression of the weak and economic exploitation.[1] The Quran replaced, supplemented or modified earlier tribal practices and laws. For example, the exploitation of the poor and orphans, female infanticide, murder, theft, usury, false contracts, fornication and adultery were condemned absolutely. Many of the Quran's other directives comprise regulations or moral guidance that limit or redefine existing practices. For example, slavery was not prohibited but slave-owners were encouraged to emancipate their slaves.

Muslims affirm the belief that the Quran and the Prophet have laid down eternal norms and principles on which Muslim life, both individual and collective, is to be patterned. Therefore, Muslims are not only to know and believe, but also to act and implement. Belief and action should be joined. The Quran enjoins upon Muslims to strive to realise God's Will in history.

> You are the best community that hath been raised up for mankind. Ye enjoin right conduct and forbid indecency ...[2]

This universal mission to spread the message of Islam throughout the world was the driving force behind Muhammad and the early Muslims who established a religio-political community (*umma*) in Madina.[3] After its advent in seventh century Arabia, Islam swept across the Middle East, Europe, Asia and Africa, and within a hundred years of the Prophet Muhammad's death, produced a mighty empire. The Quran itself and this admirable early history are seen by Muslims as the perfect example of God's Will being implemented in the world.

The Islamic state was a community of believers whose common religious bond replaced individual tribal allegiances, based on blood kinship. God was the sovereign of the state and Muhammad, his messenger on earth, served as Prophet and leader of the community. During his lifetime the Prophet, through the Quranic revelations and by his own conduct and words (*sunna*), was the exclusive source of religious and political guidance. The divine revelation of the Quran remained after his death, but his personal guidance ceased. The Quran is the primary sourcebook of Islamic principles and values. However, besides the detailed pronouncement on the law of inheritance and the laying-down of punishments for crimes such as theft and adultery, which are not defined legally, there is little in the Quran that can be termed legislative.[4] For each generation of Muslims, the continued formulation and implementation of Islamic principles has been a formidable challenge.

The first four Caliphs, in the light of the Quran and the Prophetic teachings, applied their own judgement to resolve the ever-arising issues. Succeeding generations of Muslims have regarded the time of the Prophet and his immediate successors as the ideal period, and the structure of state and society which prevailed then as the ultimate model of the Islamic way of life.

In the centuries to come, an organic, holistic approach developed, in which religion was intimately intertwined with politics, law and society. From the early days of Islam, law has been regarded as flowing from or being part of the concept of the *Shari'a* (lit. 'path leading to water', meaning the divinely ordained pattern of human conduct). The Quran, being the final and most consummate revelation to man, became the primary and indeed the sole director of human life and source of law. A fresh, comparative and interpretative application of the Quran to any given new situation had to consider the method and practice of the Prophet (*sunna*), to whose conduct belonged a unique religious normativeness. This living example (*sunna*) of the Prophet became the second source of Islam. Subsequently the *sunna* was materially extended to include the precedents established by the first four Caliphs and the agreements of the Companions of the Prophet, or at least, of a large number of them, because they were regarded as the living embodiment of the Prophetic *sunna*. The term *sunna* was not further extended to include subsequent generations of Muslims; rather, this is called *ijma* ('consensus'). The agreed practice of the Companions is known both as *sunna* and as the *ijma* of the Companions. Thus, the term *sunna* ends with the Companions and the term *ijma* begins with them.[5] Though no future generation was supposed to be capable of contriving new *sunna*, both the terms *sunna* and *ijma*, were applied to a large body of material produced by the 'Successors' ('the generation which immediately followed the Companions'), through direct deduction and application by individual thinkers. In the ninth century, the *sunna* of the Prophet was compiled in six works that came to be known as *hadith* or Tradition. The *hadith* at this point effectively replaced the living *sunna*, and was accepted as the authoritative second source of the content of Islam besides the Quran. This was accomplished in the name of *ijma* and the epithet 'agreed upon' was attached to it.[6]

Soon after the period of the first four Caliphs numerous differences on legal and dogmatic details had begun to appear. During the Umayyad administration the task of legislation was performed by the recognised religious leaders and jurists of various regions, who largely employed the method of personal opinion (*ra'y*) on the materials of the Quran and the *sunna*, and produced a vast body of uncoordinated religious and legal opinion. As a result separate and diverging rules of law were applied in different cities and provinces, based on independent interpretations of local jurists and teachers. The situation was complicated further by survival of customary law and administrative regulations. Theological sects and a sort of religious methodology began to emerge. Almost simultaneously with this free, individual legislative activity another movement was going on – a drive for coordination and unification that transformed the mass of individual opinions into systematic analogical reasoning (*qiyas*). The term *qiyas* means concluding from a principle embodied in a precedent that a new case falls under this principle or is similar to the precedent, on the strength of a common essential feature called the reason or *illa*. The term is also used for syllogistic reasoning. The movement of thought from the explicitly known to the explicitly unknown is evident in both cases. Later the concept of *ijtihad* ('systemic original thinking') took the place of *qiyas* and became a powerful principle of original thought in Islam. The principle of *ijma* began as a natural process for solving problems and decision-making, and as a check on individual opinion. It is linked with *qiyas*, which is to be performed in preparation for *ijma*. Early schools of law[7] gave the principle of *ijma* an overriding and absolute authority, making it the final and conclusive argument on every issue. *Ijma* acquired this authoritative status not only because it discerned right from wrong in the present and the future, but also because it established the past. For *ijma* was used to determine what the *sunna* of the Prophet had been, and what was the right interpretation of the Quran. In short, both the interpretation of the Quran and the *sunna* were authenticated through *ijma*. Thus *ijma* is an organic process, which creates, assimilates, modifies and rejects at the same time.[8]

The inner structure of Islam has developed in such a way that the Quran has its own identity but the other three principles – *sunna*, *qiyas* and *ijma* – are intimately interwoven. We have seen how *sunna* and *ijma* although distinct, historically pass into one another. *Qiyas* constitutes the inseparable link, since it is a process common to both. This principle of systematic reasoning (*qiyas*), was used not only to interpret the Prophetic *sunna* into law but also to integrate into *sunna* the new social and administrative practices. On the other hand, opinions, the results of *qiyas* activity, by conflict, compromise and adjustment, are gradually precipitated into *ijma*, which has the ultimate decisive authority.

After the ninth century, the *sunna* began to be represented by *hadith* alone, instead of the living *sunna* and *ijma*. *Qiyas* was therefore dislodged from its intermediary positions: between the Quran and the *sunna*, and the *sunna* and *ijma*.[9] In the medieval Muslim theory of jurisprudence, the Quran, the *sunna* of the Prophet, *ijma* and *qiyas* constituted the foundation of Islamic law. Instead of being at the service of *ijma*, and preparatory to it, as had been the case in the past, *qiyas* was put outside it. The orthodox insisted that disagreement, not consensus, would be the necessary result of *ijtihad* and considered that efforts to reach consensus through analogical thinking were vain pretensions. Around the tenth century, both dogma and law took on a definite shape, and the *ijma* arrived at amongst the schools at that time was declared final. Qualifications were established which defined who could exercise *ijtihad*, and on what subjects: these conditions were extremely rigorous and humanly impossible of fulfilment; the door of *ijtihad* was closed.[10] As a result one of the most dynamic and creative epochs of intellectual history came to a sudden end. Islamic law and dogma have developed very little since.[11] The power of *ijtihad* was abolished, and instead a restricted *ijtihad* was allowed: meaning one could either interpret law within one's own school of law or compare law of different schools and find some scope for limited expansion in detail. Throughout the medieval centuries, this state of affairs held sway; occasionally, bold and creative spirits such as Ibn Tamiya (d. 1328) claimed the right to *ijtihad*, but their recognition remained limited.

In the nineteenth century, Muslim reformist thinkers reopened this question by attacking blind observance (*taqlid*) of the authority of the schools and advocating instead the right to *ijtihad*. This reformist approach sprang from within Islam, but the challenge of the West and the permeation of its influence, through political structures, the administrative and judicial machinery, the army, the press, modern education, modern thought, and last but not least, direct contacts with Western society itself, played a role which should not be understated.

The Muslim world realised the need to adapt Islam to modern life after failing in its initial attempts at catching up materially with the West.[12] The immediate expression in the early nineteenth century of this need to adapt in the face of the Western challenge was a call for the revival of early, unadulterated Islam – a return to the golden age of the Prophet Muhammad and his first four Caliphs. This in fact meant going behind medieval authorities to the original sources of Islam. The first reformist movements of this period, for example Wahhabism in Arabia, were revivalist, ultra-conservative, puritan and literalist. Besides reasserting the equality of man under God, they recognised only two authorities: the Quran and the *sunna* of the Prophet, including the precedent of the Companions. They attacked the blind acceptance (*taqlid*) of the authority of the medieval schools in religious matters in general, and instead insisted upon the right to *ijtihad*. They even rejected *qiyas* as a means of interpreting the Quran and the *sunna*. Their insistence on the text of the Quran and the Hadith resulted in absolute literalism and socially ultra-conservatism. On the other hand, by encouraging the exercise of (*ijtihad*), as opposed to the limited exercise of analogical reasoning, with regard to problems not directly covered by the text, the door was opened for more liberal forces to interpret the Quran and *sunna* more freely.[13] The rejection of traditional authorities and the insistence on *ijtihad* by these revivalist movements directly contributed to the intellectual regeneration of Islam.[14]

Revivalism was followed, in the later part of the nineteenth century, by modern and liberal reformism. These reform movements, like Wahhabism, were critical of the contemporary state of Muslim society: its stagnation and degeneration. However, the terms of the efforts at rethinking had changed: revivalist movements, while removing traditional authority, offered very little new material to be integrated into the Islamic legacy and called for a return to pristine Islam, leaving the field empty where *ijtihad* should have worked. This empty field was now filled by the intellectual, political, scientific and technological achievements of modern civilisation. The objective of the reformists was power for Muslims, to be achieved by their political, cultural and spiritual regeneration. This regeneration could be achieved by spreading modern and scientific education and this is why we find movements in Muslim countries advocating reform in the system of education. Emergent nationalism was inseparably bound up with such reformism. Without repudiating the religious foundation of Muslim society, the reformists tried to modernise its very structure, thus applying the spirit of the European Renaissance, though of course in a different form.

Such movements can be observed in almost all the Muslim countries. Thinkers such as Sir Sayyid Ahmad Khan (1817–1898) in India, Jamal al-Din al-Afghani (1838–1897) in Afghanistan, India, Iran, Turkey and Egypt, Muhammad Abduh (1849–1905) in Egypt and Ismail Bay Gasprinskii (1851–1914) amongst Muslims in Russia, nurtured these movements.[15] They all believed in the necessity of acquiring modern education and a knowledge of science for Muslim community.

In Bukhara, Ahmad Makhdoom Donish (1827–1897), a scholar, poet, musician, doctor and court astrologer/astronomer to the Emir Muzaffar, in many respects paved the way for reform. Having visited Russia three times as a member of Bukharan embassies to St. Petersburg, he had realised the need for political, educational and cultural reforms in Bukhara. In his discourse with fellow Bukharan intellectuals, he praised the scientific, technological and cultural achievements of Russia, and tried to encourage a scientific world-view amongst Bukharans by explaining the scientific causes of natural disasters such as earthquakes and natural phenomena such as solar and lunar eclipses.[16] He exposed the ignorance, fanaticism and corruption of the *ulama* and the rulers. Well-known *jadid* such as Abdul Vahid Burhanov and Sadradin Aini attended gatherings in Donish's house; Aini wrote that before reading Donish's writings they had not even been able to imagine that the world could be changed. (For details of Donish's views and reform project, see Chapter Two).

ORIGINS OF THE *JADID* MOVEMENT

We have already discussed in the previous chapter the modernisation of means of communication and economic transformation brought by Russia in Bukhara, which led to the emergence of new social forces and also created a space in the society for people such as booksellers, publishers, translators and professional school teachers to exist. Without this economic transformation and modernisation of the means of communication (rail, postal and telegraph services), the emergence of the reformist movement in Bukhara would have been impossible. The postal system allowed subscription to newspapers, books and magazines and remitted money to distant places. It played a significant role in linking Bukhara to Muslim regions of the Russian empire.

The Russo-Japanese war of 1904 and the Russian Revolution of 1905, which represented challenges to the established order, stimulated the interest of the progressive circles in Turkistan and Bukhara in political and social issues.[17] The 1905 revolution, though unsuccessful, strongly influenced the politically backward Slavs of European Russia, as well as the Turko-Tatar peoples, in that it led to the emergence of several revolutionary and nationalist groups and parties. Its echoes were felt even in remote areas such as Turkistan and the semi-independent states of Bukhara and Khiva. The Tatars of central Russia, the Crimea and the Caucasus, and Muslims of Azerbaijan, politically the most advanced of the Russian Muslims, exerted a major influence on cultural and political developments in Central Asia. Their press, especially newspapers such as *Tarjuman* ('The Translator'),[18] *Vaqt* ('The Times')[19] and the satirical journal from Azerbaijan *Mulla Nasiruddin*,[20] played a significant role in spreading progressive ideas of national liberation amongst the people of Central Asia. Even the terms *jadid* (from Arabic, 'new'), which stood for the progressive forces, and *qadim* (from Arabic, 'old'), which stood for the traditional or reactionary forces, were borrowed from the Tatars.[21] S. Aini confirms the spread of a significant quantity of Persian-language newspapers and periodicals in the Emirate, such as *Habl-al Matin* ('Firm Rope'), published in Calcutta, and *Chehranuma* ('Mirror') from Iran and *Parvarish* ('Upbringing'), published in Egypt.[22]

Other liberal and progressive periodicals, discussing social, political and educational issues concerning Central Asian Muslims, which could have reached Bukhara in the first decade of the present century from neighbouring Turkistan included: *Taraqqi – Orta Azyaning Umr Guzarlighi* ('Progress – Central Asian Life'), edited by I. I. Geier, published in 1906 in Tashkent; *Taraqqi* ('Progress'), edited by Ismail Abidi (Gabitov), published in 1906 in Tashkent; *Khurshid* ('Sun'), edited by Munnawar Qari, published in 1906 in Tashkent; also *Tojjor* ('Merchant'), published in 1907 by Sayyid Karim Bey; *Shuhrat* ('Fame'), edited by Abdullah Avloni in

December 1907; and *Azya* ('Asia'), edited by Muhammadjan Bektemirov in April 1908, all published from Tashkent.[23]

Besides discussing social, political and cultural issues concerning Muslims of Central Asia, such as the unity of Muslims and reform of schools, these periodicals propagated amongst Muslims the need for learning science and enlightenment.[24] An article written by a well-known Turkistani intellectual Munawar Qari entitled, '*Bizin Jahalat, Jahli Murakkab*' (Our ignorance, Our misfortune), published in *Taraqqi* in 1906, criticising parents for not sending their children to school to learn science and modern education can be cited in this regard.[25] The Turkistani writer, Mehmud Khoja Behbudi, who had a close relationship with Bukharan *jadid*, in his numerous articles published in *Taraqqi*, also stressed the need for Muslims to acquire knowledge of modern sciences.[26] None of the independent newspapers which were published from Tashkent survived for more than a year either because of official intrasigence or because of a lack of subscribers. However, during their short span of life each one of them did much to stimulate the cultural awakening of the indigenous population. Under these influences people like Buri Bai Effendi, Mir Khan Parsa Ogli, Qari Burhan and Mirza Muhauddin Mansur Ogli began associating themselves with the reform movement in Bukhara, and called themselves progressives.[27]

Gradually, individual groups of free-thinking and progressive people began to form cultural groups and enlightenment societies in Bukhara, Tashkent, Farghana and Samarkand. Later these loosely coalesced; they came to be known collectively as the *jadid* movement.[28] At first these societies spoke of the need for reform in the existing schools and called for the introduction of modern educational methods. In Turkistan, they evolved into an officially sanctioned movement for culture and enlightenment, which also demanded administrative reforms. Later, after the 1917 Russian Revolution, they came together under the banner of an autonomous Turkistan. In Bukhara, which was still a nominally independent state, they began by demanding reform of the system of taxation, but soon turned into a secret society with a large number of members, which enjoyed considerable sympathy amongst various sections of the population.[29] According to F. Khodzhaev, the different paths adopted by the national liberation movements in Russian-controlled Turkistan and Bukhara were the result of differences in their economic and political conditions.[30] In Turkistan, owing to the relatively better-developed economy, the presence of a greater number of Russian workers, and the activities of Russian political parties, the situation was more favourable for the development of progressive ideas than in Bukhara, which in many ways was still medieval and suffered under the dual exploitation of Czarist capitalism and the Emir's despotism. The opportunities for open political and cultural activities in Turkistan allowed the *jadid* reformers to act within the law, while the obstacles created by the Emir's oppression compelled the Bukharan *jadid* to form a secret society. Thus, having originated from a common source, Bukharan and Turkistani *jadid* evolved separate organisational structures, and followed different paths of political development. Nevertheless, since their basic ideas were similar, Turkistani *jadid*, such as Mahmood Khoja Behboodi (1874–1919), contributed much to the achievement of common goals.[31]

The issue of educational reform amongst the Muslims of Russia dates back to 1883, with the appearance of the newspaper *Tarjuman*, edited by Ismail Bay Gasprinskii. Having realised that there was an educational crisis within the Muslim community, Ismail Gasprinskii evolved a new (*jadid*) method of teaching. By method, he meant both the technique employed for teaching the Arabic alphabet, and the complete system of education in use in the old (*qadim*) schools. After many years of training, the pupils in such establishments were often still practically illiterate. Gasprinskii aimed at providing instruction in religion effectively and concisely and thereafter, giving pupils the skills, languages and information required in the contemporary world. The fundamental innovation in teaching methods was that the Arabic alphabet was taught not merely as a series of individual letters, but as building blocks for the formation of words. Pronunciation of the alphabet showed its use in actual words in native languages, and writing practice was stressed. The size of classes, curricula and the physical environment of the schoolroom also received consideration.[32]

Under Tatar influence, new-method schools appeared in Russian-controlled Turkistan at the end of the nineteenth century. The first new-method school in the Emirate of Bukhara was established in Pustinduzan by *mulla* Jurabai of Pirmast *tumen* in 1900. However, it was soon closed owing to the pressure of the *ulama*.[33] In 1902–3 a Tatar school-teacher, Kaipov, opened a new-method school in *Novaya* Bukhara but it could not function long and was soon closed. However, the idea of new-method schools won many sympathisers in Bukhara amongst the Tatar merchants, officials and other educated individuals who had come there from Russia.[34] In 1907, a Tatar *mulla*, Nazim Sabitov, opened a new-method school in Bukhara for Tatar pupils, to which Bukharans were also admitted. In 1908 Gasprinskii, on a visit to Turkistan, met the Bukharan and Tatar progressives, including Sabitov, and discussed the question of new-method schools. It was agreed that Sabitov's hitherto private school should be transformed into an official school for Tatars and Bukharans. A formal request was made for grant of state premises to Sabitov's school. Gasprinskii suggested that the school should be named *Muzaffaria*, after the late Emir Muzaffar. However, despite negotiations with Emir Abd-al Ahad and his officials by Gasprinskii, neither premises nor permission to open the school was granted.[35]

In October 1908 a *jadid* school for Bukharans was opened in the house of Abdul Vahid Burhanov in Bukhara. Many more were opened later. The significance of Burhanov's school was that although it used Tatar books for instruction, it tried to impart instruction to its pupils in Farsi (Tajiki) as well. Aini translated the lessons into Farsi.[36] In 1909, Burhanov and Nizametdin's new-method school held its final examinations in the presence of the pupils' parents, the *ulama*, and other noted citizens. Around a hundred people were invited to the ceremony. A dispute arose amongst those who attended the ceremony about the appraisal of the new schools and the subjects being taught in them. One group, under the leadership of *mulla* Ikram,[37] maintained that the new schools were useful both in form and content. They did not find anything in them contrary to the interests of religion or the state and considered such schools vital for the progress and development of the country. Like the *jadid*, they were in favour of reform in the national system of education, including *madrasa*. The opposing group, led by *mulla* Abduraziq, considered the new-method schools harmful, anti-religious and anti-state, and called upon the people and the government to resist them.[38] They argued that both the form and content of the new education was un-Islamic. It resembled the Russian or European type of education since pupils sat at desks, read and wrote at once, etc. Moreover, the religion taught in *jadid* schools was perverted. Subjects such as arithmetic, geography and natural sciences were taught which absolutely contradicted the Islamic world-view. This was the first serious confrontation between reformism and conservatism in Bukhara. Almost every section of Bukharan society participated in the debate and two distinct groups, *jadid* and *qadim*, emerged.[39] In the event, *jadid* schools were banned and supporters of this system persecuted. Burhanov fled from Bukhara and went into hiding in Qarshi.[40]

The progressive elements in Bukhara were dissatisfied with the medieval despotism of the Emir and the *ulama* but initially lacked any organisational structure; they were little more than isolated dissenting intellectuals. Around 1909, however, the *jadid* movement took organisational shape, under the influence of the Turkish[41] and Persian[42] revolutions, which fired the Muslims of the East with revolutionary and nationalist inspiration.[43] Initially, a nine-member *Shirkat Bukhara-i-Sharif* ('Union of Bukhara the Noble') was created to provide books for the new-method schools and to defend them from the attacks of the *ulama*.[44] In Allworth's words 'men like Usman Khoja-oghli [Usman Khodzhaev], Ahmadjan Mahdum, Mirza Abdul Vahid [Burhanov], Haji Rafik, S. Aini, Mirza Muhauddin Mansur Oghli [Mansurov] and Fazilidin Maksum laid the foundation of the future Young Bukharan Party.'[45] In late 1909 a group of Bukharan exiles in Istanbul founded the Bukharan Society for the Dissemination of Knowledge (*Bukhara Tamim-i Maarif Jamiati*), whose aims were to found schools in Bukhara and to finance the sending of Bukharan students to Istanbul.[46]

In 1910 the *jadid* formed a secret society called *Jamiyat-i-Tarbiya-i-Atfal* ('The Society for the Education of Children'), comprising thirty members, mostly progressive merchants, teachers, members of the *ulama* and artisans.[47] The society succeeded in establishing a number of secret new-method schools in Bukhara[48] and sending students abroad for higher education to places such as Orenburg, Kazan, Ufa, the Crimea and Turkey, including thirteen students to Turkey in 1911 and thirty in 1913.[49] By the year 1914 the number of secret schools, according to Aini, had increased to six.[50] Moreover, by 1912 the *jadid* were publishing two newspapers, *Bukhara-i-Sharif*[51] ('Bukhara the Noble') and *Turan*,[52] in Tajiki and Uzbeki respectively. An eminent Muslim from Azerbaijan, Mirza Jalal Yusufzade, headed the editorial board. The newspapers were financed by a joint-stock company which almost immediately raised 9,000 Roubles.[53] On January 2, 1913, the papers were banned by the Russian Political Agent on the Emir's request. In 1914 the *Shirkat Bukhara-i-Sharif* opened the bookstore *barakat* ('blessing') and the library *marifat* ('knowledge').[54]

The beginning of the reign of Emir Alim [1910–1920] was an era of great expectations in Bukhara. He had studied for three years in a military academy in St. Petersburg, learned Russian well and took an interest in Russian literature. In 1910, on his accession to the throne, he announced a manifesto to eliminate the most serious abuses.[55] To put an end to corruption at all levels he forbade presentation of gifts (*tartuk*) by anyone to himself, to court dignitaries, or to officials; banned the *qazi* from fixing the price of legal deeds at will; forbade officials to impose or increase taxes; promised to increase the salaries of soldiers, civil servants and the *ulama*. This manifesto created tremendous good will in all sections of the population towards the Emir. Students wrote to him, denouncing the state of the *madrasa*, the excesses of the teachers, and urging the Emir to reform them. The Emir initially responded favourably by ordering the *Qazi-i-Kalan* to prepare for transformation. But the *ulama* opposed the reforms and the Emir annulled them.[56]

The *jadid* primarily represented the interests of the city.[57] There was almost no support for them in the rural areas. The most progressive members of the urban population were those belonging to the service class, though excluding high and privileged officials. The *jadid* numbered among their supporters members of the middle and poorer sections of the intelligentsia, the petty bourgeoisie, students at the religious schools, small shopkeepers, and minor officials. They received some material support from a small number of rich and influential merchants such as Mansurov and Yakubov, and there were a few *ulama*, like *mulla* Ikram, who sympathised with their views, but these were the exceptions rather than the rule. Of the founders of the *jadid* organisation, Sadradin Aini was a student in a religious school; Abdul Vahid Burhanov, a minor official; Fitrat, a poet and a student.[58] Usman Khodzhaev was the son of a *mulla* (who was also a small-scale, part-time merchant), while Jurabai, in whose house the first new-method school was opened, was a farmer from Vobkent.[59]

THE OBJECTIVES OF THE *JADID*

Initially, the ideological objectives of the *jadid* were to combat religious fanaticism through the dissemination of new religio-secular literature published by Turks and Tatars; the introduction of secular, new-method schools of the European type instead of the old-style religious schools; and the relaxation of censorship and at least partial freedom of the press. They also worked for lower taxes and legal guarantees of life and property against the local officials and tax collectors. Their goal was the introduction of a constitution in Bukhara, following the pattern of the Young Turks.[60] In other words the *jadid* of Bukhara sought to reform the state.

The *jadid* in Bukhara also represented the aspirations of the emerging trading class of Bukhara. In 1911 the traders and merchants of Bukhara sent a delegation to the *Zakatchi Kalan* of Bukhara, Mirza Nizamiddin Khoje, demanding certain reforms necessary for the development of trade and industry.[61] Their demands included: the establishment of a stock exchange for traders; repair of the old, and construction of new bridges on the trade routes inside Bukhara; strict vigilance over weights and measures; regulation of water distribution in the city of Bukhara, and the prohibition of festivals which contravened the *Shari'a*. The government granted only one of these demands: it established a centre for traders in Bukhara.[62] Though most of their concerns were related to the development of trade, the repair and construction of bridges also served the interests of the peasants. Bukharan traders and merchants realised the need for the modernisation of communication routes as well as other civic facilities for the development of trade and industry. The *jadid*, too, demanded the lowering of taxes, the establishment of exact norms for taxation, and an ordered system of tax collection, so as to check the rapacity of the *bek*. It was for this reason that forward-looking traders such as Mansurov and Yakubov provided financial support for the *jadid*.[63]

By 1915, the *jadid* organisation, owing to repression by the Emir and the *ulama*, had to work in semi-underground conditions. Some ten cells were functioning in the Emirate by this time. The most active were those of Bukhara, Kerki and Marshauz. Possibly because of this repression, the *jadid* of the Emirate of Bukhara were more politicised than those of Turkistan. They produced a considerable amount of revolutionary literature. During 1909–1915 several works critical of the existing political order appeared. These included Fitrat's *Bayanat-i-Sayyah-i-Hindi*, *Saiha* and *Oila*.[64] (See Chapter Four for details). Newspapers played a very important role in raising political consciousness, as did the new-method schools. After the closure of Bukharan *jadid* newspapers, Mahmud Khoja Behbudi, in May

1913, brought out first the newspaper *Samarqand* and then a weekly magazine *Ayna* ('Mirror'), both from Samarkand. The former was closed owing to financial difficulties in September after 45 issues, while *Ayna* dragged on till May 1915 and collapsed after 68 issues.[65] Other liberal and reformist periodicals of this time included: 123 issues of *Sada-i-Farghana* ('Voice of Farghana'), edited by Abidjan Mahmudov, published from April 1914 to June 1915 in Khiva and 67 issues of *Sada-i-Turkistan* ('Voice of Turkistan'), edited by Ubaidullah Khojaev, published from April 1914 to May 1915 in Tashkent. Many contributors to *Ayna*, especially its editor Behbudi stressed the need for reform of the schools, opening of the new-method schools, trade houses and trade companies, industry and banks. He also highlighted the need for Muslim doctors, engineers, planners, trade agents, heads of trade houses, state officials, judges, notaries and bank workers.[66] Pointing out the cultural and economic backwardness of the Emirate of Bukhara, *Ayna* advocated the spread of education, cultural and political reforms, as well as the opening of a trade school in Bukhara.[67]

When in 1913–14, following the demand of the *ulama*, the Emir closed the *jadid* schools, Fitrat and Ata Khodzhaev left the city of Bukhara and organised a chain of new-method schools in various other towns of the Emirate. The local population was sympathetic to the cause of the new schools, and despite the orders of the Emir, the local authorities were unable to shut the new schools at Kerki and Shahr-i-Sabz.[68] These schools played a significant role in preparing the political struggle against the Emir by organising the elements opposed to the government, and by involving the pupils' parents in their work. Khodzhaev reports that 'Our comrades, parents and pupils gathered in the schools of Usman Khodzhaev, Burhanov and others, where discussions on various topics began, which led to criticism, initially timid, but later open, of the Emir and his government. Major topics of discussion were the enslavement of Bukhara by the Russians, the backwardness, lack of culture and ignorance of the *ulama*, the depravity and luxury of the Emir's court, the oppression of the rulers, the heavy burden of taxation and many others.'[69] Hence, those opposed to the existing order gathered around the new-method schools.[70] The broad mass of the population did not join the *jadid* camp at this stage. However, a nucleus emerged. Slowly and imperceptibly, the cadres of the future Young Bukharan Party were prepared. Persecuted by the authorities and lacking the support of any powerful social group, impeded, too, by strong religious prejudices, the *jadid* movement grew fairly slowly. Petty prejudices, the patriarchal, authoritarian structure of the family, practical concerns about loss of service and trade, and anxieties about personal material well-being weakened the movement from within.[71]

The *jadid* movement faced a crisis in 1914–15, when its newspapers and bookstore were closed. This came at the time when the students who had been sent abroad by the *jadid* were returning after completing their studies at Orenburg and Istanbul. Most of them had been abroad for three to four years. They now disagreed with their senior comrades, not only on the aims of the movement, but also on the methods to be used for political struggle. They demanded the concrete formulation of a political programme and the launching of a mass struggle to reduce the burden of taxes on peasants. They were critical of the oppression by state officials and wanted the *jadid* to work to limit it. In short, they wanted to give the movement a more broad-based character. Owing to these differences of opinion, two wings developed in the *jadid* movement. One, headed by Burhanov, restricted its activities to the cultural field, while the other, more left-wing, comprising mainly the youth and headed by Fitrat, advocated radical policies. Nonetheless, they maintained a superficial unity.[72] A twelve-member Central Committee was formed, including Abdul Vahid Burhanov (President), Fitrat (Secretary), Usman Khodzhaev (Treasurer), Muhauddin Rafa't, Musa Saidjanov, Ata Khodzhaev, Ahmadjan Abdul Saidov, Faizulla Khodzhaev, Hamid Khoja and others.[73]

Up till this time the *jadid* activities were focussed mainly in the cultural field: the dissemination of new-method education and propagation of reformist ideas through print media. In this Turkistani *jadid* Muslim newspapers and liberal Muslims of the Russian empire rendered considerable support and cooperation to the *jadid* of Bukhara. However, political events in Russia introduced a new dimension into the *jadid* struggle for cultural and political reform in Bukhara.

THE INFLUENCE OF THE RUSSIAN FEBRUARY 1917 REVOLUTION

The February 1917 Revolution in Russia, the overthrow of the monarchy, and the proclamation of the Russian Republic furthered the cause of reform in Bukhara. The *jadid* pinned their hopes on the new Provisional Government in Russia. However, although the Provisional Government was established in the centre, the Soviets of Workers' and Soldiers' Deputies, dominated by Mensheviks, Socialist Revolutionaries, or, occasionally, Bolsheviks, often exercised the real power. After a meeting on 8 March 1917, the railway workers of *Novaya* Bukhara refused to support the Provisional Government, liquidated local police organs, and freed the political detainees. On 12 March, a thirty-member Executive Committee of the Provisional Government for *Novaya* Bukhara, composed mostly of workers, was elected. It chose Mensheviks and Socialist Revolutionaries as its leaders.[74] The Bukharan *jadid* hoped that the new Russian government would support the progressive forces in Bukhara. However, the Russians were too busy with internal problems. Not only did they not urge the Emir to reform his autocratic regime, but they also failed to change the Czarist diplomatic apparatus in the Emirate. The Political Agent, Miller, who, in F. Khodzhaev's view, was sympathetic to the Emir, remained at his post.[75]

After the February 1917 Revolution in Russia, the divisions within the *jadid* organisation sharpened. The moderate *jadid* hoped that under the influence of the Russian Revolution the Emir would agree to the reorganisation of the system of government and the establishment of people's representation, which might control at least the local governors (*bek*) and senior officials, if not the Emir himself. They decided that further underground political activity was useless, since it could misrepresent the organisation and frighten the Emir. The more radical wing feared that the Emir might enter into a long-term agreement with the Provisional Government in Russia, and that if he introduced any reforms they would be very insignificant. Therefore, open political activity was premature and dangerous. Eventually, a Central Committee was formed which united these two groups. However, differences of opinion on new issues soon appeared. These focused on a new manifesto proposed by Emir Alim (for details see pp. 102–104). In F. Khodzhaev's view, these differences led to the virtual disintegration of the Central Committee.[76] It continued to exist in name but had little control over its members. It was 'at this stage that the organisation, which was later known as the Young Bukharan Revolutionary Party, originated', claimed Khodzhaev.[77] However, it did not take formal shape until some time later.

After 1917 the movement spread amongst the intelligentsia and working people. To maintain secrecy and protect it from the agents of the Emir, a cell system was adopted, whereby under every member of the Central Committee there were twelve other members; every member of the twelve-man cell (Russian *duzhin*) was authorised to form a new cell, etc. According to F. Khodzhaev, 'the organisation widened enormously. In the city of Bukhara alone there were up to 50 units'.[78]

To seek help for their reform programme from the new Russian government, the *jadid* sent a telegram to the Provisional Government and the Petrograd Soviet of Workers' and Soldiers' Deputies, in which, after congratulating the new regime, they pointed out the historical relations between the two peoples, and requested the Provisional Government to pressurise the Emir into carrying out reforms in the Emirate.[79] The government despatched prompt replies to Miller and the Emir. The Petrograd government expressed its desire for speedy reforms in the Emirate, stating that, now that there was a new regime in Russia, a state where people had no rights must not and should not exist in its neighbourhood. However, reforms did not follow.[80]

After some time the *jadid* sent another telegram to Petrograd, yet again requesting the Russian government to exert pressure on the Emir. The telegram was drafted by F. Khodzhaev and signed by Fitrat and Saidjanov. The telegram had to be sent from Samarkand (under Russian rule) because the contents of any telegram being sent from Bukhara would be conveyed to the Emir. The *jadid* also decided to send a delegation, comprising Fitrat and

Usman Khodzhaev, to Petrograd. The delegation had two aims: to inform the Provisional Government of Russia about the real situation in Bukhara and to tell the Muslims in Russia about the aims of the Bukharan *jadid*. When Fitrat and Usman Khodzhaev reached Orenburg, they learnt that a Russian commission was on its way to Bukhara to resolve the dispute between the *jadid* and the Emir. The delegation therefore remained at Orenburg. According to F. Khodzhaev,

> without Russian help, the introduction of even partial administrative, legislative and educational reforms in Bukhara would have taken many painstaking years of preparation. To overthrow the Emir of Bukhara was even more difficult.[81]

THE REFORM MANIFESTO OF THE EMIR: THE *JADID* REACTION

The efforts of the *jadid* to persuade the Russians to bring pressure to bear on the Emir to introduce reforms in Bukhara were not wasted. Miller, following directives from Petrograd, held long consultations with the Emir and the *Qushbegi*. He also met with various representatives of the Bukharan population in order to assess the situation, and finally invited *jadid* leaders such as Burhanov, Usman Khodzhaev and others to a personal meeting. To preserve the secrecy of the organisation, Burhanov and other *jadid* leaders put forward their points of view individually, not as a group. The following demands were presented: I) Reform of the administrative system, including people's representation at the central administrative level as well as at local levels. II) Abolition of all taxes except those required by the *Shari'a*. III) Freedom of education, press and publication. IV) Dismissal of certain fanatical and reactionary officials.[82] Miller argued that the demands of the *jadid* were substantial, but too idealistic. In his view, the *jadid* lacked the strength to compel the Emir to accept their demands. Moreover, he frightened the *jadid* leaders by showing them a list of their members which he could only have obtained by using his agents to infiltrate the organisation.

However, on March 17/30 Emir Alim made public a new and long-awaited manifesto, which did include some elements of reform. The ceremony was held in the Emir's palace in the presence of religious dignitaries, ministers, high officials and prominent citizens. Miller's colleagues Shulga (the author of the manifesto) and Vvedenski, delegates from the Kagan and Samarkand Soviets of Workers' and Soldiers' Deputies, Mahmud Khoja, and a few other progressives also attended the ceremony. Some 200 persons were invited to participate.

> The Emir sat in the middle of the hall. Behind him were seated the *Qazi-i-Kalan* and the administrator Sharifjan Maksum (who had recently replaced the

reactionary Burhanuddin). Sharifjan Maksum read the manifesto on behalf of the Emir. The audience approved it, Mahmud Khoja congratulated the Emir and everyone present for the reforms; copies of the manifesto were distributed amongst the attendants. Besides Sharifjan Maksum certain *Rais* were appointed from the progressives

reported Faizulla Khodzhaev, who was present thanks to the influence of his uncle Latif Khodzhaev.[83]

The manifesto envisaged modest reforms but was ambiguously worded. The salient points were:

(i) The Emir's readiness to carry out extensive reforms of the administration to suppress irregularities and injustices, through the principle of election.

(ii) Reforms would be based on the Holy *Shari'a*.

(iii) The judicial system and the collection of taxes such as *kharaj* and *zakat* would be reformed.

(iv) Steps would be taken for the development of industry in the Emirate, and particular attention would be given to encouraging trade with Russia.

(v) Officials and civil servants would receive fixed salaries and be forbidden to accept any other reward for their services.

(vi) Measures to spread education and sciences in the Emirate, in strict accordance with the *Shari'a*, would be introduced.

(vii) An elected council of respected citizens would take charge of public sanitation and health in the city of Bukhara.

(viii) A state exchequer would be created and an annual budget, stating precise income and expenditure, would be set up.

(ix) A printing press would be established to print books and newspapers.

(x) In future the affairs of the public and government would be decided through consultation and consensus.

(xi) Freedom would be granted to all those presently held in prison.[84]

However, the manifesto did not satisfy the demands of the *jadid*.[85] On the other hand, it annoyed the reactionaries, who, through the *ulama*, started agitating against it and against the *jadid*.

On the day of the reading of the manifesto, the *jadid* held a meeting at the house of one of their members, Ahmad Naim, to discuss the situation. Representatives of the Samarkand Soviet of Workers' and Soldiers' Deputies were also present. The participants unanimously agreed that the manifesto was a first step towards the liberation of Bukhara, but they were divided over their future course of action. The majority of the moderate *jadid*, grouped around Abdul Vahid Burhanov, were for gradual and slow reform without revolution and bloodshed. They wanted to hold meetings to explain the meaning of the manifesto to the population, but were against a popular demonstration. They argued that this would provoke the conservative elements in society, who might then rally around the Emir and cause bloodshed. If they organised their movement on solid foundations, time would compel the Emir to enact the manifesto and even widen it.

The left-wing *jadid* maintained, however, that conflict with the Emir was inevitable. He might well use the *ulama* to stir up the ignorant, fanatical masses against the *jadid*, on the pretext of danger to religion; he also had the support of the army, financial resources and the state apparatus. If the *jadid* delayed now, they might weaken the momentum of support for reform. They were therefore in favour of a popular demonstration to show enthusiasm for the reforms. Even in the event that the demonstration failed, the advantages were many. It would enable the *jadid* to assess the strength of their forces; to enter into contact with the broad masses; to conduct real propaganda and agitation for the first time; and to rid the organisation of unreliable members and provocateurs. The organisation would be purified and strengthened and their supporters would be invigorated, argued Fitrat, Usman Khodzhaev and Faizulla Khodzhaev.

They decided to consult the Russian Resident, Miller. Accordingly, a delegation, comprising Mahmud Khoja, Bakhshulla Khan, Mirza Ghulam, Mirza Izatulla Giakhojaev and Faizulla Khodzhaev, met Miller to seek his opinion. He advised against the demonstration.[86] Fazmitdin Maksum, Muhauddin Raf'at, Mirza Shah, Mirza Izatulla, Aini and Hamid Khoja also opposed the demonstration till the end. According to Faizulla Khodzhaev,

> he had to put a great deal of effort into persuading the comrades in various regions to prepare for the demonstration.[87]

The left-wing view prevailed and the demonstration took place on 8 April.

Around 150 people, including Burhanov and Fazmiddin Maksum, two of the opponents of the demonstration, gathered at about eight o'clock in the morning near the bookstore *barakat*. The opponents of the demonstration asked Khodzhaev whether Miller had agreed to the demonstration. Khodzhaev was evasive. Around 1,000 people, including some of the Jewish, Persian and Lezghi minorities, to whom the manifesto promised equal rights, began a march towards *Registan* (lit. 'desert', the name of the square in front of the Emir's palace in Bukhara). The participants carried red banners inscribed with the slogans, 'Long Live Freedom', 'Long Live the Reform' and 'Long Live the Liberator Emir'. On the way they gathered new recruits. The demonstration passed through the main cotton market and reached Gaukushan where some of the activists went to the home of the *Qazi-i-Kalan* and requested him to welcome the demonstration. More and more people joined the procession. At Khayaban the demonstration was welcomed by Shi'as and Persians with flowers. A large meeting was held there. By the time the procession reached *Registan* it was 5,000 to 7,000 strong, according to Khodzhaev.[88] There it encountered a crowd of 7,000 to 8,000 well-armed counter-demonstrators who had been mobilised by the conservative elements in the *ulama*. Two battalions of the Emir's infantry, whose intentions were not clear, were also present. The leader of the *jadid*, Burhanov, ordered the demonstration to disperse peacefully so as to avoid a bloody clash. A delegation comprising Ata Khodzhaev, Mirbaba and Usuf-Zade was sent to the *Qushbegi* to explain the peaceful intention of the demonstration.[89]

Despite these peace overtures, the Emir, under pressure from the *ulama*, decided to deal with the *jadid* sternly and took immediate measures against them. Around thirty people, including the members of the delegation sent to the *Qushbegi*, as well as Sadradin Aini, Mirza Nasrulla and Mirza Sahbabai, were arrested. The detainees were severely beaten on the Emir's orders. Aini received 75 lashes and Mirza Nasrulla 150. Abdul Vahid Burhanov, fearing a massacre by the *qadimi*, asked the Russian authorities for asylum in Kagan on behalf of the *jadid*. Faizulla Khodzhaev had to flee Bukhara before the receipt of a positive answer from the Russian Resident. Most of the *jadid* fled to the Russian settlements of the Emirate, which henceforth became the centre of their activities.[90]

THE *JADID* IN EXILE

The *jadid* who had fled to *Novaya* Bukhara gathered in the Russian Muslims' club to map out their future strategy. The most immediate task was to help the detainees and reorganise the *jadid* forces. A twofold strategy was evolved: to agitate in Bukhara and if possible, organise a protest demonstration there; and to carry out propaganda amongst the Russian workers and Russian population and call on the revolutionary organisations of Turkistan for help. Meanwhile, the Executive Committee of the Kagan Soviet wrote a note of protest to the Emir. It also demanded that the Russian Resident move troops from Samarkand to restore order in the Emirate.[91] On the directives of the Tashkent Soviet, a commission from Samarkand, headed by S. R. Chernivoi, was sent to *Novaya* Bukhara. A joint meeting of the representatives of the Soviet and the *jadid* was held, addressed by Faizulla Khodzhaev on behalf of the *jadid* and by Bekberdiev and Arif Karimov on behalf of the Russian Muslims. A letter from Shulga, the First Secretary of the Russian Residency, to the *Qazi-i-Kalan*, which had been intercepted by the *jadid*, was read out. In the letter Shulga warned the government of Bukhara about the spread of the *jadid* movement and advised the Emir to deal sternly with them, offering all possible help. As a result, the workers and soldiers, and the *jadid* present at the meeting, demanded the arrest of Shulga, who was then put under house arrest.[92]

On 8 April the Kagan Soviet and the *jadid* informed Tashkent, Samarkand and Kerki about the situation in Bukhara and asked for help.

The Provisional Government did not act, but the Kagan Soviet sent soldiers to Bukhara. The representatives of the Provisional Government at Tashkent directed the political authorities at Kagan not to allow the soldiers to enter Bukhara. The soldiers were stopped at the gate of the city, but on 9 April, after hearing that the detainees in Bukhara had been given barbaric punishments, the Kagan Soviet made it clear that their soldiers would enter the city to save the prisoners. Only then, to avoid an armed confrontation, did the political authorities demand their release. The Emir promised to comply, but the soldiers insisted on doing it themselves. Around fifty soldiers entered Bukhara and released the detainees,[93] who, along with the injured *jadid*, were then taken to *Novaya* Bukhara. The next day Mirza Nasrulla died as a result of the punishment he had received. A large funeral was held for this first martyr of Bukhara's liberation, attended by the *jadid*, revolutionary organisations from Turkistan, and Russian workers and soldiers.[94]

The group of moderate *jadid*, led by Burhanov, Fazmitdin Maksum and Muhauddin Raf'at, who had opposed the demonstration, reasserted their authority. They blamed the left-wing *jadid* for the setback, and called for a reorganisation of the party. They held a meeting, to which they invited Muhauddin Mansurov, the wealthy Bukharan businessman who had funded the *jadid*, and had previously fled Bukhara after disagreements with the Emir over trading concessions, but had subsequently joined the *jadid* organisation, along with his two sons. Burhanov stressed the need to hold negotiations with the Emir and the Russian Resident, and urged the formation of a new Central Committee to fulfil this goal. He proposed Mansurov as President, arguing that he was an intelligent and influential man who commanded respect amongst the Russians. Mansurov did indeed have good personal contacts with Russian business circles and the Russian Residency. The nomination was accepted. The new Central Committee now consisted of Muhauddin Mansurov as President, his son Abdulkadir Muhauddinov, Muhauddin Raf'at, Abdul Vahid Burhanov, Usman Khodzhaev, Arif Karimov, Mirza Isam Muhauddinov, Musa Saidjanov, Mukhtor Saidjanov, Faizulla Khodzhaev and a few others. Later, Fitrat and Ata Khodzhaev, who had been members of the old Central Committee, also joined. In Faizulla Khodzhaev's account, 'though formally these elections were not valid because most of the branches of the *jadid* organisation were not present, and many members did not approve of the new Central Committee, due to the precarious situation of the party they decided to avoid inner party struggle and to accept these decisions.'[95]

The new Central Committee considered two lines of action: (i) to obtain an amnesty from the Emir, using the good offices of the Russian government; this would mean an end to the general persecution of the *jadid* and the creation of conditions for peaceful, lawful political work; (ii) to prepare for active struggle by secretly arming the party and organising guerrilla warfare in the provinces. The second proposal was intended to accommodate the left-wing view. Mansurov himself was categorically opposed to armed struggle and the use of force, and favoured the former path. After long consultations with Miller, Mansurov decided that they must negotiate with the Emir through the Russian Resident. Despite some reservations from Faizulla Khodzhaev, a committee comprising Mansurov, Abdulkadir Muhauddinov, Isam Muhauddinov, Musa Saidjanov, Burhanov, Ata Khodzhaev, Abdul Sattar Khoja, Mukhtar Saidjanov and F. Khodzhaev was elected to conduct the negotiations. The Central Committee authorised them to seek agreement with the Emir to allow the *jadid* to conduct political work legally, in conformity with the Emir's manifesto. Mansurov and F. Khodzhaev met Miller, who arranged an audience with the Emir. Consequently, the *jadid* delegates, along with some deputies of the Soviet of Workers and Soldiers, accompanied by Miller and Vvedenski, arrived in the city of Bukhara on Friday 14 April.[96]

A hostile reception awaited them. The Emir's officials carried the delegates in open carriages through the bazaars of Bukhara at a time when the faithful were coming out of the mosques after the Friday prayers. The crowd, some 5,000 strong, gathered at *Registan* and hurled themselves upon the carriages, showering the *jadid* with abuse and stones. After this rough treatment the delegates finally reached the throne room. There, officials and the *ulama* abused the *jadid* and called them traitors.

> Mansurov began his speech, 'We, lovers of the motherland and the existing system, citizens of Bukhara, although we criticised the shortcomings of the manifesto of His Highness which did not correspond to our aims, now extend our hand to the high officials of the government to realise the Emir's will ...'. His speech was interrupted by shouts of 'traitor' and 'infidel'. The Emir intervened, saying, 'You are all my subjects, there exists some misunderstanding between you. Calm down, it will be cleared up, all will remain as it was in the past' and he left the room.[97]

> The mob meanwhile gathered outside the palace gate, demanding the trial of the delegates. The *jadid* now realised that they had been tricked by the Emir and Miller, who hoped to destroy the *jadid* once and for all.[98]

It was at this moment that an alliance between the revolutionary elements of Central Asia and the workers and peasants of Russia emerged which later liberated Bukhara, claimed F. Khodzhaev.[99] The treacherous role of the Russian Provisional Government and its Residency at Bukhara became evident to the *jadid*. Having no other option, they clung to the deputies of the Soviet of Workers and Soldiers. Although Miller tried to persuade the deputies to leave, they stayed with the *jadid*. The next day the delegation was freed by soldiers from *Novaya* Bukhara. After this debacle the left wing reasserted itself. A new Central Committee was elected, comprising

Abdul Rahid as President and Rahmat Rafiq, Fatkhulla Khoja, Fitrat, Faizulla Khodzhaev, Tatsev, Faizaldin Maksum, Musa Saidjanov, Atbarov, Usman Khodzhaev, Ata Khodzhaev and Haji Mirbaba. The organisation, renamed the Young Bukharan Party, established contact with all the other *jadid* groups apart from the supporters of Mansurov and Muhauddin Raf'at.[100]

The summer of 1917 was a difficult time for the *jadid*. After the failure of the demonstration and the audience with the Emir, they found themselves in exile in the Russian settlements. The social base of their organisation narrowed again. Influential Bukharan merchants, although opposed to the existing system in Bukhara, feared open conflict with the Emir and therefore abandoned their support for the movement. The backing of the more progressive members of the *ulama*, under the leadership of *mulla* Ikram, also ceased. The peasants showed no interest in the movement. The Russian Provisional Government and the Residency at Bukhara concluded agreements with the Emir. The *jadid* realised that they must regroup their forces, and assigned Fitrat to formulate a new programme, aimed at taking into account the interests of the diverse social groups who were dissatisfied with the Emir's government, in the hope of uniting them under the Young Bukharan Party. However, since a more radical programme could at that time have caused a split in the organisation, 'it touched on neither the constitutional question nor the monarchy. It envisaged an enlightened monarchy of the European type and a state based on the rule of law instead of oriental medieval despotism; a strengthening of the Emirate, politically, economically and militarily.'[101] (For details of this programme see pp. 154–156). In 1918 the Central Committee of the Young Bukharan party adopted a slightly amended version of Fitrat's programme, but it was not published until 1920.

CONSEQUENCES OF THE BOLSHEVIK REVOLUTION IN BUKHARA

In October 1917, the Bolshevik Revolution took place in Russia. The Young Bukharan Party initially did not understand the nature of this Revolution.[102] The Emir, on the other hand, was quick to realise that there could not be any friendship with the new government in Russia. He made friendly overtures to all manner of counter-revolutionary forces, and to Afghanistan. In Tashkent, the Bolsheviks had proclaimed on 22–27 November 1917 the formation of Soviet government in Turkistan, but had not yet consolidated their success. The Emir did not recognise the new Soviet government and tried to prevent the Soviets from taking over in the Russian settlements of the Emirate.[103] The existing Soviets, dominated by Socialist Revolutionaries and Constitutional Democrats, cooperated with the Emir against the Bolsheviks. The Bolsheviks, meanwhile, convened a regional conference of the Soviets of Russian settlements in the Emirate on 15 December 1917. Taking power into their own hands, they created an executive organ, the Soviet of People's Commissars of the Russian Settlements of Bukhara.[104] The Russian Residency in Bukhara was renamed the *Kollegiya Po Bukharskim Delam* ('Board of Bukharan Affairs'), and was staffed by V. S Utkin, M. A Preobrazhenskii and B. M. Barzhanov, the representatives of the *Novaya* Bukhara, Chaharjui and Termez Soviets respectively. The Board represented not only the Russian settlements, but also the Turkistan Soviet of People's Commissars (Sovnarkom).[105] F. I. Kolesov (1891–1940), President of the Turkistan Soviet of People's Commissars, wrote an official letter to the Emir of Bukhara in January 1918, confirming the transfer of all the functions of the former Russian Residency to this body.[106] Such acts of hostility aggravated the already strained relations between the government of Bukhara and the Soviets. Meanwhile, on 13 December 1917 the Fourth Extraordinary Muslim Congress declared the formation of the Autonomous Government of Turkistan. The jurisdiction of this government was confined to the Farghana valley.[107] Khodzhaev reports that Bolshevik workers in *Novaya* Bukhara such as Preobrazhenskii, Utkin and Poltoratskii maintained close contacts with the Young Bukharans and explained to them the nature of the October Revolution. Consequently, the *jadid*, with no one else to turn to, established links with the Bolsheviks.[108]

In December 1917, F. Khodzhaev and Preobrazhenskii (representing the Soviet of the Russian Settlements in the Emirate), went to Tashkent to talk with the Soviet government of Turkistan on the formation of a united front against the Emir of Bukhara. There, Khodzhaev met Kolesov, President of the Turkistan Soviet of People's Commissars.[109] Ishanov and Iskandarov claim that in order to secure the help of the Bolsheviks against the Emir, Khodzhaev assured them that he could muster 30,000 men, 4,000 of them armed revolutionaries.[110] Both the Bolsheviks and the Young Bukharans were probably trying to use each other for their own ends, the former to secure recognition from the Emir of Soviet power in the Russian settlements and the Board of Bukharan Affairs, the latter to introduce democratic reforms in the Emirate.

Faizulla Khodzhaev presented his plan, approved by the Young Bukharans, to Kolesov, advocating that preparations for an armed insurrection in Bukhara and Kerki should be started as soon as possible. The uprising in Bukhara was to take place at night, starting with the capture of government establishments, followed by the arrest of the Emir and his ministers. The arrest of the Emir was necessary in order to isolate him, but he was to remain the head of the state and the *ulama* and to accede to the demands of the *jadid* in the form of a manifesto. Kolesov agreed with the plan, but owing to problems on the Kokand front, proposed a delay of two months. However, he promised arms and the assistance of the Red

Army.[111] The *jadid*, it would appear, still entertained the idea of a constitutional monarchy and sought reforms under the leadership of the Emir.

In February 1918 Soviet forces successfully liquidated the Autonomous Republic of Farghana.[112] Thereupon, the Emirate of Bukhara became a sanctuary for all kinds of counter-revolutionary elements, including officers of the White Guard, former government officials and fleeing capitalists. Cossacks demobilised from the Caucasian front supplied the Emir with a substantial quantity of arms; he also bought weapons from other sources, and strengthened his army with the help of White Guard officers. Soviet Turkistan was alarmed by these developments, and, intoxicated by his victory over Kokand, Kolesov decided to intervene in Bukhara.

At the end of February 1918, on his way back from Ashkabad, Kolesov briefly stayed in *Novaya* Bukhara and met the Young Bukharans under the leadership of Khodzhaev.[113] He informed them about the armed action that he intended to take five days later. The Young Bukharans demanded weapons; Kolesov promised to deliver them on the day of the operation. Meanwhile, a Revolutionary Committee comprising Fitrat, Ata Khodzhaev, Burhanov, Atbarov, Pulatov, Fazmidin Maksum and Faizulla Khodzhaev (as President) was elected by the Young Bukharans. Kolesov reached *Novaya* Bukhara on 1 March and in the evening distributed arms to the Young Bukharans. The Revolutionary Committee, along with Kolesov, decided to deliver an ultimatum to the Emir demanding immediate reforms, but assuring him that if he agreed to their demands, he could retain his position. He was given 24 hours in which to send written agreement to the proposals, and then to disarm his army. The Emir's first reaction was evasive. He expressed his readiness to introduce reforms, but wrote that since the ignorant and fanatical masses opposed reforms he requested them not to insist upon immediate implementation, but rather to do it gradually.[114]

Before the attack on Bukhara the Emir sent another letter, agreeing to every clause of the ultimatum if (i) the troops did not enter the city; (ii) the Young Bukharans did not organise any demonstration in the city; (iii) the reforms could be introduced at an opportune moment. The letter was not signed by the Emir and had no official stamp. The next day Kolesov's forces, with 200 Young Bukharans and 200 workers from *Novaya* Bukhara, moved on Bukhara. The first skirmish took place near the city walls. The Emir's regular troops avoided an encounter and quickly retreated. However, the *ulama*, though poorly armed, fought desperately. As Kolesov's forces were advancing towards the city, representatives of the Emir arrived bearing the revolutionaries' proposals, signed by the Emir. The attack ceased and the Soviet-Young Bukharan forces returned to Kagan. Negotiations with the Emir's delegation, comprising Usmanbek Qushbegi, Haji Zakria and others, were held in Kolesov's train compartment. The

Young Bukharans were represented by F. Khodzhaev, Fitrat, Burhanov and Fazmidin Maksum. A truce was proclaimed, and Kolesov and the Young Bukharans agreed to send a delegation to supervise the disarming of the Emir's troops.[115]

During this respite, the Emir's forces were able to cut the telegraph link and the railway line connecting Chaharjui and Qarshi with Samarkand and Merv, to tear down the electricity poles, destroy the water mains and tanks and collect a sizeable army. All the members of the delegation sent by the *jadid* save two were massacred. Indiscriminate killing of the Russian inhabitants of the Emirate began. Kolesov tried to regain control of the situation by using his superior firepower. The chief aim was to stop the Emir's offensive and create panic amongst the people. Kolesov's artillery bombardment continued for 36 hours, but achieved nothing: not a single shell hit the target. This fact was interpreted by the *mulla* as proof that God and the Prophet Muhammad were defending Holy Bukhara against the gunfire of the infidels. Lack of contact with Tashkent prevented the arrival of reinforcements, and since Kolesov was short of munitions he decided to retreat to Samarkand. On their way back the insurgents were chased and harassed by the Emir's forces. Finally, they were rescued by troops arriving from Tashkent. On 25 March 1918, peace was signed at Kizl Teppe. The independence of the Emirate was recognised by the Soviet of People's Commissars of Turkistan, in return for which the Emir pledged to disarm his troops and not to support forces hostile to the Bolsheviks.[116] Thus, the Young Bukharans' first armed attempt to dislodge the Emir failed miserably.

Faizulla Khodzhaev gives the following reasons for the failure of the uprising: (i) Kolesov was unable to provide the Young Bukharans with a sufficient quantity of arms when needed, preventing them from organising an uprising inside Bukhara; (ii) since the Young Bukharan forces were too weak to initiate an uprising inside the city, the impression was created of an attack by the Red Army on Holy Bukhara, instead of an internal revolution; (iii) the *ulama* whipped up a nationalist fervour to rally the population around the Emir; (iv) the Young Bukharans overestimated their strength, owing to their successful political work amongst artisans, cartsmen and the army of the Emir; (v) the party lacked unity; (vi) equipment was short and Kolesov's troops provided insufficient support.[117] As to the question of why the Young Bukharans joined the armed insurrection under these circumstances, Khodzhaev thought that they had no other option.

The defeat of the Young Bukharans was followed by even greater persecution of the *jadid*, their sympathisers and progressive people in general.[118] Those who could, escaped to Soviet Turkistan, where they made Samarkand and Tashkent their centres of activity. The former centre was led by Rahmat Rafiq and Ata Khodzhaev, the latter by Atbarov, Burhanov, Fitrat and Faizulla Khodzhaev. The movement was in disarray. Rafa't and

Maksum died. Ata Khodzhaev, Pulatov and Qori Ghulam created a new faction, sympathetic to the left wing of the Socialist Revolutionaries, Fitrat took a job in the Afghan consulate at Tashkent, Pars Khodzhaev went to Kashgar, Aslan Khodzhaev to Persia, Rahmat Rafiq joined the *Mussavat* ('Equality') group in Baku.[119] Faizulla Khodzhaev, as President of the Revolutionary Committee which had led the failed attack on Bukhara, was subjected to severe criticism by some members. Consequently, he resigned and the Central Committee became ineffective.[120]

Meanwhile, in April 1918 the central government in Moscow sent P. A. Kobozev (1878–1941) to Tashkent as Commissar-General to review Russian policy in Central Asia and to win the support of the local population for the Bolshevik Soviets.[121] He convened the Fifth Congress of the Soviets of Central Asia, which on 30 April proclaimed the creation of the Turkistan Autonomous Republic within Soviet Russia.[122] A 26-member Turkistan Executive Committee containing ten Muslims, several of them *jadid*, was created. This gave the Young Bukharans an opportunity to work in the new order.

On 20 April 1918, the Russian Communist organisation in *Novaya* Bukhara organised a joint meeting with the *jadid* to create a Muslim Communist organisation.[123] The vast majority of Young Bukharans in exile in Soviet Turkistan took a keen interest in politics, especially the new recruits, such as deserters from the Emir's army and artisans. They joined the army and attended short political courses. This created a favourable climate for the creation of a Communist faction among the Young Bukharans. The Bukharan Communist Party was founded by Mukhtar Saidjanov, Yakubzade, Azimjan and other *jadid*. Soon they were joined by Hussainov, Aminov, Akchurin and many others.[124] The Communist organisation paid special attention to the training of the Bukharan emigres: they attended Party schools in Tashkent and other cities, some joined the Russian Communist Party, and some volunteered to join the Red Army in Farghana or on the Trans-Caspian front. The Communist faction also published a newspaper, *Qutulush* ('Liberation').[125]

REVOLUTION IN BUKHARA

In January 1920 Faizulla Khodzhaev and his comrades organised the Turkistan Bureau of the Revolutionary Young Bukharan Party. This Turkistan Bureau, parallel to the Bukharan Communist Party, according to Khodzhaev, was aimed at mobilising against the Emir all the revolutionary forces who could not come to terms with the Communists, for example, petty merchants, artisans, small and middle-ranking officials and others. The Revolutionary Young Bukharans brought out a newspaper entitled *Uchkun* ('The Spark'),[126] in which they called for the overthrow of the Emir and the proclamation of a democratic republic in Bukhara.

The Revolutionary Young Bukharan Party adopted the programme formulated by Fitrat in 1918, but they now advocated the abolition of the Emirate and the proclamation of a People's Republic.[127]

Khodzhaev's idea of transforming Bukhara into a republic may have taken shape during his stay in Moscow from October 1918 to November 1919. There, he was exposed to the ideas of 'scientific Socialism' by observing the October Socialist Revolution and meeting revolutionaries such as Sverdlov, Frunze, Kuibyshev and Rudzutak.[128]

Prominent members of the Turkistan Bureau included Pulatov, Usman Khodzhaev, Mukammil Burhanov, Muinjan Aminov and Issatulla Aminov. The Party had Committees in all the cities of Turkistan bordering the Emirate and underground organisations inside the Emirate, such as those at Kerki, Chaharjui and Shahr-i-Sabz. In the city of Bukhara, besides underground cells, it enjoyed the support of sympathisers from almost every section of the population.[129]

The Communist faction, on the other hand, by organising cells amongst share-croppers, small peasants, agricultural workers and petty shopkeepers, claimed in 1919 to have established 43 organisations, comprising 5,000 members.[130] They asserted that the democratic stage of the revolution had passed and demanded the immediate abolition of the Revolutionary Young Bukharan Party and the submission of all Bukharan revolutionary groups in both Turkistan and the Emirate to the authority of the Communist Party of Bukhara.[131]

Both groups, Communists and Revolutionary Young Bukharans, wanted the overthrow of the monarchy and the establishment of Soviet government in Bukhara. The Young Bukharans expressed their readiness to merge with the Communists on certain conditions. They proposed the formulation of a mutually acceptable plan of action; this would provide an opportunity to act together, postponing a formal merger until the victory of revolution in Bukhara. The motives for this proposal were: (i) the realisation that unification under a Communist banner would alienate the Bukharan emigrants who did not share Communist ideas, and thus exclude them from the ranks of the revolution at a time when solidarity was essential; (ii) the realisation that unification under a Communist banner would frighten those of the propertied classes who were opposed to the Emir's rule but not sympathetic to Communist ideas; (iii) the fear that twenty years of struggle by the *jadid* was in danger of being ignored in the cause of revolution.[132]

Tension between the two groups reached such a point that it paralysed their political work. At this stage the Turkistan Commission[133] intervened in an effort to restore unity. On the initiative of Mikhail Frunze, both the groups were invited to a meeting. Mirza Buhran and Arifov represented the Communists, Muinjan Aminov, Pulatov and Faizulla Khodzhaev the Revolutionary Young Bukharans. Kuibyshev, Turyakulov and Gopner of the Turkistan Commission also attended the meeting. The leaders of the

Communist faction agreed that the programme of the Young Bukharans could serve as a basis for the struggle, but objected to the fact that they mentioned religion and *Shari'a*. For them, this was incompatible with the demands of reform. Khodzhaev, however, felt that this was an indication of their ignorance of the history of the revolutionary movement in Bukhara, and stressed the importance and tactical need for such a programme in Bukhara.[134] He expressed his readiness, in principle, to work for the realisation of the Communist programme as an ultimate goal, but proposed postponing unification into a single Communist organisation until the victory of the revolution. The Turkistan Commission accepted this demand for the independent existence of the Turkistan Bureau of Revolutionary Young Bukharans and proposed the commencement of concrete revolutionary work.[135]

The formal reconciliation of the two groups was achieved at the 1920 Chaharjui conference of the Communist faction of the Bukharan *jadid*, on the basis of a resolution of the Russian Communist Party, which stated that the Young Bukharan party was a progressive factor which would facilitate the overthrow of the despotic power of the Emir.[136] The selection of Chaharjui for such an event was not accidental. The majority of the population were Turkmen, bitterly hostile to the Emir's officials, who were mostly Uzbeks. This was especially true of the poor, land-starved peasants, burdened by increased irrigation costs and taxes. Both groups of Bukharan revolutionaries sent their representatives to Chaharjui. These included political workers and soldiers who had deserted from the Emir's army.

Anticipating the events in advance, Frunze ordered the Red Army, together with the Regiment of the Eastern Muslims (consisting mostly of deserters from the Emir's army and Bukharan peasants) to move on Bukhara via the railway line. Meanwhile, Chaharjui fell to rebelling peasants and revolutionary forces on the night of 28 August 1920. The Revolutionary Committee called the entire population to join in the struggle against the Emir and an appeal for aid was sent to the Red Army.[137] They responded immediately. Frunze ordered his troops to march into Bukhara on the morning of 29 August 1920.[138] The fortress of old Bukhara fell after an attack lasting 26 hours. The Emir and his officials fled to eastern Bukhara and later to Afghanistan. Two new state organs, a Revolutionary Committee and a Soviet of People's *Nazir* ('Commissars'), were formed on 2 September 1920.[139] The Revolutionary Committee comprised Abdusaidov as President, Aminov, Akchurin, Arifov, Yusopov, Imburhanov, Haji Hasan Ibrahimov, Faizulla Khodzhaev and Kul Muhammadov. The Soviet of People's Commissars included Faizulla Khodzhaev as President, Pulatov, Muhauddinov, Mukhtar Saidjanov, Usman Khodzhaev, Hussainov, Ibrahimov, Burhanov and Shehabuddinov.

On 11 September 1920 the Revolutionary Young Bukharan dissolved their organisation and its members joined the Bukharan Communist Party en masse. Consequently, the membership of BCP rose to 14,000.[140] On 6 October 1920, the newly-formed Congress of Representatives of the People of Bukhara abolished the Emirate and proclaimed the People's Soviet Republic of Bukhara.[141] A delegation was sent to Moscow to discuss friendship and mutual aid, which concluded a 'Treaty of Union' with RSFSR on 4 March 1921. This treaty significantly curtailed the Bukharan right to act independently in financial and economic affairs. Russian consent was required, before granting trade concessions to any other foreign state or to carry on trade on a commodity-exchange basis with Soviet Russia. In addition, a single customs union was formed by abolishing all internal customs barriers between Bukhara, Khwarezm and Soviet Russia. Moreover, on 21 September 1921 an agreement on the distribution of Amu Darya flotilla was concluded between RSFSR, Khwarezm and Bukhara.[142]

On 25 September 1921 the Constitution of the People's Republic of Bukhara was adopted at the Second Congress of Bukhara Soviets. This fundamental document did not mention the 'Right of the Toiling and Oppressed Peoples' or the dictatorship of the proletariat.[143] Instead, Article 26 declared that no published laws of the Republic can be in contradiction with the basic tenets of Islam.[144] Article 5 guaranteed the right to own property in all circumstances and guaranteed the citizens the unfettered right to use and dispose of their movable and immovable goods.[145] Article 7 and 8 of the constitution guaranteed the freedom of conscience, speech, press, assembly and the inviolability of person and of home (Article 9). Article 10 defended the population against the arbitrary action by the government. Article 58 guaranteed the right of vote to adults of both sexes, however, Article 59 deprived of civic rights those individuals who had served the former regime as well as big landowners and capitalists.[146]

The republic survived for four years and leading *jadid* such as Faizulla Khodzhaev, Fitrat and Usman Khodzhaev served in key posts. The new government did not implement its promise of agrarian reform, credit to the peasants and judicial reforms. They, however, declared Uzbeki as the state language. Schools having *vaqf* incomes were transformed and secular knowledge was introduced. The government faced problems in this area because there was a shortage of trained teachers and *mulla* were not equipped to teach chemistry or mathematics.[147] To speed up the training of teachers seventy students were sent to German universities in 1922 and the foundation of a modern university was laid in Bukhara.

The establishment of soviet form of government, the merger of the Young Bukharans with the BCP, the conclusion of mutual alliance and military-political agreements with Soviet Russia extended communist influence in Bukhara. On 2 February 1922 the Politbureau of the Central Committee of the Russian Communist Party resolved to merge the communist parties of Bukhara and Khwarezm with the Russian Communist

Party. To facilitate this the Russian Communist Party on 18 May 1922 reorganised its Turkistan Bureau into the Central Asian Bureau of the Central Committee of the Russian Communist Party.[148] Following the initiative of 23 January 1923 of this Central Asian Bureau the republics of Turkistan, Khwarezm and Bukhara decided to set up a Central Asian Economic Council on 5 March 1923. A nine member presidium was elected comprising one from Soviet Russia, four from Turkistan and two each from Bukhara and Khwarezm.[149] Though the purpose of the Central Asian Economic Council was to facilitate the speedier economic reconstruction of Central Asia, it restricted the freedom of action of the Central Asian governments in economic decision making to a great extent. Disputes, whether a certain issue carried a significance for only an individual republic or for Central Asia as whole, arose. Moreover, Central Asian Economic Council extended its sphere to other activities. For example, it suggested to the governments of Bukhara and Khwarezm to carry out reforms in land, tax structure, system of agricultural taxes and private trading. To resolve national friction inside Bukhara and Khwarezm, measures such as eradication of economic inequality among Uzbek, Turkmen and Kazakh populations were also stressed by the Council.[150]

The objection by the Bukharan communists and the government against the merger of their party and against the Council were overruled. The reluctance of Bukharan communists and Young Bukharans to fall in line with the policies framed by the Central Asian Bureau of the Central Committee of the Russian Communist Party resulted into expulsion from the party and denunciation of their leaders. As a result of purges 15,000 members lost their party cards in Bukhara. Some left the party voluntarily, especially the Young Bukharans Revolutionaries, and joined the Basmachi camp. Prominent among those were Mirza Abdulqadir Muhauddin, Muhauddin Makhdum (he was chief of the police and joined the Basmachi camp with 300 policemen), and Usman Khodzhaev, the well known *jadid* activist and the first *nazir* of finance in the government of Republic of Bukhara.[151] A year later, after the national delimitation of Central Asia, new Soviet republics were formed. (See pp. 14–15).

CONCLUSIONS

Jadidism was a movement which began as a response to the challenges of the West. Initially, it was aimed at reforming the existing system of education. By furnishing Muslims with the modern knowledge and skills it wanted them to catch up with Western progress. However, it did not reject Islamic values. On the contrary, it drew on Islamic tradition to bring about change. The rigorous opposition of the orthodox *ulama* to any innovation in the system of education gave birth to the first *jadid* organisations which primarily evolved around new-method schools. The movement later adopted a wider agenda, calling for political and administrative reform under the leadership of the Emir, though the overwhelming perspective remained Islamic. The activists of the movement, because of the persecution of the Emir and the orthodox *ulama*, had to flee Bukhara to Russian Turkistan. There, in Soviet Turkistan, after the Russian revolution, the *jadid* renamed their organisation as the Young Bukharan Party. They accepted help from the Bolsheviks, but their armed campaign still aimed at carrying out reforms in Bukhara under the leadership of the Emir and Islam was to play a pivotal role. Following the failure of the attempts, both peaceful and armed, to persuade the Emir to carry out reform in Bukhara, a more radical worldview began taking root among the Young Bukharans. Its culmination point was the emergence of communist faction among the Young Bukharans which advocated the overthrow of the Emir and undermined the role of Islam. The reformists responded by organising the Turkistan Bureau of the Revolutionary Young Bukharan Party. This organisation accepted the idea of overthrowing the Emir and the proclamation of a democratic republic in Bukhara, but still stressed the role of Islam. An alliance of the communists and Young Bukharans, supported by the Red Army overthrew the Emir and established the republic of Bukhara. The Muslim reformists served in the key posts of the new government and the constitution of the new republic guaranteed a role to Islam. Later, however, the struggle of Muslim intelligentsia for reform was taken over by Western Soviet Russian Revolutionaries. A new, more revolutionary frame of reference instead of Muslim reformist was introduced leading to abolition of Bukhara as a country and creation of various Soviet Socialist Republics.

Chapter Four

Abdal Rauf Fitrat

Journalist and political activist, Abdal Rauf Fitrat (1886–1938) was one of the leading thinkers of Bukharan *Jadidism*. His literary legacy was also significant. In Tajik prose, Ahmad Donish's *Navadir-ul-Voqai* is often cited as a model of simplicity of language and clarity of thought.[1] However, Sadradin Aini paid tribute to Fitrat's contribution to the modernisation of Tajik when he commented that 'with the prose [writings] of Abdal Rauf Fitrat, the Tajik language acquired a new literary form.'[2]

Very little was written about Fitrat until the late 1980s. The main reason for this taboo was the negative assessment of *Jadidism* by the Soviet establishment, illustrated by the use of such terms as 'anti-revolutionary', 'anti-people', 'bourgeois nationalist'. This prevented any objective study of Fitrat's work being undertaken. Even after the collapse of the Soviet Union, he was still regarded with some reserve. It remains difficult to find many of his works in the libraries of Central Asia other than a few examples in Russian translation of *Qayamat* ('The Day of Judgement'),[3] entitled in Russian *Strashnyi Sud* ('The Dreadful Judgement'), or sometimes *Sudnyi Den* ('Judgement Day'). During the Soviet period, this book achieved a certain notoriety since it was used for the promotion of atheistic propaganda. This is evident from the introduction to the 1964 edition, where the reader is warned:

> If you are a believer and want to know what the holy scriptures promise you in the life hereafter, you should read this book without fail. This story is drawn by the author on the basis of relevant verses of the Quran and other books of Muslim theology. If you are not a believer, it offers you rich material to struggle against the narcotic of religion.[4]

BIOGRAPHICAL SKETCH

Fitrat was born into a family of petty Bukharan merchants in Bukhara in 1886; his father, Abdu Rahim had travelled extensively in the Ottoman Empire, Iran and Chinese Turkistan.[5] Fitrat graduated from the *Mir Arab*

Madrasa in Bukhara and then for a brief period also taught at a *madrasa* (which one is not known). Later he proceeded to Turkey to obtain higher education (1910–14), there he studied at the *Darulvaizin Madrasa*.[6] It is sometimes suggested that he fled to Turkey to avoid persecution by the authorities after the sectarian Shi'a-Sunni conflict which erupted in Bukhara on January 9, 1910, on the day of the *Muharram* festival.[7]

In Turkey Fitrat established himself in Istanbul where, along with other Bukharan emigres, he participated in the activities of the *Bukhara Tamim-i Maarif Jamiati* ('Benevolent Society of Bukhara for the Dissemination of Knowledge among the Masses').[8] His first book, *Munazara* ('The Debate' or 'The Dispute'),[9] a discussion between a Bukharan *madrasa* teacher (*mudarris*) and a European about new (*jadid*) and old (*qadim*) schools, was published in Istanbul in 1909–10 (1327 AH).[10] Originally written in Farsi (Tajiki), the *Munazara*, a 61-page pamphlet, was translated into Russian in 1911, by Colonel Yagello,[11] and into Turki/Uzbeki in 1913, by Shukrullah Samarkandi.[12] Both translations were published in Tashkent.

In the words of Edward Allworth,

> Abdalrauf Fitrat used a traditional Central Asian and Middle Eastern style of imaginary travel account in dialogue form. Set in Hindustan, it pits a visiting European against a Bukharan Madrassah teacher on his way to Mecca for a religious pilgrimage. The contents and flavour of The Dispute – insistent didacticism and repetitive argument rather than brilliant wit and literary flair – aim at persuading by reason and familiar example rather than by literary invention.[13]

Munazara was very popular in Bukhara and Turkistan. Sadradin Aini reports that the progressive new-method teacher Abdulqadir Makhdum alone distributed 150 copies of the work. He personally delivered copies to such cities as Shahr-i-Sabz, Kitob, Chirakchi and Yakkabagh. He himself would read the book to the illiterate.[14]

Fitrat's second book, *Bayanat-i-Sayyah-i-Hindi* ('The Tales of an Indian Traveller'),[15] published in Istanbul in 1911, was originally written in Farsi. A Russian translation by A. Kondrateva, *Razskazy Indiiskago Puteshest-vennika (Bukhara, Kak ona est*,[16] was published in 1913 in Samarkand (at that time under Russian control). An edited version of the same translation was published in 1990 by Hamid Ismailov in the journal *Zvezda Vostoka* ('The Star of the East').[17] The book is a fictional account of an Indian traveller's visit to the major cities of the Emirate of Bukhara, where he meets a wide range of people, including craftsmen, traders, peasants and *ulama*. He holds discussions with them, and through this device Fitrat portrays the Bukhara of his time. He describes the educational institutions, the abuse of *vaqf* incomes, the corruption and ignorance of the *ulama*, the belief in superstition, the state of agriculture, trade, industry, health care and the armed forces.

After his return from Turkey in 1914, Fitrat took active part in the struggle for social, religious and political reform in Bukhara, especially the struggle to establish the new-method schools. He also led the left wing of the Bukharan *jadid* movement.[18]

His book *Rahbar-i-Najat* ('The Guide to Salvation')[19] was published in Petrograd in 1915. *Rahbar-i-Najat*, comprising 224 pages, is a relatively well-organised treatise in which the main themes of Fitrat's philosophy are set out: the purpose of human life, the role of intellect and reason, the causes of the downfall of Islam in general, and of Bukhara in particular, and the importance of acquiring knowledge and a modern education. The book was written in Tajiki, and as far as is known, has not been translated into Russian. His other works in Tajiki include *Mukhtasar Tarikh-i-Islam* ('A Short History of Islam'),[20] written for the pupils of new-method schools, *Aila* ('The Family'),[21] and *Saiha* ('The Cry'),[22] a collection of patriotic poems. These poems, which clearly express the idea of Bukharan independence,[23] 'had a lightning effect on the readers, as powerful as an electric shock'.[24] The work was smuggled into Bukhara and circulated secretly. 'In this period, Fitrat's literary work revolutionised ideas in Bukhara', notes Sadradin Aini.[25]

After the February 1917 revolution in Russia, Fitrat became the editor-in-chief of the Uzbek newspaper *Hurriyat* ('Freedom'), which was published in Samarkand. Fitrat began writing in Uzbeki at this time, probably because of his Pan-Turkic sentiments. It is well-established that during his stay in Turkey, he was attracted to Pan-Turkic and Pan-Islamic ideas.[26] His Pan-Turkic inclinations were further strengthened after meeting Faizulla Khodzhaev (1886–1938) in Bukhara in 1916.

> After the February revolution [in Russia], the reform movement [in Bukhara] was led by *jadid* such as Fitrat and Usman Khodzhaev, who after their return from Turkey, where they acquired their education, started propagating Pan-Turkism. They talked in Ottoman Turkish not only amongst themselves, but also to the inhabitants of Bukhara, the majority of whom could not speak even Uzbeki,

reports Sadradin Aini.[27] Fitrat played a prominent part in the abortive pro-reform demonstration held in Bukhara in 1917 and consequently had to flee to Russian Turkistan.

At the end of 1917 the *jadid* organisation assigned Fitrat to work out a new programme. Within two months, Fitrat presented his draft to the Central Committee, which approved it, with minor amendments, in January 1918. The programme (*muromnama*) was written in Uzbeki and advocated amongst other things a constitutional monarchy in Bukhara (for description of the work see: p. 154–156). The programme was published in 1920.[28]

In 1918, Fitrat founded a literary circle of young Turkistani writers and poets in Tashkent, called *Chaghatay Gurungi* ('Chaghatay Conversation').

One of their main objectives was to modify the Arabic orthography then in use in such a way as to show all the Uzbek vowels, thereby facilitating the teaching of reading and writing in the vernacular. However, the *Gurungi* came in for severe criticism from the pro-Soviet faction who dubbed it an 'anti-revolutionary bourgeois nationalist organisation'.[29] Subsequently, the *Chaghatay Gurungi* was banned in 1923.[30]

During his stay in Turkistan, Fitrat worked for the Afghan consulate at Tashkent in 1919.[31] He wrote a pamphlet entitled *Sharq Siyasati* ('The Eastern Politics')[32] probably in 1919. In this work Fitrat denounced imperialist Europe and its civilisational record, and atrocities committed by British imperialism in India. He advocated a strategic alliance between Muslim world and Soviet Russia.[33] Fitrat joined the Bukharan Communist Party (BCP) in June 1919 and became a member of its Central Committee.[34] He worked for the party press and taught in the first Soviet schools and institutions of higher education. He taught higher mathematics at the Institute of Enlightenment in Tashkent.[35] He later (9 April – 15 May 1920) edited the Uzbeki socio-political and literary-scientific journal *Tang* ('Dawn'), published by the BCP.[36]

After the formation of the People's Soviet Republic of Bukhara in 1920 Fitrat became the head of the *Vaqf* Department, *Nazir* ('Minister' or 'Commissar') of Foreign Affairs (1922), *Nazir* of Education (1923) and Vice President of the Council of *Nazirs* as well as of the Central Executive Committee.[37] He also remained Vice President of the *Sovet Truda* ('Council of Labour') in the government of the People's Soviet Republic of Bukhara.[38] In 1923 he was accused of misuse of power and removed from office. He was offered, and accepted, a Professorship in the Institute of Oriental Languages at Moscow.[39] His works from this period include *Qayamat* ('The Day of Judgement'),[40] published in Moscow in 1923, and *Uzbek Adabia-i Namunalari* ('Specimen of Uzbek Literature').[41] Later, in 1927, Fitrat reverted to Tajiki, writing a play entitled *Shorash-i-Vosey* ('The Uprising of Vosey').[42] This work was written in Tajiki after a gap of almost a decade.

Fitrat was often accused of promoting Uzbek nationalism, because he openly defended his views on Central Asian literary identity. In 1938–39 he was executed by the Soviet secret police, for his so-called bourgeois nationalism.[43] Most of the Soviet sources record 1938 as his year of death but are silent about the circumstances. He was partially rehabilitated in the late 1980s.

PHILOSOPHICAL VIEWS

A fairly coherent picture of Fitrat's philosophical and political views is given in the three books he wrote before the Bolshevik revolution in Russia and the overthrow of the Emir of Bukhara, namely, *Munazara*, *Bayanat-i-*

Sayyah-i-Hindi and *Rahbar-i-Najat*. Although Fitrat started by analysing the social and moral crisis in Bukhara in concrete detail (the *Munazara* and *Bayanat-i-Sayyah-i-Hindi* are mainly devoted to this topic), he later realised that the central issue was the crisis of Islam in the twentieth century. *Rahbar-i-Najat*, his third major work, addresses this broader subject and in so doing provides the philosophical framework for his earlier political, social and educational views. It is therefore an important starting point for an evaluation of his philosophical outlook.

The *Rahbar-i-Najat* is very much in the classical Islamic tradition. Fitrat frequently quotes relevant verses from the Quran, the Traditions and the works of Ghazali to substantiate his points. He demonstrates an excellent knowledge of the Quran and traditional Islamic disciplines. This, paradoxically, belies the impression created by his earlier works such as *Munazara* and *Bayanat-i-Sayyah-i-Hindi* that the education imparted in the traditional Bukharan *madrasa* was worthless. Fitrat himself, like other well-known Bukharan intellectuals such as Donish and Sadradin Aini, had graduated from a Bukharan *madrasa*. It is possible that his criticism of the old system of education was a little exaggerated. Nevertheless, it should be kept in mind that, throughout the history of Islam, many great thinkers emerged from outside the official places of learning. Moreover it should not be forgotten that in spite of the fact that he was leading the left wing of the Bukharan *jadid* movement, just two years before the Bolshevik Revolution in Russia, Fitrat's world-view remained strictly Islamic. In his view, Islam was fully capable of providing adequate answers to all the problems that Muslims were facing.[44]

Fitrat believed that Muslims had moved away from the commandments of God, i.e. from real Islam. They faced problems precisely as a result of their own misdeeds. He identified the moral bankruptcy and hypocrisy of the Muslim world as the primary cause of its decline. Part of this bankruptcy was the tendency to renounce the terrestrial world for the sake of the world hereafter or, indeed, vice versa, which Fitrat strongly criticised. In his view, Islam advocated the pursuit of happiness in both worlds. He argued that human beings were distinguished from animals because the Lord of the universe had designed a higher objective for human beings to which they would progress. In *Rahbar-i-Najat* he identifies three essential qualities. The highest of these was *ghaya* (lit. 'purpose'/'objective') as he called it, namely the pursuit of happiness in this world as well as in the world hereafter (*sa'dat-i-darain*). This objective could be achieved with the help of *aql* ('intellect'/'reason') – the greatest blessing of God upon human beings, which elevates man above the stature of animals. Fitrat stressed that no reform was possible without action upon the inner being (*nafs*) of the individual. To regenerate the Muslim community he tried to revive the true meaning and understanding of Islam, insisting upon the reform of *nafs* ('self') and acquisition of knowledge. Fitrat's writings thus consistently emphasise the role of reason, the worth of the individual and his role in the community. The key concepts of his philosophy are the meaning of intellect (*aql*) and knowledge, the nature of self (*nafs*) and the purpose of life (*ghaya*).

Key Concepts

Ghaya: The cardinal principle of Fitrat's philosophical thought is that 'there is a purpose (*ghaya*) to human life'.[45] In the view of the *mutakallimin* ('scholastic theologians'), life implied motion, feeling and sensation. Classical scholars (*hukama-i-qadim*) considered that life was a function dependent upon the mental states of sensation and perception. Scholars contemporary to Fitrat, however, held that life resulted from the combination and collection of *ajza-i-fardah* ('smaller particles'). According to this theory, there was no body which did not have life. Finally, popular wisdom attributes life to a body which has sensation and motion; but according to this interpretation, human beings cannot be distinguished from animals.[46]

Fitrat's position was close to the last view, but he drew a distinction between animal and human life. To demonstrate it, he used the example of man's evolution.[47] Man at the time of creation was weak, naked and highly dependent: he had to endure hunger, thirst, heat, cold and natural calamities. He was the weakest and most dependent of all creatures. But God granted him *aql* – a tool with which he could conquer the whole world. When man began to use *aql* he gradually overcame all hardships: he built houses to protect himself from cold and heat, developed weapons to defend himself against other animals, acquired control over nature.[48] In short, in the language of the Quran, he 'conquered the whole universe'.[49]

Fitrat concluded therefore that believed that the Lord of the universe had designed a higher objective for human beings, and that the heavenly religions were there to guide them towards that purpose.[50] He was convinced that the purpose of life (*ghaya*) could be found in the definition of religion.

> Religion consists of the commandments of God (*Ahkam-i-Ilahiya*); it guides those who follow it towards the pursuit of *sa'dat-i-darain* ['happiness in this world as well as in the world hereafter', henceforth abbreviated: 'happiness']. Therefore, the essence or purpose of a human life is the pursuit of happiness in both worlds.[51]

That is the fundamental difference between animal life and human life.

> Human beings have the capacity for the pursuit of 'happiness' while animals are devoid of that capacity. Whoever does not strive for the pursuit of 'happiness' cannot be distinguished from animals,

123

declared Fitrat.[52] This, according to Fitrat, is the real interpretation and essence of the Quranic verse:

> Surely We created man of the best stature.[53]

Since *ghaya* and *samra-i-zindagi-i adam* ('the fruit of man's life') are the pursuit of 'happiness' in both worlds, whoever considers himself a human being should attempt to seek happiness and fortune in this world and in the world hereafter.[54]

> 'The perfect Muslim (*musalman-i-kamil*) is the one who seeks happiness in both worlds'.[55] God praises those who seek happiness in both worlds in these words: 'And of them (also) is he who saith: Our Lord! "Give unto us in the world that which is good and in the Hereafter that which is good and guard us from the doom of fire".'[56] 'For them there is in store a goodly portion out of that which they have earned. Allah is swift at reckoning'.[57]

There is no other way to attain 'happiness' but to fulfil one's moral duties (*vazaif-i-akhlaqia*), i.e. satisfy one's conscience.

> *Vazaif* [sing. *vazifa* lit. 'duty'] are deeds that human beings have to perform at any time and in any place because they are human beings.[58]

Fitrat divided moral duties (*vazaif-i-akhlaqia*) into three types: (i) duties to the self (*vazaif-i-nafsia*), (ii) duties to the family (*vazaif-i-alia*) and (iii) duties to mankind (*vazaif-i-noiya* or *insania*). They were integrated in such a way that if anyone of them was ignored it would affect the others.[59]

Nafs: Fitrat defined *vazaif-i-nafsia* as the duties that human beings have to perform for the preservation and development of their *nafs* ('self'). It is obligatory for human beings to strive for the perfection of their *nafs*, which is the essence of being. Perfection of *nafs* is doing that which is useful and beneficial for the individual as well as for other human beings: it arises out of performing right deeds and refraining from wrong deeds. Islam ascribes great importance to this. The Quran almost always mentions *amal-i-saleh* ('right deeds') in conjunction with *iman* ('faith'). The scholars of the Traditions consider *amal-i-saleh* part of *iman*. Therefore, achievement of the perfection of *nafs* is not only a moral obligation but also a religious duty for Muslims. To urge the *nafs* to prefer *amal-i-saleh*, we should reform the *quwa* ('power', 'faculty') of the *nafs*.[60]

Nafs ('self') has three faculties in classical ethics: (i) *quwa-i-aqlia* ('faculty of reason'), (ii) *quwa-i-shahwania* ('faculty of lust' or 'instinct') and (iii) *quwa-i-ghazabia* ('faculty of emotions'). Reform or training of *quwa-i-aqlia* results in *hikmat* ('wisdom', 'knowledge') which distinguishes truth from falsehood, right from wrong, and benefit from harm. Development of intellect (*quwat-i-aql*) results in performing right deeds and refraining from wrong. Reform of the *quwa-i-shahwania* results in *iffat* ('purity', 'chastity'), whose product is health of the body, and hence, preservation of the species. From the reform of *quwa-i-ghazabia* comes *shuja'at* ('courage'), which is useful for the protection of human dignity, honour of the nation and preservation of *nafs*. The harmony of the above three faculties produces a fourth quality: *adalat* ('justice'). Therefore, scholars of ethics divided *nafs* into four units: (i) Knowledge, (ii) Chastity, (iii) Courage and (iv) Justice.[61]

Aql: In keeping with this classical analysis of the structure of the self, Fitrat saw *hikmat* ('knowledge', 'wisdom') as the product of *aql* ('intellect', 'reason').[62] Knowledge, he argued, was not possible without the reform of the faculty of intellect, which is the greatest blessing of Allah to man, the guide for the pursuit of 'happiness' in both worlds.

> Intellect made human beings stronger and enabled them to become rulers of the earth. Had human beings not been granted intellect, they would have been destroyed by the stronger creatures, since in life it is the stronger that rule and defeat, and defeat is the first step to destruction. Human beings would have been destroyed without intellect. Therefore, it follows that the guide to 'happiness' in this world is intellect.[63]

Fitrat acknowledged that the Prophet had been chosen by Allah to guide the Arabs, through reason and intellect, to worship One God. Some of them accepted the words of the Prophet and embraced Islam. They abandoned the religion of their forefathers because Islam was *haq* ('truth') and their former beliefs false. Through *aql* they had acquired the ability to distinguish right from wrong. Therefore, they abandoned the wrong and accepted the right.

> The mirror of the intellect and reason (*aql-vo-tafakkur*) of those who rejected the teachings of the Prophet was blinded by the flame of jealousy and animosity. Therefore, they could not distinguish truth from falsehood. Hence, they remained ignorant. Had not human beings possessed reason, or if their intellect had been blinded by jealousy, animosity or ignorance, nobody would have embraced Islam. It follows that the guide to salvation in the hereafter is also intellect and reason.[64]

It is evident that reason guides human beings in the pursuit of 'happiness'. Had there not been reason, the pursuit of 'happiness' would not have been possible. Since the only difference between animals and humans is the capacity of human beings to pursue 'happiness', human beings without reason, or those whose reason is blinded by jealousy, ignorance or animosity, fall to the status of animals. This is why Islam attached so much importance to *aql*. The Quran stresses *ta'qqul* and *tafakkur* ('think and contemplate') and condemns the infidels for not using reason.[65] Fitrat quotes,

'... And expoundeth thus his revelations to mankind that haply they may remember'[66] '... Thus Allah maketh plain to you (His) revelations, that haply ye may reflect.'[67] '... And sendeth down water from the sky, and Thereby quickeneth the earth after his death. Lo! herein indeed are portents for folks who understand.'[68] 'He hath revealed unto thee (Muhammad) the scripture with truth, confirming that which was (revealed) before it, even as He revealed the Torah and the Gospel. Aforetime, for a guidance to mankind; and hath revealed the criterion (of right and wrong). Lo! those who disbelieve the revelations of Allah, theirs will be a heavy doom ...'[69]

Many interpreters here take the word *furqan* as synonymous with the Quran. But Fitrat insisted that in this verse, it means *faraq kuninda* ('the criterion of right and wrong') i.e. a synonym of *aql*, since it is *aql* which distinguishes right from wrong.[70] (To emphasise the virtue of *aql* Fitrat quoted from the Traditions, see Appendix 2, a)

In this regard, Fitrat also referred to a section in Imam Ghazali's book *Mizan-al-Aml*, quoting,

> The greatest of man's powers is *aql*. For the proof of the greatness of *aql*, there are rational arguments as well as arguments from experience and the senses. Such is the argument from the *Shari'a*: The Prophet said, 'God created *aql* prior to all other creatures and ordered it to come forward. It came forward. Then ordered it to go back, it went back'. (Meaning it obeyed the order). Following that God said, 'O reason, I swear upon my honour, I did not create anything greater than you. I judge human beings on the basis of you and pardon human beings on the basis of you'.[71]

Ghazali's rational argument runs:

> What leads to *sa'dat-i-darain* is reason. The thing which leads to happiness should be the best of all creation. Reason is the greatest because through it human beings come closer to God and become His vicegerents, and under its guidance complete their religion. That is why the Prophet said, 'If someone lacks reason he lacks religion' and 'Never be satisfied with the Islam of a person unless you know the degree of his intellect'. The Prophet said to Ali, 'Though people try to get closer to God by paying alms and charity, you try to come close to God through reason. In this way you come close to the people in this world and God in the world hereafter will grant you status'.[72] The argument from the senses is the following: 'Although human beings are the weakest of all the creatures, all other animals are frightened of them. It follows that in human nature there is a hidden power which makes them stronger and superior to other animals. That power is reason. The thing which gives human beings power and success is the greatest blessing of the Almighty'.[73]

Fitrat also referred to Imam Ghazali's book *Ahya-i-Ulum* ('Revivification of Sciences') and quoted from Ghazali two sayings of the Prophet:

Aisha narrated that 'I asked the Prophet, "what is virtuous for human beings in this world?" "Reason", replied he. I asked "In the hereafter?" "reason", he rejoined'. According to Abi Saeed Khadri, the Prophet said, 'everything has to depend upon something; the believers depend upon reason, their piety will be according to their intellect. The adulterers, while entering hell, will say, 'Had we done the right deeds and used our reason we would not have found ourselves in hell.' Therefore, it is clear that the greatest blessing of God, the guide to happiness and closeness to God is reason.[74]

Having discussed the proofs of the greatness of *aql* Fitrat distinguishes two types of *aql*: (i) *aql-i-fitri* ('natural reason') and (ii) *aql-i-kasbi* ('acquired reason'). *Aql-i-fitri* is granted by God at the time of creation to every human being. *Aql-i-kasbi* is acquired by man through education and experience. In other words, if one develops *aql-i-fitri* according to the laws of knowledge, it expands on the basis of experience and becomes acquired reason (*aql-i-kasbi*). Fitrat illustrates this with an example. A child has the potential to write but cannot write. As he grows up, he goes to school, he makes an effort and his writing potential becomes actual. Similarly, everyone by nature has the potential to understand facts, but in reality may not do so. However, in time one makes an effort and learns from knowledge and experience. Natural reason thus converts into acquired reason.[75]

The purpose of human life is the pursuit of 'happiness', and the guide to 'happiness' is perfect reason; perfect reason is acquired reason and the means to acquire it is *ilm* ('education', 'knowledge'). Therefore, it follows that it is necessary to acquire knowledge, there is no other way to pursue 'happiness' but by acquiring knowledge.[76] Fitrat illustrates the importance of knowledge by citing verses of the Quran and sayings of the Prophet. For example, 'Are those who know equal to those who know not?'[77] 'The erudite among His bondsmen fear Allah alone.'[78] 'Say (Muhammad), "O Lord! enhance my knowledge".'[79] According to Ans, the Prophet said, 'The lack of knowledge and grip of ignorance, drinking of alcohol and adultery are signs of the approaching Judgement Day'.[80]

For Fitrat, 'order and system in this world depend upon knowledge and morality. If knowledge and morality disappear the world will be destroyed.'[81] He quotes from the Traditions to support this assertion. Abi Zar reported a saying of the Prophet that

> Anyone who sets a step in the direction of attaining knowledge, God creates a path to paradise for him.[82]

Abi Horera noted this saying of the Prophet:

> The best charity for a Muslim is the acquisition of knowledge and its transmission to others.[83]

There is another well-known saying of the Prophet that

> The pursuit of knowledge is a duty of all Muslims.[84]

According to Hazifa the Prophet said,

> I prefer greatness in knowledge to greatness in worship.

According to Abi Imama the Prophet said,

> The superiority of the men of knowledge over the pious is such that the Lord, his angels, those of the heavens and the earth, even worms and fish, pray for the one who gives good teaching.[85]

Fitrat took this as proof that the Prophet praises the *alim* who guides people in the right direction; followers of Islam must strive to attain knowledge.[86]

Branches of Knowledge

In *Rahbar* Fitrat divided knowledge or sciences into *ulum-i-aqlia* ('rational sciences') and *ulum-i-naqlia* ('traditional sciences').[87] *Ulum-i-aqlia* are further divided into: (I) *ulum-i tabi'a* ('natural sciences'), which are subdivided into (a) *ilm-i tababat* ('medical sciences') (b) *ilm-i hikmat tabia* ('physics') (c) *ilm-i nabatat* ('botany') (d) *ilm-i hayvanat* ('zoology') (e) *ilm-i ma'dan* ('mineralogy'); (II) *ulum-i ryazia* ('mathematical sciences'), which consist of (a) *hisab* ('arithmetic') (b) *jebr* ('algebra') (c) *handsa* ('numbers') and (d) *hyait* ('geometry'); (III) *ulum-i falsafia* ('philosophical sciences'), comprising (a) *ilm-i ahwal-i ruh* ('science of the soul') (b) *ilm-i akhlaq* ('science of ethics'), (c) *ilm-i Ilahi* ('science of God') and (d) *mantiq* ('logic').[88] According to Fitrat, *ulum-i-aqlia* are the result of the collective enquiry of humankind. These sciences are general, not particular. It is therefore wrong to label them as Christian or Muslim sciences. Rather, they are human sciences. All human beings, irrespective of sex or religion, deal with the truth of these sciences.[89] He strongly urged the Muslims to learn all the rational sciences.[90]

Ulum-i-naqlia are subdivided into: (I) *ulum-i-dinia* ('religious sciences') and (II) *ulum-i-dunyavia* ('worldly sciences').[91] *Ulum-i-dinia* include: (a) *ilm-i tafsir* ('science of Quranic exegesis'), (b) *Ilm-i Hadith* ('science of the Tradition') (c) *Ilm-i fiqh* and *usul-i fiqh* ('Science of Islamic jurisprudence and principles of jurisprudence') (d) *ilm-i kalam* ('scholastic theology'). *Ulum-i-dunyavia* consist of (a) *ulum-i lisania* ('linguistics') (b) *ilm-i tarikh* ('history') (c) *jughrafia* ('geography').[92]

Fitrat advocated the learning of both the religious and the worldly sciences.[93] However, he makes a distinction between knowledge that is useful and knowledge that is useless. As the saying of the Prophet is reported by Jabir, 'Seek from God beneficial knowledge and take refuge in God from useless knowledge'.[94]

During the lifetime of the Prophet the Quran had been committed to memory by many people. Contemporary Arabs were obviously completely conversant with Arabic grammar, lexicography and the Arabic idioms of the time. They were also aware of the backgrounds of the Quranic revelations, known as 'occasions of the revelation'. In the event of any difficulty in determining the correct meaning, the Prophet was there to solve it for them. After the death of the Prophet, for some time there were no guides for deducing meaning from the Quran. Gradually, the Islamic community realised the need to compile books of interpretation.[95] With the expansion and development of Muslim civilisation, sciences such as grammar, lexicography and literature, as well as rational sciences, progressed. Human reason began to play a greater role in deducing meaning from the text. Such interpretations were termed *tafsir bil-ra'y* ('interpretation based on [personal] opinion').[96] Since the directives of the Quran guide one to the pursuit of 'happiness', the acquisition of knowledge of *tafsir*, which enables one to deduce meanings from the Quran, is thus useful and a necessity. Fitrat noted with sorrow that some Turkistanis spent twenty years of their life in study but did not learn this noble skill.[97] Fitrat considered *ilm-i hadith* a useful science and necessary for Muslims on similar grounds.[98]

Fitrat argued that man is a social being. Owing to their social nature, human beings enter into relationships and transactions with other men. He lists four types of human transactions: *mu'amilat* ('secular affairs'), *a'qubat* ('punitive affairs'), *munakahat* ('marital affairs', i.e. family affairs) and *ibadat* ('religious affairs').[99] During the period of the Companions and Successors, Muslims had deduced laws from the Quran and the Traditions to deal with these transactions. However, with the passage of time the situation of Muslim people changed, and the *ulama* had to take into account their changing needs. Therefore, the instrument of *ijtihad* (systematic original thinking) was developed. 'Laws had to be deduced from the Quran and Traditions with the help of *qiyas* and *ijma*, hence, *ilm-i fiqh* was developed.'[100] In Fitrat's view, *fiqh*, too, is a useful science; he advocates learning the principles of *fiqh* because without knowing them one may only follow *taqlid*.[101]

He argued that knowledge of *kalam* was not necessary for every student since it was invented to refute heretics and dissenters who no longer existed.[102] He was critical of those who denied themselves the opportunity of studying religious sciences by spending too much time learning Arabic linguistics. To him, it was tantamount to indulging in ablutions for far too long and missing the obligatory prayer.[103] Hence, for Fitrat, knowledge which is useful neither in this world nor in the world hereafter becomes irrelevant. *Blahat* ('ignorance') and *khab* ('intellectual treachery'), which both occur owing to impairment of the faculty of *aql*, i.e. the absence of wisdom, are prohibited by the *Shari'a*.[104]

It is clear from his work *Rahbar-i-Najat* that Fitrat appreciated the necessity and importance of modern knowledge. Modern sciences, in his view, were compatible with Islam. He substantiated his case by referring to the Quran, the Traditions and the works of Ghazali. He laid out in detail his reasons for believing in the necessity of acquiring knowledge of religious, natural and social sciences.

POLITICAL AND SOCIAL VIEWS

Fitrat's views on contemporary political and social issues are interspersed throughout his writings. His general thought on the crisis of the Muslim world is mostly contained in *Rahbar*. In this work he expressed his deep admiration for and commitment to Islamic values. However, *Munazara* and *Bayanat-i-Sayyah-i-Hindi*, his other works, deal with the concrete political and social issues of Bukhara in minute detail.

The Crisis of the Muslim World

Fitrat was deeply impressed by the fact that a small Arab community, having embraced Islam under the Prophet's guidance, had defeated the two great powers of the time, Persia and Byzantium. He described how Muslim rule was extended from China to India, and from Egypt to Andalusia, during the reign of the Umayyads. The Umayyads and Abbasids founded great seats of learning and gathered people of science, art and skill irrespective of gender and religion in Baghdad and Andalusia. These two great Muslim caliphates became, in a short span of time, such great centres of learning that not only the Muslims of Turkistan but the *nasrani* ('Christian') Europeans were attracted to them for the pursuit of knowledge and skill. Fitrat wondered what had happened to this greatness. Why did the Islamic world, with the nobility of knowledge and learning, descend to such a level of ignorance and poverty?[105] The answer, he believed, lay in the violation of God's commandments.

> The Abbasid caliphate did not perish until it started spending all its time in extravagance and foolishness. The Sultans of Andalusia did not vanish until disunity became their driving force. The Persians did not enter the era of decline until they ignored the Quranic commandments. The Muslims of India did not become weaker than even the *majusi* ['Zoroastrians'], until they sacrificed the truth of Islam for superstition and the myths of Bani Israel.[106]

Fitrat believed that

> the Quran is such a social canon [and] any *millat* ['nation'] that follows it fully achieves glory, happiness, wealth, and greatness.[107]

Fitrat found further evidence for this theory in the early history of Islam, as the following incident, which he narrates in some detail, indicates:

'During the battle of *Uhad*, Muslim forces under the cover of a mountain faced the forces of the infidels. There was a small pass on the left side of the Muslim army. To prevent a possible attack by the enemy through this pass during the height of the battle, the Prophet deployed a force of fifty bowmen there under the leadership of Abdulla bin Jamir, and instructed them not to leave the pass in any eventuality. After the initial defeat of the enemy, most of the fifty bowmen, setting aside the instructions of the Prophet, left their positions at the pass and engaged themselves in collecting war booty from the deserted enemy tents. Khalid bin Walid, who up to that time had not embraced Islam, took advantage of this opportunity, and attacked through the said pass at the head of 200 horsemen. After killing Abdulla bin Jamir he stormed the remaining Muslim troops and defeated the army of Islam'.[108]
'The companions of the Prophet were very distressed by this event and said, "God had promised us victory: why were we defeated this time?"'[109] God revealed the answer: 'And was it so when a disaster smote you, though ye had smitten (them with a disaster) twice (as great), that ye said: How is this? Say (unto them, O Muhammad): It is from yourself. Lo! Allah is able to do all things'.[110]

These verses of the Quran, wrote Fitrat, show that

the real reason for our intense humiliation and insignificance is our own misdeeds. We consider ourselves Muslims but have abandoned totally the important commandments of Islam. If we look towards the Almighty and seek guidance from him, and from now onwards consider the Quran our only guide, there remains a hope.[111]

Fitrat cites another verse of the Quran to support his contention:

'Whatever of good befalleth thee (O man) it is from Allah, and whatever of ill befalleth thee it is from thyself ...'.[112]

It was obvious to Fitrat that the Islamic world lagged far behind the Western world, and that within the Islamic world, the Turkistanis were the most demoralised and backward of all. This view was shared by the great majority of the Turkistani intellectual elite of the time. There were two schools of thought regarding the causes of the situation. One faction ascribed it to lack of education and inertia. The other felt that

Our state of confusion and dissolution is God's will. God has created the world a paradise for infidels (*kafir*) and a hell for the Muslims. The 'Day of Judgement' is approaching, so Islam is being gradually eroded in this world. According to the saying of the Prophet 'every forthcoming day will be worse for the Muslim than the previous one'.[113]

Fitrat agreed with the former group, but believed that there must also be a deeper reason for the problems.[114] The verse 'Lo! Allah changeth not the condition of a folk until they (first) change that what is in their heart; ...'[115] encapsulated the dynamism of thought that had enabled Islam to spread to Arabia, India, China, Tataristan, Turkistan, Afghanistan, Persia and Andalusia. Fitrat noted that

> The earth had trembled before the followers of Islam, who were imbued with honour, glory, wealth, grandeur and might. Such was the might of Islam, that the gunfire of the Muslim rulers of Andalusia was capable of destroying French forts and Russian serfs were in the shadow of Timur's horses. The Persian and Turkish rulers were able to make the world of Islam superior to that of the Europeans. Eighteen great Muslim rulers formed a continuous line of sovereigns of India.[116]

He came to the conclusion that since all Turkistanis were Muslims and that the Holy Book was their Guide, it was to the Quran that they must turn for solutions to these problems.[117]

The Crisis of Bukhara

Although Fitrat occasionally refers to the specific problems of Bukhara in *Rahbar*, he gives a far more detailed critique of these problems in *Munazara* and *Bayanat-i-Sayyah-i-Hindi*.

> There was a time when our own country was recognised as the 'rising dawn of civilisation' and 'the source of the river of knowledge'. Scholars such as Farabi, Bukhari, Bu Ali, Ulughbek and others were introduced to the world by our motherland. It was our country, which through our great scholars, spread the message of our dignity to the whole world. Our crafts achieved such a level that the Abbasid Caliphs, despite all their grandeur and might, borrowed their style of dress from our country.[118]

The Bukharans' ancestors, argued Fitrat, had realised the importance of learning, as illustrated by the Quranic verse:

> Are those who know equal to those who know not?[119]

and had constructed over 200 *madrasa*. He described how in the past Bukharans had had great respect for knowledge and gave alms to support scholarship.[120] Yet, he pointed out, though 'Bukhara was the dominion of powerful scientific forces, which trained 400,000 scholars and spread them to every nook and corner of the world, this

> 'sky of the Sun of civilisations', 'paradise of humankind', 'well-organised home of sciences of the world', 'auditorium of cognition of the universe' is being strangled by mountains of sad stupidities and hobbled by the chains

132

of contempt. This lifeline of the East, despite the presence of all these resources for progress, has allowed death to seize it by the throat. All these places of blessings and constant flow of great sums of money have gone into the despicable hands of a few usurpers who fear not God. Their low and spoiled acts have turned society into a society of the gluttonous.[121]

The Bukharans' ancestors, realising the importance of the acquisition of knowledge had built useful institutions to further this aim. However,

> gradually, the world changed. Efforts and knowledge gave way to *susti* ['laxity'] and *taqlid* ['imitation', 'blind following']. *Nawishtan* ['writing'] became confined to immoral compilations. *Arbab-i-faiz* ['men of letters'] did not display any competence except in writing *qasida* ['song of praise'] and presenting them to the rulers. Even after fifty years, if a *sahib-i qalam* ['man of letters'] wrote something, it was a *divon* ['collection of poetry'], which could not benefit readers in the religious or temporal worlds,

argued Fitrat.[122]

> There was now hardly an educated person in the city who could read and explain appropriately a single page of *tafsir* of the Quran or the Traditions, or could read two or three simple Arabic poems, a matter of shame and disgrace for the noble tribe,

wrote Fitrat.[123]

Reasons for Decline

Fitrat identified the moral bankruptcy and hypocrisy of the Muslim world as the basic causes of its decline:

> We consider ourselves Muslims but knowingly ignore God's commands and fearlessly do what has been forbidden by God. We do not stand united, do not cultivate piety, do not consult each other, do not take a single step in the cause of truth, but accept *riba* ['usury'] and bribes, drink alcohol, indulge in gossip and jealousy. In short, we indulge in all the prohibitions of the *Shari'a* and are in the grip of bad morality. Despite all these shortcomings we consider ourselves 'perfect' Muslims and call those who try to stop us from committing these injustices, infidels. We boast seventy times in a single breath of being Muslim but do not act like perfect Muslims at all.[124]

He accused those who uttered, 'I believe in God and His Angels ...' but did not act according to the faith of hypocrisy.[125] To emphasise his point he referred to the Tradition of the Prophet:

> Faith and actions are interrelated, neither is right without the other.[126]

133

A practical example illustrated this even more pithily:

> You believe in the existence of the *mirshab* of Bukhara, and that he may imprison those who disobey his orders. If the *mirshab* ordered you not to come out of your homes after sunset, would anybody dare to leave his home, violating the orders of the *mirshab*? Surely not, because you believe in the existence of the *mirshab* and the jail. You have faith that anybody acting against the orders of the *mirshab* will be jailed. Had the Bukharans faith in the existence of God and the reality of the Day of Judgement as much as they have in the existence of the *mirshab* and the jail, if they had given importance to the commandments of God equal to that of the orders of the *mirshab* of Bukhara, they would not have acted against the commandments of God.[127]

Fitrat was critical of three tendencies prevalent amongst the Muslims of his age, especially the Bukharans. Firstly, there were those who considered eating and sleeping the only purpose of life. If they had water to drink, a piece of bread to eat and a bed to sleep in they did not worry about anything else. All that concerned them at night was tomorrow's food, and during the day, a bed for the coming night. In short, they could not think of anything except worldly comforts. The intellect of this group was very low and they lowered themselves from the stature of humans to that of animals. Fitrat argued that they should not be admitted to human society because they were very harmful to the community of human beings. God would deprive them of happiness in the hereafter.[128] He quoted the Quranic verse in support of his view:

> ... But of mankind is he who saith: 'Our Lord! Give unto us in the world'. and he hath no portion in the Hereafter.[129]

Secondly, there were those who would not act at all to secure happiness in this world. Such people believed that only infidels pursued this goal, since the world was a paradise for them, but a hell for the Muslims. Yet,

> 'to renounce the terrestrial world and to seek the world hereafter alone, is not in conformity with the holy *Shari'a*',[130]

claimed Fitrat. To prove his point he quoted the following verses of the Quran:

> 'He it is who created for you all that is in the earth ...'[131] 'See you not how Allah hath made serviceable unto you whatsoever is in the skies and whatsoever is in the earth and hath loaded you with His favours both without and within?'[132] 'And hath made of service unto you whatsoever is in the heavens and whatsoever is in the earth; it is all from Him. Lo! herein verily are portents for people who reflect.'[133]

As these verses clearly indicate, it was misguided to assume that 'the terrestrial world is hell for the Muslims and paradise for the infidels', and ascribe it to God's commandments.

Do we understand God's commandments better than the Prophet who spent all his life in effort and hard work? ... The Prophet who worked as a shepherd, traded, became a teacher, preached, led the prayers, was a soldier and a general, sometimes acted as a speaker and sometimes as a doctor. Is not all this effort and endeavour? And if effort is an obligation then why have we made inaction and laziness our maxim?

asked Fitrat.[134]

Another argument that Fitrat brought forward to support this view was the duty to give alms. The Quran enjoins,

'Who believe in the unseen, and establish worship, and spend of that We have bestowed upon them.'[135] 'These depend upon the guidance from their Lord. These are the successful.'[136]

Fitrat argued,

note that God's guidance and salvation is reserved for those who possess three qualities, of which one is giving alms. It is evident that alms can only be given if one is affluent. Look! which religion encourages its followers towards affluence to such an extent? Those who reject the terrestrial world for the sake of the world hereafter, or vice versa, are wrong.[137]

To further substantiate this point he quoted from the holy Traditions:

According to Ans, 'Best amongst you are those who do not abandon the world hereafter for the sake of the terrestrial world and abandon not the terrestrial world for the sake of the world hereafter, and do not become a burden on others'.[138]

Thirdly, there were those who believed in the pursuit of happiness in both the worlds, but did not act in such a way as to attain these goals. Fitrat argued:

If one asks them, 'You seeker of happiness in both worlds, why do you not make an effort in that direction?' Their answer is *Allah karim* ['God is Gracious']. They call their laziness and inaction *tawakkal* ['trust in God']. Despite their exasperation at their poverty and destitution they go to a mosque or *mazar* [holy place, 'tomb'] and pray. Such prayers of the Turkistanis will not be granted because, after having a good night's sleep and wasting the day in useless activities, we go to a mosque or a *mazar* to pray and seek favours from the Lord, and return only to engage in unworthy and useless activities. We never make an effort to achieve our aims. Such prayers are not acceptable to God and will never be granted. Anyone having an objective must first try to make an effort, and then should pray.[139] To the objection that if we make an effort to achieve a certain aim, there is no need for prayer, since we can achieve our goal by effort alone, he answered, 'This is not an appropriate way, you have misunderstood. Many people try very hard but still cannot achieve their objective and all their efforts and hard work are wasted. We pray so that our efforts are not wasted.'[140]

He gave the practical analogy of a farmer, who, instead of tilling the field in time, spends the night in a mosque and prays to have a good yield. Obviously such prayers will not be granted. At the same time, if the farmer tills the field in time and provides everything needed for a good yield, it does not necessarily follow that he will get a good yield because floods may destroy his land or locusts may attack his crop. Therefore, in order to repel such dangers, it is necessary that the farmer prays, and hopes that the Almighty fulfils his prayers.[141] (Two more analogies stated by Fitrat to explain his point can be seen in Appendix 2, b)

Fitrat identified the paradox inherent in a mistaken understanding of *tawakkal*. For example, if one asked a merchant why he was buying leather carelessly; a retailer why he opened his shop only once a week; a *dehqan*, as spring was approaching, where his implements were; or criticised a porter, saying, you do not have a piece of bread to eat at night, why do you sleep all day, they would answer unanimously '*tawakkal ba Khuda*' ('trust in God'). For Fitrat,

> this has nothing to do with *tawakkal*. It is sheer ignorance, laziness and inaction ... *Tawakkal* devoid of action is like prayer devoid of action. Hence, of no use.[142]

As revealed in the Quran,

> ... and consult with them upon the conduct of affairs. And when thou art resolved, then put thy trust in Allah. Lo! Allah loveth those who put their trust in (Him).[143]

To Fitrat, this meant that God advised his Prophet first to consult with the people, then, after reaching a unanimous decision, to act, leaving the rest to God.[144]

Fitrat was highly critical of superstitious beliefs, including the practice, prevalent in Bukhara, of visiting the mausolea of saints. Abd al-Wahab held similar views, and Fitrat was familiar with them. He wrote extensively on this subject. As he explained, the Prophet allowed visits to cemeteries only to arouse fear of the Day of Judgement. Abi Horera instructs,

> pay visits to the graveyard, since it reminds you of the Day of Judgement.[145]

Fitrat argued that human beings commit sins because they lack faith in God and the Day of Judgement; full faith in the existence of God and the Day of Judgement prevents human beings from committing sins. If someone commits a sin unintentionally he will sincerely repent. Some people, due to ignorance and negligence or haughtiness and pride, forget about the Day of

Judgement, lose their fear of God, commit sins and do not repent. For these people, visiting a cemetery might be beneficial because it could remind them of the Day of Judgement. The torments of that Day might instil in them the fear of God and consequently deter them from committing sins. For this reason the Prophet allowed his followers to visit the cemetery. And yet, people visited the *mazar* of the *avlia* to seek help, although the Quran says,

> ... And beside Allah there is for you no friend nor helper.[146]

The *Shari'a* has forbidden visiting of the *mazar*. By visiting *mazar* one becomes a sinner, maintained Fitrat.[147]

He regarded as idolatrous the practice, which he had observed at the mausoleum of Baha'uddin, of bowing to the flag planted at the head of a holy man's *mazar*, which he equated with the Christian practice of bowing before the cross.[148] According to a Tradition related by Aisha,

> God curses the Jews and the Christians for turning the graves of their Prophets into mosques [by praying there].

Jabir reports,

> God may destroy the Jews for turning the grave of their Prophet into a mosque.

Jandab-bin-Abdullah recalls that the Prophet said,

> Pay attention to those nations who came earlier to you and turned the graves of their Prophets and *avlia* into mosques. Beware, do not turn my grave into a mosque. Do not pray at anybody's grave, I forbid that.[149]

In answer to the argument that people do not pray at the *mazar* to seek help, but rather to explain their situation to the Lord, Fitrat explained that

> 'The very act of finding intermediaries [between God and man] is seeking help – a contravention of the *Shari'a* and therefore a sin.'[150] As the Quran says, 'They worship beside Allah that which neither hurteth them nor profiteth them, and they say: These are our intercessors with Allah. Say: Would you inform Allah of (something) that He knoweth not in the heavens or in the earth? ...'[151] also, 'Say: Unto Allah belongeth all intercessions. His is the Sovereignty of the heavens and the earth. And afterward unto Him ye will be brought back'.[152]

Fitrat believed that by treating saints as intermediaries and praying to them, the difference between monotheism and polytheism was eroded. He quoted the story about Umar that once, during pilgrimage, he was going around the *Ka'ba*. He reached the *hajr-i aswad* ('black stone'), kissed it and then said,

> I know that you are a stone and cannot harm or benefit anyone. Had not I seen the Prophet kissing you I would not have kissed you at all.[153]

Fitrat saw the world as a battlefield, an arena of perpetual struggle. Each person and each nation has to struggle to obtain a livelihood. Without struggle and effort nothing will be gained. If a person sits hungry and thirsty at home and does not go out to work to earn his bread, food will not appear from the roof and he will die of hunger and thirst. If *tawakkal* without effort could be of any use, the Prophet, Fitrat pointed out, at the time of the Battle of the Trench (*khandaq*) would not have dug the trench with his own hands.[154] Fitrat argued that the fatalistic approach advocated by the *qadim* faction was contrary to Quranic teachings because:

> Allah never changeth the grace He hath bestowed on any people until they first change that which is in their heart.[155]

He felt strongly that

> the problems we face are caused by our own misdeeds.[156]

As the Quran says,

> Lo! Allah wrongeth not mankind in aught; but mankind wrong themselves.[157]

> Whatever of misfortune striketh you, it is what your right hands have earned. And He forgiveth much.[158]

Fitrat argued that Muslims, by remaining unmindful of the sacred guidance of the Quran and Traditions, had plunged themselves into the well of ignorance, disunity, superstition, inactivity and decline:

> The Prophet Muhammad, who is wiser than you [the Bukharan *ulama*], never left matters to God, (Who is higher than Baha'uddin) alone. He endured all the pains of travel, the discomforts of journeys, the torment of hunger and participated in battles in person. In the face of an all-round attack on Islam by infidels, how may His *Shari'a* permit you, a handful of *ulama*, lovers of comforts, to enjoy sumptuous food, not thinking of saving the precious religion of Islam, and even pronouncing it the duty of Baha'uddin? Moreover, has God Almighty given command for waging *jihad* ['holy war'] to defend Islam, in many verses of the Quran, to the living or the dead? Why do you pronounce the duty of defending Islam, which God obviously entrusted you, the living, a duty of the dead?[159]

Fitrat was here alluding to the belief prevalent in Bukhara at that time (and encouraged by the *ulama*) that the tomb of Baha'uddin would defend the state if it were threatened by any outside aggression.

In Fitrat's view, Bukhara had lost its independence to the Russians. The Emir received instructions from the Russian Emperor, and the *Qushbegi* from the Imperial Political Agent. It could be said that the instructions were friendly advice, but if so,

Then why does the Emir in turn not give such instructions to the Russian ruler?

asked Fitrat.

If Bukhara is taken by the Russians, why does Baha'uddin not liberate it?[160]

Fitrat warned his fellow-countrymen of dire consequences if they did not mend their ways:

If we continue to follow our old ways, do not learn the lesson from our miseries and misfortunes, and do not act according to God's will, the worst may happen ...[161]

As stated in the Quran,

'And when We would destroy a township, We send commandment to its folk who live at ease, and afterwards they commit abomination therein, so the word of (doom) hath effect for it, and We annihilate it with complete annihilation'.[162] 'And how many a township did I suffer long though it was sinful! Then I grasped it. Unto me is the return.'[163] 'Say: O mankind! I am only a plain warner unto you'.[164] 'So, when they angered Us, We punished them and drowned them every one.'[165] 'And We made them a thing past, and an example for those after (them)'.[166]

These verses were a clear indication to Fitrat that disobedience to God had been the cause of the destruction of his people.[167]

Decline of Education in Bukhara

One of the most important reasons for the decline of Bukhara was the state of its education system. Fitrat particularly singled out the lack of scientific education, and opposed wasting a long time on learning Arabic. He wrote,

it is a well-known fact that our forefathers were distinguished scholars in almost every field of knowledge, especially in science and ethics. Their knowledge of science and ethics did not consist of mere polemics, rather they knew and applied the important principles of science well.[168]

Realising the importance of learning, the Bukharans had built numerous *madrasa* and allocated fixed *vaqf* for them.[169]

The *madrasa* were divided into higher, secondary and lower seats of learning. Fitrat made a detailed list of the 33 institutions of higher learning in Bukhara. Collectively, they were allocated *vaqf* worth 2,815,000 *tenga* (422,250 roubles) per annum. The amount of *vaqf* allocated to a *madrasa* depended upon its size. For example, *Madrasa J'afar Khoja* was allocated the largest *vaqf*, worth 250,000 *tenga* (37,500 roubles), and *Madrasa Ibrahim Akhund* the smallest, worth 40,000 *tenga* (6,000 roubles). A *vaqf* worth 150,000 *tenga* (22,500 roubles) per annum was allocated to the *Madrasa Kukaltash*, which comprised 140 rooms for students, a lecture theatre, library, mosque and communal kitchen. Thousands of *tenga* went to the library, 24,000 *tenga* were taken by the *mudarris* and the rest were distributed amongst the *imam*, *sufi*, yard-keeper, water-carrier, barber and the owners of the rooms.[170]

Fitrat also catalogued the 39 seats of secondary learning in Bukhara, with an annual allocation of *vaqf* worth 961,000 *tenga* (144,150 roubles). *Madrasa Ir Nazar* received the largest amount, 35,000 *tenga* (5,250 roubles), and *Madrasa Jura Bek* the smallest, 12,000 *tenga* (1,800 roubles). There were also more than a hundred lower *madrasa*, with a collective *vaqf* of 500,000 *tenga*. These *vaqf* varied from 1,000 to 5,000 *tenga* per *madrasa* per annum. Besides *madrasa*, there were more than 300 *maktab* in Bukhara.[171]

An annual *vaqf* worth 43,100 *tenga* was allocated to the eleven big libraries collectively. These *vaqf* varied from 18,000 *tenga* (2,700 roubles) for the library *Jafar Khoja* to 800 *tenga* (120 roubles) for *kutab khana* ('library') *Mirza Ulugh Bek*.[172] There were twenty big and twenty small community dining halls, each having an allocation of *vaqf* worth 10,000 to 40,000 *tenga* and 4,000 to 9,000 *tenga* respectively. In addition, there were five or six Quranic schools and forty communal baths which had a significant amount of *vaqf* at their disposal.[173]

Despite all these educational establishments and their vast resources, the standard of education had fallen to such an extent that, according to Fitrat, there was hardly a man in the town who could pronounce the name of God correctly: they would say *avah* or *ablah* instead of Allah.[174] Fitrat claimed that

students in Bukhara spent 39 precious years in vain.[175]

'Children at school learned how to steal, beg and be ill-mannered.'[176] 'The *maktab* and *madrasa*, instead of teaching erotic poems, which fatally influence the morals, and senseless investigation of the mystical laws of the Quran, should have occupied themselves in the correction of morals'

wrote Fitrat.[177]

In Fitrat's view, the basic cause of the decline of education in Bukhara was unnecessary engagement in irrelevant complexities and declensions of the Arabic language at *maktab* and *madrasa*.[178] The decline had begun some 200 years ago (i.e. at the beginning of the eighteenth century), with the arrival of Mirza Khan of Shiraz, when the Bukharan *ulama* began limiting their studies to the explanation of words, in marginal notes written on the books.

They engaged themselves in this useless exercise to such an extent that they completely forgot about the useful sciences.[179]

Turkistanis, who often acquired their education at Bukhara, fell with the Bukharans into this fathomless stupidity and negligence. Consequently, 'the shining star of heavenly civilisations', 'the brightest page of human history', (i.e. Turkistan) 'found itself in such a dismal situation that it is shameful to discuss it with either friends or foes.'[180]

Despite the heavy emphasis on learning the Arabic language and grammar, Bukharans could hardly speak Arabic.[181] Fitrat illustrates this fact in his book *Bayanat-i-Sayyah-i-Hindi*, when the Bukharan *mudarris* consults a dictionary to understand a few everyday sentences uttered by the fictional Indian traveller.[182] Fitrat argued that science was the path to progress. As he explained,

'Science is such a powerful means that its possession enabled the wild Americans to reach their contemporary high level of civilisation and grandeur, and its absence amongst the civilised Persians hastily plunged them into servility and disgrace. Science is the means that enabled a handful of islanders-Englishmen [to become] masters of India, Egypt, Baluchistan and part of Arabia, and uncivilised Russians, the rulers of Tatar, Kirghiz, Turkistani and Caucasian Muslims; finally, it is the lack of science in Turkey that has been responsible for the loss of its vast territories to the French.'[183] 'If the Muslims of Turkistan continue with their old system of education and deprive themselves of learning the useful sciences, in a few years, Islam will totally disappear from Turkistan except for names in the history books.'[184]

The Role of the *Ulama*

Fitrat blamed the *ulama* for the moral and intellectual decline of Bukhara.

The Bukharan *ulama*, having captured all paths leading towards progress, plunged the well-being and the very existence of the nation into flames.[185]

He described them as

people who have attained high positions in Bukhara but do not have any conception of the modern sciences. After twenty years of learning and twenty years of teaching they become *mufti*. Finding books written in Arabic difficult, they turn to the books of the *Shari'a* in Persian. They consider that religious matters depend upon their opinions and aims, so they interpret the verses of the Quran according to their wishes and freely re-invent the Traditions.[186]

Fitrat ridiculed them:

O you who know not God, who live all your lives in Bukhara and know nothing even about Samarkand, how can you talk about the fourth heaven? This is not religion; where has the sweet talk of religion gone? ... The vile acts of the Bukharan clergy are the fundamental cause of the spiritual extinction of the nation.[187]

More specifically, Fitrat claimed

> had not you [the *ulama*] shut the door against the progress and enlightenment
> of Islam; had not spread undisguised savagery; had not limited the
> acquisition of armaments to the bow and cold steel; had not held soldiers
> in the army until they were seventy; had not you forbidden the production of
> cannons, weapons, bombs, dynamite and military science; had not you
> divided the united and a powerful Muslim nation into sects like Shi'a, Sunni,
> Zeydi, Wahhabi etc., and created hatred and animosity amongst them; had
> not you distorted most of the Quranic verses to suit your passions; had not
> you helped usurpers to deny the rights of the people through servility and
> flattery; then Islam would not have found itself in such an appalling
> situation.[188]

Fitrat was outraged by the corrupt practices of religious officials. For
example, the *Qazi-i-Kalan* recommended flatterers, irrespective of merit
and qualification, to the Emir for appointments as *alim*, *mufti* and *mudarris*
etc.[189] These were extremely lucrative posts. An *alim*, for example, might
receive 30,000 *tenga* from his *madrasa*, 20,000 for similar work, and
another 12,000 *tenga* when distributing the *vaqf* money allocated for the
students (*juz-jeshi*)[190] by defrauding them.[191] A *mufti* earned up to 30,000
tenga from the *madrasa* and more again for putting the official seal on legal
documents. Despite having such highly remunerative jobs, the Bukharan
ulama demanded money from the students to start teaching any new book.
Such abuses were commonplace; the reasoning of the *ulama* was,

> nobody moves without self interest in this era.[192]

The problem was not unique to Bukhara. Fitrat pointed out that for the last
three centuries the *ulama* throughout the Muslim world had been engaged
in all forms of malpractice. Until very recent times, the majority of Turkish,
Tatar, Indian and Persian scholars, like their Bukharan counterparts, had
sucked the blood of their own people. However, having realised the gravity
of the situation earlier than the Bukharans, these other nations had acted to
overthrow them. In a very short time they were able to distinguish authentic
scholars from selfish Mulla-worshippers. They gave respect to the former
and crushed the latter.[193] It was the duty of scholars and clerics, argued
Fitrat, to direct people towards the path of unity and agreement; to
stimulate the people to learn modern sciences; and to help in the opening of
new schools for the progress of Muslims.[194]

Rulers and People

Fitrat accused the ordinary people of contributing to their own misfortune
and the decline of Bukhara through their ignorance and blind subservience.
As he put it,

People should always remain people and should not descend to the level of animals.[195]

He reminded his readers that the Quran states unequivocally that

Surely we created man of the best stature.[196]

It was man's duty to make full use of all his faculties and all the opportunities that existed in the world since, as the Quran teaches, the Lord

'hath made of service unto you whatsoever is in the heavens and whatsoever is in the earth'.[197] 'If everything that exists in the heavens and the earth had not been for the service of humankind, the Europeans would not have invented balloons and aeroplanes to fly. How could human beings, who, according to the Quran, are the highest beings, to whom heaven and earth are subservient, whose hands can mould iron into wax, and can move mountains, turn into a flock of sheep?'

demanded Fitrat.[198]

He described the Bukharans as

The nation which has been deprived of every right, but is still obedient, bowing down before their oppressors as though it were an honour. The nation which, having fallen into the blind well of ignorance, calls their redeemers *kafir*; how can one place one's hope in such a nation?[199]

He continued,

O poor people, your legal rights have been usurped and you have become the adherents of the usurpers; your blood is being sucked, your property is confiscated, your honour and reputation is set on fire and you do not realise it.[200]

However, Fitrat reserved his greatest scorn for the *umara* ('rulers'), who, without exception, had attained their high posts owing to blind luck. He identified two categories. Firstly,

the illiterate sons of rulers, who, during the rule of their fathers, engage in all manner of stupidities and misdeeds; they lack any trace of admirable human qualities. Secondly, shopkeepers and merchants, for whom filling their stomachs is the most desirable act in this world or the next. They consider education superfluous and are not interested in the progress of the country.[201]

The Emir of Bukhara, he argued, was an exception, since he cared a great deal about his subjects:

Our Emir is just himself, but the majority of his officials have never even heard of justice. This is the basic cause of the downfall of our country, and if the system remains the same we can never rise again.[202]

In the introduction to *Munazara*, Fitrat addressed the Emir as

dear father of Bukhara, saviour of the World,[203]

believing that reforms were possible in Bukhara under the leadership of the Emir. In the first years of his reign, Emir Abd-al Ahad (1885–1910) had acquired a reputation as a reformer who, though under Russian pressure, formally abolished slavery on his accession, closed the infamous underground prison in the citadel at Bukhara, ended executions by impalement or hurling from the top of the sixty-metre Great Minaret, and prohibited exhibitions by *bacha* ('dancing boy').[204] However, the effect of these reforms was trivial, since slavery lingered on in the form of debtor's bondage and inhuman penal conditions continued, at least in the *valayat*. The system continued to ignore the needs of the population at large in order to enrich the Emir and his administrators. After the death of Abd-al Ahad in 1910, Emir Alim, on his accession to the throne, announced a manifesto to eliminate the most serious abuses.[205] To put an end to corruption at all levels he forbade anyone to present gifts to officials, court dignitaries, or to himself; forbade officials of lesser rank to impose taxes; banned the *qazi* from fixing the price of legal deeds at will; and promised that real salaries would be paid to civil servants. The new Emir also announced that, unlike his predecessors, he would not personally trade in cotton and *karakul*. (Emir Abd-al Ahad used to buy cotton and *karakul* from farmers at very low prices and sell them to Russian merchants at a vast profit.) His refusal to indulge in this trade brought some relief to farmers from the oppression of the agents who bought cotton for the Emir. Though the manifesto remained a mere declaration and was never implemented, such measures emboldened the reformists, including Fitrat, who hoped that they might win over the Emir to the cause of reform.

FITRAT'S REFORM AGENDA

Although Fitrat was acutely aware of the problems of the Bukharan state, he was not entirely without hope that the situation could be retrieved, since the situation in Europe during the Middle Ages had been worse than in contemporary Bukhara. Fitrat illustrated this point with numerous references to European history. He argued that at that time in Europe the masses were ignorant and oppressed, while the rulers and the clergy acted as tyrants; the clergy owned huge tracts of land and were so powerful that the state officials did not dare to enter their domains to collect taxes or arrest criminals. The rulers could not act without consulting the clergy. In 1077 Pope Gregory VII excommunicated the German ruler King Henry IV because the latter had failed to consult him. Such wild offences, shameless, Godless acts, Fitrat argued, were contrary to Divine and human law and could not last long.

With God's help, human effort and resolution agitated like an ocean and washed away their foundations. During the tenth century [AH], societies opposed to the clergy emerged in various parts of Europe. These societies campaigned against the clergy and flourished further in the twelfth century. These Protestant societies translated the Bible into vernacular languages and urged people to read it. They criticised those actions of the clergy which were not in conformity with the Bible. For example, they criticised the clergy's excessive accumulation of wealth while they continued to instruct people to give up worldly wealth. The Protestant societies became so popular that some members of the clergy also joined them. Such societies were very successful, firstly because they wrote their basic charters in very clear language and spread it amongst the people. Secondly, they did not recognise the authority of the Pope and when compelled to do so, they exposed the sins of the clergy. Another significant reason which helped the cause of these societies was the war of the Christian nations against the Muslims to recapture the Holy Land [1090–1492].[206]

Fitrat argued that the Europeans had benefited enormously in both material and spiritual terms from their contact with Muslims.[207] He cited in support a French professor, a certain Carl Siniubus,[208] who wrote,

In the eleventh century, the Muslim world was totally different from that of the European. European cities were small and miserable, the villages, comprised of hovels, were ruined, roads were not safe. The Muslim cities of Baghdad, Syria, Egypt and Spain were flourishing: they contained marble palaces, factories, schools, seminaries and rich bazaars. From Spain to Turkistan there was a constant flow of trade caravans. Realising the glory of Muslim culture, Europeans came to these cities to learn scientific knowledge. The Muslims acquired knowledge and science from the Greeks, Persians, Indians and Chinese, developed it further, and then handed it over to the Europeans.[209]

The Europeans had learned from the Muslims in many fields. In agriculture, for example, they learned to cultivate green wheat, saffron, the mulberry tree, rice, dates, palms, lemons, cotton, coffee and sugar-cane. They imported luxury items such as fine Syrian textiles, brocades, glass, mirrors, paper and various sweets. In the field of science they acquired the knowledge of algebra, geometry, trigonometry, chemistry and numbers. The Europeans, ignoring their clergy, studied in Baghdad and Egypt to learn science from the Muslims. The clergy severely punished those who created controversies, who studied in Muslim schools, or who wore new clothes on Friday, but at last the opponents of the clergy won.[210] Thus, the Europeans were highly indebted to the Muslims for their progress. However, continued Fitrat, the *ulama* derided as infidels those Muslims who moved in the direction of recovering their lost culture and civilisation, and put hurdles in their way.[211]

Fitrat stressed:

'The present prosperity of idol-temples is due to our disunity; Islam is in essence the same as it was, every defect comes from us, who claim to be Muslims. Islam is our faith, Islam is our honour, Islam is our happiness, Islam is the reason of our rise, and of peace. We are entrusted with Islam by the Prophet. Holy Bukhara is our fatherland, kind Bukhara is our mother, dear Bukhara is our object of love, Bukhara is our beloved, Bukhara is ours, we are Bukhara's'.[212] 'Sitting idle, careless and ignorant in the face of this total disgrace any longer would destroy our faith and ruin our holy fatherland, which the Shari'a disapproves. The intelligent people of the world would curse us and exclude us from mankind. Brothers! come to your senses a little. Man is superior to all other creatures on earth; unlike other creatures man is capable of progress and regression. Wise men have identified three states of progress and regression: (a) the animal state (b) the mineral state (c) the human state. Those who maintain their human capabilities at the same level abide in the animal state; those who transfer their human capabilities from a higher level to a lower level fall into the mineral state; those who develop their human capabilities achieve the human state. Wise men call them human beings. In short, why do infidels progress and we regress? Infidels are considered human beings by wise men and why do they consider us minerals? The infidels become wealthier and we poorer and more wretched. It is a matter of shame that Christians display their thousands of talents by constructing railway lines, ships and telegraph lines, and our skills are limited to carts and mud pottery. In these ill-fated days we should blush with shame to the doorway and walls [i.e. 'to the roots of our hair']. At the time when the most insignificant Christian states have hundreds of thousands of regular troops, we have 10,000 robbers gathered around us; in other words, we have undertaken a child's play [i.e. are extremely foolish]. O those who read this book! If you love religion, the fatherland, life, property, your children, if you want means for saving religion and spreading the Shari'a, the flourishing of fatherland and happiness, the primary means is to attain knowledge. Send the most capable students to the capital of the Muslim Caliphate [Istanbul], the less capable to Bukhara, and render help to open new-method schools. The second means is the unity of all the Muslim societies: consider all those Muslims who say 'there is no god but God and Muhammad is His Prophet', regardless of the sect to which they belong; precisely speaking, stop the Shi'a-Sunni conflict. Those who hinder unity are traitors to Islam. Do not be deceived by them. I beg [to assert that] not learning modern sciences and disunity between Muslims are illegal'.[213]

Reform of the System of Education

Fitrat believed that the solution to the problem of decline lay in the acquisition of modern, European-style sciences. Modern education was not, in his view, incompatible with Islam and could only be taught effectively, according to Fitrat, in the new-method schools. To prove this Fitrat gave a comparative account of new and old schools and in his work *Munazara* have explained and answered the objections raised by the *qadim ulama* to new-method schools:

Firstly the *qadim ulama* believed that new-method schools would turn their children into infidels.[214] They thought that by teaching the *Shari'a* in schools the new-method teachers were presenting themselves as well-wishers of Islam, and once Bukharans yield to their deception they will start converting children into infidels.[215] The conservatives also objected that pupils in *jadid* schools would learn such European ways as sitting on chairs and argued:

> since the Prophet said, 'Everyone imitates their own people': Russians sit on chairs, so if our pupils also sit on chairs they would become Russians.[216]

A third objection to the new-method schools was that

> the new education system will harm Islam since our old system of education, which educated our *mujtahid* [lit. 'renewer'], scholars, fathers and forefathers, would disappear, and a new system invented by the infidels would replace it.[217]

Still another objection was that opening *jadid* schools would be *bida* ('innovation').[218] The decision to ban these schools, in their view, represented the consensus (*ijma*) of the *ulama* and Muslim community. According to the Tradition of the Prophet, once the consensus is reached there is no room for vacillation.[219]

The new-method schools, wrote Fitrat,

> admit the child at the age of six, and by the time he is nineteen, he grows into a devout patriot, a friend of religion, a friend of the nation, upright, just, obedient to the commands of Islam and a well-bred, educated man. The period of education at the new schools is thirteen years, as opposed to thirty years at the old *madrasa*. In the old system, the pupils spend ten years in dark, disgusting buildings, resembling a prison or bestial (lit. 'quadrupedal') dwellings. They get two lessons a day from the teacher – 'angel of death'; nobody cares whether have they learnt their previous lesson or understood the current one. In the new schools, students are given instruction three times a day by well-mannered, angel-like teachers, in high, bright buildings, constructed in the middle of flower-filled gardens, in conformity with hygienic requirements. Students have a break of fifteen minutes after each lesson and can breathe fresh air. Advantages of the old system: during thirty years of study, the students do nothing else; they often live in poverty and are in debt. Due to poverty they cannot marry. After graduating from the *madrasa* at the age of 37, they have to spend another three years looking for work. Instead of serving Islam and guiding people to the way of the faithful they bargain away

their dignity to obtain an insignificant post of *mudarris*. Many of them die without marrying, due to poverty and debt. Hence, the population of Muslims has decreased. In the new schools, education is free for the poor while the rich have to pay. Students are prepared to take up a range of occupations such as the army, trade, agriculture, crafts and industry. Moreover, in the old schools, due to the length of study women cannot be educated. In the new schools, girls join at the age of six, are educated until they are aged between fourteen and eighteen and then marry. Obviously the old schools will disappear but it will not harm Islam.[220]

Fitrat's reply to the first objection was that:

Firstly it is said in the Traditions, that whoever says, 'there is no god but God will not fall into Hell.' Secondly, if such an insignificant resemblance [sitting on the chair] was sufficient to become infidel, when your *ulama*, like fire-worshippers, fasten gold and silver around the necks of their horses, they may also become fire-worshippers. Thirdly, the Lord made your eyes and ears like the Russians, but has that brought any harm to your religion? Fourthly, the Russians did not invent sitting on chairs, *bek* Abi Sufian, one of the greatest courtiers of the Caliph Mua'via, first sat on a chair. Fifthly, if someone reads the Quran not sent to the Prophet Muhammad [i.e. anything but the Quran], sitting on earth or grass, will he become a Muslim? Or if a Muslim reads the Quran with full respect sitting on a chair, will he become an infidel? Sixthly, if you disallow Muslims new-method schools because children sit on chairs, why do you not forbid the Russo-native schools, where children not only sit on chairs, but also learn the Russian language?[221]

In Fitrat's view, the old system had to disappear. However, he argued that its disappearance would not bring any harm to Islam. Firstly, because the old system was not invented by *mujtahid* or other great Muslims. Secondly, the new system was not a creation of the infidels. Even if the new system had been invented by the infidels, Muslims should adopt it, since it was easy and useful.[222] He illustrated this point with two analogies:

'Your forefathers, officials and *mujtahid*, who intended to perform the *Haj* at Mecca, rode a horse or donkey for six months from Bukhara to reach Baghdad or Bombay and then sailed in a boat for another year to reach Mecca. They returned to Bukhara after four years. Now, the infidels have invented the railway and ships. The Muslims have abandoned the old means to perform *Haj* and reach Mecca in 25 days, using the railway and ships constructed by infidels. Neither has this harmed their faith, nor was the world destroyed. Rather, thousands of Bukharans now travel every year to perform the *Haj*, instead of twenty as in the past. The question of education stands thus: the old system deprived all women of education, kept most of the men illiterate and produced hardly two or three great scholars in a century. The new system of education, due to its easy method of teaching, educates both men and women'.[223] 'Similarly, during the life of the Prophet and his companions, the Quran was written on sheep's bones using *kufi* script. Now that centuries have passed, people write on paper using *naskh* script [i.e. they adopted a simpler and easier script than *kufi*]'.[224]

To answer the objection that opening *jadid* schools would be *bida*, Fitrat drew a distinction between two types of *bida*: benevolent innovation and ill-starred or corrupt innovation. Writing the Quran using *naskh* script on paper instead of bones, travelling on ships or trains to perform the *Haj*, and allocation of *vaqf* to open new schools were benevolent innovations. Extortion of money from students, the decoration of horses with gold chains, the wearing of European velvet gowns, and visiting Russian brothels, Fitrat considered corrupt innovations. He deemed the production of cannon and guns essential for the defence of Islam, hence a benevolent innovation.[225]

To refute that there was a consensus (*ijma*) in the Muslim community to ban the new schools Fitrat pointed out that

the Bukharans alone do not constitute Muslim community; wherever Muslims reside there is a Muslim community. The Muslims of India, Afghanistan, Turkey, Arabia, the Tatar lands and Persia have unanimously recognised the necessity of such schools. If you are opposing them, it must be clear by now which side the majority of Muslims supports.[226]

He also used the argument that

Such schools have been functioning in Istanbul, Baghdad, Egypt, India, the Tatar lands and the Caucasus for many years. Nobody there, till now, has been turned into an infidel. Rather, graduates of these schools have attained high standards in religious learning as well as in the sciences. Pay attention to the fact that, at a time when Christians use all means for the refutation of Islam and to achieve this purpose publish innumerable books daily, scholars in Istanbul, India and Egypt are busy ceaselessly compiling and publishing books to refute them. But I have never heard that Bukharan scholars have written even a single line to refute them. Presently, in 1329 AH. [i.e. in 1912],[227] new schools are being opened in Afghanistan and in luminous Madina, the city of the Prophet. In Madina especially, the opening of this school is being celebrated as a great national occasion. Nobody has said that it is illegal or will convert their children into infidels. What right do you have to say so?[228]

The principle of *ijma* in Islam, as pointed out in Chapter Three, began as a natural process for solving problems and decision-making, and as a check on individual opinion. It is linked with *qiyas* (analogical reasoning), which is to be performed in preparation for *ijma*. Orthodox schools of law[229] gave the principle of *ijma* an overriding and absolute authority, making it the final and conclusive argument on every issue. *Ijma* acquired this authoritative status not only because it discerned right from wrong in the present and the future, but also because it established the past. For *ijma* was used to determine what the *sunna* of the Prophet had been, and what was the right interpretation of the Quran. In short, both the interpretation of Quran and the *sunna* were authenticated through *ijma*. Thus *ijma* is an organic process, which creates, assimilates, modifies and rejects at the same time.[230] The issues at stake in Bukhara were the right interpretation of the faith, and whether to assimilate modern knowledge or reject it. These issues were debated by Fitrat within Islamic parameters.

Fitrat considered the education of women absolutely vital for the progress of the country. He referred to the Tradition of the Prophet that

it is the duty of every Muslim to seek knowledge

and to American and French writers who considered women equal to men in matters of reason. He argued that if women were not educated they could not educate their children.[231] Fitrat made the point that it was an indication of quite how far the Bukharans had strayed from the teachings of the Prophet and Quran that they were now afraid of the spread of knowledge.[232] In short, Fitrat's argument was that

modern European sciences should be learnt. To save Islam the only course left is the opening of new-method schools.[233]

Reform of Health Care, Trade and Industry

Fitrat also addressed the issues of health care and the economy in Bukhara. Medical and sanitary facilities were very poor.[234] *Hauz-i Divon Begi* ('the Pond of the Divon Begi') was the chief source of drinking water in the city, but the water was contaminated and harmful for health. Almost half a *man* (1 *man* = 8 *pud*) of dirt was thrown into the pond by Bukharans daily.[235] Fitrat emphasised cleanliness and the importance of better hygienic conditions, with the help of the Traditions and verses from the Quran.[236]

Fitrat urged the government to convert one of the biggest *madrasa* into a medical school and recruit teachers from St. Petersburg or elsewhere in Europe to teach there.[237] He also tried to persuade the government to send some of the most capable students abroad to study medicine.[238] According to him the annual cost of sending ten students abroad would be 5,000 roubles. For this purpose 40,000 *tenga* (6,000 roubles) of *vaqf* allocated to the *Madrasa Dar-u-Shafa* (lit. 'House of Health') could be used. After returning home, the successful students could replace the European teachers.[239] There could be no harm in sending students abroad, since, according to the Tradition,

Seek [knowledge] even if you have to proceed to China.[240]

In support of his argument, Fitrat quoted examples from history of the great Muslim rulers who had invited foreign, non-Muslim doctors to their capitals and deputed Christian scholars to translate learned books.[241]

Fitrat advocated the modernisation of crafts, trade and industry, stressing the need for the replacement of small-scale production units with large-scale factory production. He feared that local businesses would be annihilated by the growing competition from cheaper European factory products.[242] Fitrat both recognised the superior qualities of local work and had the foresight to see that these skills could vanish forever. Fitrat makes one of his characters comment on the output of an *alacha* ('famous Bukharan hand-made cloth') manufacturer at Qarshi:

> 'Your workshop is better than others in Qarshi and your *alacha* is finer and more graceful. In fact, your *alacha* is superior to most Russian materials, because though their material is finer and prettier, it is not durable in the wearing, as yours is. About the fineness and durability of your *alacha* I have heard a story which I shall narrate to you. A Bukharan pilgrim went to the *Haj* and took a few pieces of this material to grant in charity in Madina. He somehow did not use the cloth there and brought it back. At the port of Odessa the Russian customs officials mistook it for French material and demanded duty; the Haji tried to convince them that it was ordinary Bukharan cloth, but the officials were adamant, saying that there were no factories in Bukhara which could make such a fine thing and that the Haji had bought it in Istanbul. The Haji had to pay duty. The Russians were not at fault since the *alacha* was in reality very good and looked to them like a French product – in durability it was even superior to French.'[243] The Indian traveller then asked the manufacturer, 'what do you plan in the future for your craft? Will your art survive another twenty years?' The weaver replied, 'Our craft was a success in the past, and is successful now. The future is known to God alone'.[244]

Fitrat analysed the changes that were taking place in the Turkistani economy. Before the Russian penetration the Turkistanis had produced almost everything hand-made, from cloth to crockery. No foreign manufacturer was able to earn anything. Later, European industrial goods began to replace native goods, putting native craftsmen out of work. If they had planned for the future and modernised their machines, not only would they themselves have been happier, but the enormous amounts of wealth earned by the foreign manufacturers would have remained in the country. He concluded that native crafts would disappear unless the native craftsmen converted their workshops into modern, European-style factories.[245]

Fitrat argued that the *Shari'a* never forbade the development of trade and business; rather, the Quran and Traditions praise those who spread knowledge of these professions. Trade, investment and ownership of capital are essential for every nation.[246] From the point of view of the

Shari'a, two of the basic duties of a Muslim, giving *zakat* and performing the *haj*, both required wealth. Even offering prayers and keeping the fast can more easily be performed by the rich, because both require peace of mind and dedication, which a poor person is less likely to enjoy, since he has to work hard to earn his living while the rich can better fulfil these obligations. Moreover, the affirmation of the unity of God by word and by deed (the fundamental tenet of Islam) requires knowledge, and the acquisition of knowledge requires money. That is why, as Fitrat quoted, the Prophet said that 'poverty is closer to unbelief'.[247] Fitrat maintained that Islam encourages trade because it is an issue of life and death for mankind. The needs of mankind cannot be fulfilled without indulging in trade.[248]

Fitrat argued that in modern times, trade had become so important to European countries that their entire society was organised around it. They had schools devoted to commercial practice and would defend their trading interests by force, to the extent that trade was the basic cause of modern wars.[249] Fitrat even developed an analysis of European colonialism.

> Some strong countries send their people to weaker countries, where after attaining certain privileges, they open trade routes. If the natives then damage their trade interests in any way, they send their troops and colonise the land. If some other big power also has trade interests there, they also send troops to defend their interests, and a war begins. Hence, two big powers get involved in an armed conflict in a third country due to trade interests ... For example, England colonised India to secure its trade interests.[250]

In this context it was vital for Bukhara to develop its economy so as to protect itself against foreign economic and ultimately military domination.

Fitrat argued that the Bukharan merchants were engaged in trade only to fulfil their personal ambitions, whereas Europeans conducted trade which was useful. In his view, the Bukharan cotton traders, despite their better knowledge of the local situation, suffered colossal losses while the foreign cotton traders succeeded, because the native traders were disunited while the foreign traders stood together. Bukharan traders competed with each other during the purchasing season, and their basic aim was to harm fellow traders. Thus, they purchased cotton at a rate higher than that current in Moscow and consequently suffered losses. The European traders, however, after mutual consultation, fixed a rate that was lower than the one in Moscow and none of them purchased cotton at a higher rate. Another reason was that the Europeans had their own cotton-processing factories, on which the Bukharans were dependent. A third reason was that the European traders had studied modern commercial sciences, while the Bukharans had no such training. The Europeans had already taken over the cotton and silk trade from the natives, and Fitrat warned that if there was no change of attitude amongst the Bukharans, they would take over the *karakul* trade as well.[251]

Bukhara possessed other sources of wealth apart from the staple commodities. It had reserves of gold, copper, iron, coal and oil. Fitrat advocated the formation of partnerships of local businessmen to explore the mineral resources of the country and the use of modern means like machines and factories, otherwise, he argued, the Europeans would take over these fields as well.[252]

In economic matters as in the field of health care, the principal thrust of Fitrat's critique of Bukharan society was the need to make full use of modern knowledge and advance planning to compete with the Europeans.

Reform of the System of Government

The most explicit and concise expression of Fitrat's political thought is contained in the reform project which he wrote in 1917–18 at the request of the Central Committee of the Young Bukharan Party. This addressed the structure of government as well as specific policy issues. Fitrat recommended that the kernel of government should be a Council of ten Ministers: of Agriculture, *Vaqf*, War, Finance, the Interior, Justice, Police, Transport and Mines, Public Education, and Foreign Affairs, with additional Muslim advisors. The Minister of Foreign Affairs was to preside over the Council. Decisions were to be reached by common agreement. Any Minister not in agreement with a decision was to resign, and to be replaced by another Minister, appointed by the President of the Council with the approval of the Emir.

The Ministry of Agriculture would be responsible for solving such pressing questions as land and water reforms. Fitrat proposed the levying of a tax (2–3 Roubles per *tanab*) on all *amlak* and *kharaj* lands, whether cultivated or uncultivated; exempting *mulk hurr* lands from all taxes; redividing the *valayat* into between 5 and 100 districts, each to be headed by an intelligent and honest *aqsaqal*, who was to maintain a land register. The register, along with the taxes, were to be handed over to the *bek*, who was to deposit it in the state exchequer, in accordance with the entries in the register. Other measures were the abolition of taxes on buildings and horse-fodder; the improvement of water installations; the equitable distribution of water by the *mira'b*; the construction of canals from the Amu Darya; the prohibition of *hashar* ('unwaged labour for the lord') on state lands, in orchards or for construction work; the prohibition of usury; the establishment of agricultural banks with branches in each *valayat* to advance interest-free or low-interest loans to farmers; the introduction of machinery into Bukharan agriculture; the distribution of government-held irrigated lands to landless peasants and the opening of schools of agriculture. Last but not least, it was important to appoint a competent man to head the Ministry.

Fitrat advocated the creation of a Ministry of *Vaqf* Holdings to oversee the problems associated with *vaqf* property, and the establishment of a special exchequer for *vaqf* holdings, to put their revenue and expenditure in order; the aim of these bodies would be to prevent abuses by tenants and managers; to ensure that *vaqf* money was invested in commerce and the profits used to promote education and repairs of confessional and secular schools, mosques, libraries, reading rooms and refectories.

Bearing in mind the fragile nature of Bukharan independence, Fitrat recommended the creation of a Ministry of War to run military affairs. He called for the number of servicemen to be raised to 12,000, the maximum number allowed by the Russo-Bukharan treaty, as well as compulsory military service to be introduced for every adult male of 22 years of age, barring students, disabled people and members of the Emir's family. He recommended the appointment of trained personnel as commanders and the payment of fixed salaries to soldiers by the state. He also advocated the establishment of a military academy.

Fitrat's specific recommendations for the Ministry of Finance included the reorganisation of the public exchequer; the collection of taxes and customs duties by the departments of the Ministry; reform of the livestock tax; the taxation of merchants on the basis of their annual turnover; the appointment of a court treasurer responsible for the expenses of the Emir; and the introduction of an annual budget.

The Minister of Internal Affairs was to supervise the maintenance of law and order. Fitrat suggested a decimal system of administrative divisions, whereby the Emirate would be divided into up to ten *kurgan* ('provinces'), headed by a *kurgan begi*; each *kurgan* would be divided into ten *ilbegstvo* ('regions'), headed by an *ilbegi*; and each *ilbegstvo* would be divided into ten *tumen* ('districts'), headed by a *tumenbegi*. The *kurgan begi*, *ilbegi* and *tumenbegi* were to be appointed by the Internal Affairs Minister with the approval of the Emir. *Aqsaqal* and *mulla* were to look after matters concerning the people at the level of the *tumen*. *Aqsaqal* were to be popularly elected, though confirmation by the *tumenbegi* was to be mandatory. The Minister of Internal Affairs and his subordinate officials were not to meddle in judicial matters, but were to apply and implement the decisions of the *Shari'a* courts. In other words, executive and judicial powers were to be kept separate. The local night police chiefs (*mirshab*) were also to come under the Minister of Internal Affairs, though the *mirshab* of the city of Bukhara was to have ministerial rank.

A Justice minister would replace the *Qazi-i-Kalan* and oversee the administration of justice, though he would not direct judicial business himself. Fitrat's programme suggested dividing the Emirate into two or three judicial divisions. The Justice Minister was to nominate salaried *qazi* at the level of *kurgan*, *ilbegstvo* and *tumen*; each court was to be constituted by a *qazi* assisted by two *mufti*. Fitrat also proposed the establishment of an appeal court (*istenaf*). The presentation of a formal summons to call a person to attend court was to be made obligatory.

For the upkeep and construction of roads and railways and the exploitation of mineral resources such as coal, gold, ferrous ores and oil, Fitrat proposed the appointment of a Minister of Transport and Mines. A Minister of Public Education was to look after the state and *vaqf* schools, the appointment of staff, curricula, and teacher-training. The Foreign Minister, besides presiding over the Council of Ministers, was also to be responsible for relations with Russia and other states.

Besides the appointment of these ministers, Fitrat also proposed the establishment of a Communal Council for each town to oversee public order, maintaining the streets and the price of goods etc. He also advocated the establishment of two national Control Commissions. The first was to have twenty members, at least half of whom were to be Muslim jurists from Russia and the Caucasus. This Commission was to approve the budget of the ministries. The second was to be constituted by the people through the press, guaranteeing the freedom of the press.[253]

In his 1918 programme, Fitrat did not raise the issue of limiting the Emir's powers, let alone his overthrow. He still believed in the possibility of reform under the leadership of the Emir, as he had written in 1913:

> The day the Emir and *Vazir* resolve to reform schools, Bukhara will have fifty seats of higher learning, 150 preparatory schools and 360 elementary schools.[254]

In essence, this programme advocated the establishment of the rule of law, by transforming the despotic regime into a constitutional monarchy of the European type. It also advocated the strengthening of the country economically, politically and militarily, by increasing the material well-being and educational level of the people. The chief reason for Fitrat's faith in the ability of the Emir to bring about reform was that he saw no hope of change being initiated by the ordinary people. In the specific conditions of Bukhara, reforms could only be introduced from the top. He had no option, therefore, but to believe in the goodwill of the Emir. It was for this reason that Fitrat addressed the Emir in his earlier works as 'Dear father of Bukhara', 'Saviour of the World', etc.[255]

Although Fitrat continued well after the Bolshevik revolution and the failed *jadid* rising against the Emir to envisage the future of Bukhara as a monarchy, the practical expression he intended for his principles of Islamic rectitude was the emergence of an honest and unselfish class of public servants, who would act for the good of the country, not for the Emir. Fitrat believed that

> Each state official should regard himself as a servant, first to the state, then to the people and then to the ruler. They hold their offices thanks to the state

and the people. Had there not been a state or people there would be no officials. In the Emirate, local state officials, after being appointed to a region, often forget God, the people and the region and just try to please the Emir by illegitimate and legitimate means. The Emir cannot be pleased with officials who destroy the state by robbing the people.[256]

Fitrat extended this sense of public duty, which officials should have, to include responsibility for the welfare of the people. He cited the saying of the Prophet,

Each one amongst you is a pastor of his subjects and will be accountable to God.[257]

CONCLUSIONS

Fitrat was dissatisfied with the existing state of affairs in Bukhara which he believed were characterised by social decay, political weakness and economic disintegration. He believed that no remedy for these ills was possible unless a deeper reform of people's most fundamental beliefs, values and practices was undertaken, based upon strengthening individual and social morality. This reform was to lead to the eradication of the superstition and fatalism fostered by the *ulama*, and to a more positive, this-worldly religious attitude, in which otherworldly spirituality would play a less dominant role. Fitrat's thought outlined in *Rahbar-i-Najat* champions a decisively positive this-worldly shift: though he vigorously asserts faith in the transcendental truth of Islam, and in the need to seek happiness in the world hereafter, he rejects the attitude that happiness in this world should be ignored or renounced, and seeks instead the betterment of social, political and moral life in this world.

His understanding of Islam is that of a dynamic religion, one that was primarily based on reason. He stressed that Islam is not only not incompatible with reason, but that it is the only religion which calls upon man to use his own reason and investigate nature as a religious duty. Numerous verses of the Quran enjoining man to think intelligently and to study nature cited by him are witness to this. However, he agreed that the debased irrational form of Islam, which was believed in and practised by most of its adherents, was threatened by modern advances in thought and science. Therefore he rationally interprets Islam and encourages Muslims to accept the intellectualism and humanism of the modern West as having really developed from the apogee of Islamic civilisation itself, and indeed as the true message of Islam. Learning European sciences, to him, meant re-acquiring the lost heritage of Islam and restoring its past glory. The acquisition of modern knowledge from whatever source was mandatory for every Muslim, since, he argued, this knowledge was the result of the collective enquiry of humankind as a whole. He was opposed to the idea that science could be divided into Muslim and Christian. He understood that there had been cross-fertilisation of cultures between East and West and that this had been a source of progress.

Fitrat, in advocating the integration of modern ideas and institutions back into the religion from which they had originated, not only encouraged the influx of Western ideas and education, but also partly justified the existing Western intellectual impacts on Bukhara. However, the actual incorporation of Western ideas into the values of Islam could only be a long and slow process. He could do no more than provide a basis for subsequent developments on reformist lines. What was required, before all else, was an integrated educational programme. But who could accomplish this programme? The *ulama*, the traditional guardians of Islamic faith and practice, were not only incapable of fulfilling this task because of their narrow and restricted education, but could not even perceive that there was a problem. Fitrat, not only supported but also tried to devise and implement a programme. The new-method system of education, based on modern European sciences, was a means to more important ends, namely, the political and cultural awakening of the people, the modernisation of Islamic life, and the emancipation of women.

Thus, for this reason, the issue of new-method education acquired pivotal importance in his writings. The intellectual and political battle lines in Bukhara were drawn over the question of new-method education and he remained in the forefront of the battlefield for reform.

Fitrat began by advocating reform under the leadership of the Emir. His insistence at this period on the leadership of the ruler should be understood in terms of his lack of faith in the ability of the masses to overthrow the system. In a society where the bulk of the population was ignorant and blindly subservient to powerful and conservative forces such as the *ulama*, it was not possible, he thought, to launch a struggle against both the Emir and the *ulama*. He believed that retaining the Emir was necessary to protect Bukhara from anarchy. Moreover, Fitrat still had faith that Emir Alim Khan, who came to the throne in 1910, could be manipulated so as to work for the cause of reform and the spread of new-method education. Even after Russian revolution Fitrat wanted to retain the Emir as head of state, his programme of reform written in 1917–1918 for the Young Bukharan Party is witness to it. Later events led him to accept the overthrow of the Emir.

Conclusions

The development of reformist thought in late nineteenth and early twentieth century Bukhara is particularly interesting because the reformist movement here took a somewhat more political character, both in form and in content, than in other parts of the Muslim world at the time. It emerged, owing to a combination of internal and external factors, amongst a tiny layer of intelligentsia in a very traditional and conservative society, situated in a remote and isolated part of the world.

Ahmad Donish was the first and most significant Bukharan reformist thinker. He understood clearly that the impact of the Western scientific, technological and industrial revolutions would necessarily disrupt traditional Muslim societies such as that of Bukhara. The most effective way to make a constructive adjustment to new challenges, in his view, was through a critical discussion of the system of government and values. The chief cause of his country's decline, as he saw it, was the ruler's violation of the *Shari'a*. This had led to the moral and spiritual degeneration of society. He therefore insisted upon reinstating the paramount role of reason and the *Shari'a* in matters concerning the governing of the country. Reason and *Shari'a*, for Donish, were not distinct from each other. By stressing the importance of reason he restored the role assigned to human reason by the earliest Muslims. He also took a firm and progressive position on the issue of divine destination and freedom of will, maintaining that man possessed free will. The importance of Donish's ideas on human freedom of thought and action, and the progressive nature of such ideas, can be understood against this background. He believed in the need for the ruler to be accountable to the people. He also believed in the limitation of the ruler's power.

Donish stressed the need to introduce modern, European-style education in Bukharan *madrasa*, so that natural sciences, history and literature, in addition to the traditional disciplines, could be taught. He was well aware of the necessity of political reorganisation, and saw that profound political reform was impossible without social reform and economic development. Socio-economic modernisation required a new kind of education and new legislation, which depended in turn upon political authority. He therefore presented a detailed project to the Emir Muzaffar, embracing political reorganisation, socio-economic and cultural reforms.

His reform project, a blend of Islamic and European concepts, envisaged the dissemination of progressive ideas by an enlightened and just monarch, ruling with the aid of a consultative council composed of representatives of all classes, and through ministries with well-defined functions. Donish's proposed reforms encompassed most of the political, scientific, technological, cultural and educational achievements of the West. However, they in no way contravened the Islamic faith and his frame of reference remained entirely Islamic. Russia, for him, was not a model to be aped, but a useful source of knowledge and an instrument for restructuring Bukharan society. What he wanted was a remodelling of the institutions of Bukhara, without altering the Islamic framework.

The most striking quality of Donish's work is that, despite being surrounded by fanaticism and ignorance, and without much access to the work of other contemporary Muslim reformists, he nevertheless examined the prevailing conditions critically. He analysed the problems, and advocated some degree of political reorganisation, science, technology, culture and modern education as a remedy. He came to conclusions similar to those of the most radical thinkers in the Muslim world, who supported freedom of thought and action, championed the cause of science, modern education and culture, and opposed the traditional, conservative world outlook. He also prefigured some of the ideas of communist thinkers of the next century.

After the rejection of his reform project by the Emir, Donish realised that the Emir and his clique were actively obstructing reform in Bukhara. He did not then hesitate to call for the total destruction of the system and the overthrow of the ruler. This was at a time when the orthodox *ulama* still clung to the doctrine of absolute obedience to the ruler, as set out in the Quranic verse 'O ye who believe! Obey Allah, and obey the messenger and those of you who are in authority ...'.[1] They took this to mean that the ruler was as much worthy of obedience as Allah and his messenger. They failed to produce any suggestions to control the absolute power of the ruler. In this situation, Donish's idea of overthrowing the Emir was a very daring step, to say the least. However, his call was not heeded during his lifetime because, at that stage, the social and political forces necessary for a movement against the Emir's absolutism were lacking. Nevertheless, Donish's ideas had a formative effect on the younger generation and he remained a great source of inspiration for subsequent pro-reform intellectuals. They were stimulated by his opposition to *taqlid*, his implicit support for *ijtihad*, his ideas for political reorganisation and his fearless denunciation of the ignorance and corruption of the rulers and the *ulama*. He gave younger intellectuals the impetus to take action.

The beginning of the twentieth century marked a significant change in the Bukharan economy, and new social forces emerged. The Russo-Japanese war, the Russian revolution of 1905, the revolutions in Iran and Turkey, all helped to raise the political awareness of the intelligentsia. The spread of various journals and newspapers published in Persian, Turki and Arabic also contributed to a political awakening among intellectuals. Gradually, a body of philosophical, political, scientific and social thought came into being that was to serve as a frame of reference for a reformist movement in Bukhara. Abdal Rauf Fitrat was the most significant member of this group.

Unlike Donish, Fitrat travelled widely, and was familiar with the writings of Muslim reformers such as Ismail Gasprinskii (1851–1914), Muhammad Abduh (1849–1905), and Jamal Al-Din Al-Afghani (1838–1897). Fitrat, like other reformists, was immensely dissatisfied with the existing state of affairs: social decay, political weakness and economic disintegration. He believed that no remedy for these ills was possible unless a deeper reform of people's most fundamental beliefs, values and practices was undertaken, based upon strengthening individual and social morality. This reform was to lead to the eradication of the superstition and fatalism fostered by the *ulama*, and to a more positive, this-worldly religious attitude, in which otherworldly spirituality would play a less dominant role. Fitrat's thought champions a decisively positive this-worldly shift: though he vigorously asserts faith in the transcendental truth of Islam, and in the need to seek happiness in the world hereafter, he rejects the attitude that happiness in this world should be ignored or renounced, and seeks instead the betterment of social, political and moral life in this world.

Like Donish, Fitrat saw Islam as a dynamic religion, one that was primarily based on reason. Donish set out to demonstrate that reason, modern knowledge and science were not incompatible with Islam. Fitrat sought to further elaborate this position, drawing widely on religious texts for proof. He stressed that Islam is not only not incompatible with reason, but that it is the only religion which calls upon man to use his own reason and investigate nature as a religious duty. To support this view he cited numerous verses of the Quran enjoining man to think intelligently and to study nature. However, he agreed that the debased form of Islam, which was believed in and practised by most of its adherents, was threatened by modern advances in thought and science, and warned that 'If the Muslims of Turkistan continue with their old system of education and deprive themselves of learning the useful sciences, in a few years, Islam will totally disappear from Turkistan except for names from the books of history.'[2]

The chief thrust of Fitrat's discourse on the historical and cultural significance of Islam was reformist. His basic intention was to encourage Muslims to accept the intellectualism and humanitarianism of the modern West as having really developed from the apogee of Islamic civilisation itself, and indeed as the true message of Islam. He reiterated the fact that Muslim scholars had preserved and developed the Greek sciences, and that the Europeans had subsequently managed to break out of their Dark Age by drawing upon the knowledge and experience of Islam. Learning European sciences, to him, meant re-acquiring the lost heritage of Islam and restoring its past glory. The acquisition of modern knowledge from whatever source was mandatory for every Muslim, since, he argued, this knowledge was the result of the collective enquiry of humankind as a whole. He was opposed to the idea that science could be divided into Muslim and Christian. He understood that there had been cross-fertilisation of cultures between East and West and that this had been a source of progress.

Donish and Fitrat, in advocating the integration of modern ideas and institutions back into the religion from which they had originated, not only encouraged the influx of Western ideas and education, but also partly justified the existing Western intellectual impacts on Bukhara. However, the actual incorporation of Western ideas into the values of Islam could only be a long and slow process. The reformists could do no more than provide a basis for subsequent developments on reformist lines. What was required, before all else, was an integrated educational programme. The *ulama*, the traditional guardians of Islamic faith and practice, were not only incapable of fulfilling this task because of their narrow and restricted education, but could not even perceive that there was a problem. Donish had pointed out the indispensability of educational reforms, while Fitrat, along with other Bukharan reformists, tried to devise and implement a programme. The new-method system of education, based on modern European sciences, was a means to more important ends, namely, the political and cultural awakening of the people, the modernisation of Islamic life, and the emancipation of women.

The issue of new-method education for this reason acquired pivotal importance in Bukhara. In the first two decades of the present century, the intellectual and political battle lines in Bukhara were drawn over the question of new-method education. The history of political and intellectual development in Bukhara in the early twentieth century is the history of the tension between orthodox and reformist educational trends. The orthodox *ulama* of Bukhara rigorously opposed any change in the system of education, while the reformist intelligentsia began creating and spreading literature to combat the religious fanaticism and obscurantism of the orthodox *ulama*. They demanded reforms such as the relaxation of censorship and partial freedom of the press. Lack of opportunity to openly propagate their ideas compelled the reformists in Bukhara to form clandestine organisations. This gave the Bukharan movement a more political character than similar movements in other parts of the Czarist Empire. Their programme started to include demands such as people's representation and lessening of the tax burden on farmers. It is impossible to say how these efforts might have developed since revolution in Russia brought a new dimension and a new direction to reform in the region as a whole.

Fitrat began by advocating reform under the leadership of the Emir. This might seem to be a retreat from Donish's ultimate position. However, Fitrat's insistence at this period on the leadership of the ruler should be understood in terms of his lack of faith in the ability of the masses to overthrow the system. In a society where the bulk of the population was ignorant and blindly subservient to the powerful and conservative *ulama*, it was not possible to launch a revolutionary struggle. He believed that retaining the Emir was necessary to protect Bukhara from anarchy. Moreover, Fitrat still had faith that Emir Alim Khan, who came to the throne in 1910, could be manipulated so as to work for the cause of reform and the spread of new-method education. For this reason Fitrat initially addressed the Emir with such flattering phrases as 'Dear Father' and 'Saviour of the World'.

The programme and demands of the Bukharan reformists were in conformity with Islam and moderate in nature. The extreme conservatism of the rulers and *ulama*, however, did not permit even limited change. This drove some of the *jadid* to look for outside help. They turned to Russia. Initially they pinned their hopes upon the emerging Russian democracy, and their position was close to the Russian Constitutional Democrats. Later, when they fled from Bukhara to Russian-controlled Turkistan to avoid persecution by the Emir and *ulama*, all manner of ideas, from Socialist to Communist, began taking root among them. However, as late as 1917–18 the manifesto written by Fitrat for the Young Bukharan Party still does not call for the overthrow of the Emir or the abolition of the Emirate. Rather, it advocates the establishment of the rule of law by transforming the existing regime into a European-style constitutional monarchy and a system of justice based on the *Shari'a*. Even on the eve of the October Revolution, Fitrat's world-view, like that of Donish, remained totally Islamic. *Rahbar-i-Najat*, his major work, published less than two years before the October Revolution, does not even refer to Socialism or Communism. Rather, the framework of early Islam is advocated as a means of establishing good governance.

The impact of the Russian October Revolution upon Bukharan reformists was enormous. A significant number of reformists began leaning towards the Bolsheviks. The Young Bukharan Party accepted help from the Bolsheviks, but their first Bolshevik-backed armed campaign still did not aim at overthrowing the Emir. Rather, they wanted him to remain as a figure-head; reforms were to be implemented under his leadership and Islam was to play a significant role. This unsuccessful rising in favour of reform was followed by the formation of a Communist group amongst the Bukharan reformists, later named the Bukharan Communist Party. A new, more revolutionary frame of reference, advocating an epistemological break with the Islamic past, began to consolidate. In 1920, Fitrat and the other reformist Revolutionary Young Bukharans also accepted the Communist idea of liquidating the Emirate, which Donish had advocated more than twenty years earlier. However, they continued to insist on the importance of the role of Islam and the Bukharan reformist tradition for transforming Bukhara into a democratic republic. An alliance of some of the Bukharan reformists and Communists, backed by the Red Army, overthrew the Emir and established the People's Republic of Bukhara.

For four years the Bukharan reformists maintained an uneasy relationship with the Bolsheviks, but in 1924 their Republic was abolished. Bukhara was divided, and incorporated into three new Soviet republics. The frame of reference changed entirely. A revolutionary and ambitious drive for modernisation led by the Bolsheviks over-stepped Islam and rendered the Bukharan reformists simply irrelevant. Any hope of implementing reform within an Islamic framework was dashed. Reformist thought in Bukhara ended with the abolition of Republic of Bukhara and the creation of the Soviet Union. Thereafter, throughout the Soviet period, Central Asians were cut off from all Muslim reformist thought in the rest of the world.

Though it is beyond the scope of this thesis to compare Bukharan reformism with contemporary Muslim reformist movements elsewhere in the world, it can be said that Bukharan reformists pursued almost identical objectives to those of Sayyid Ahmad Khan (1817–1898) in India and Muhammad Abduh in Egypt. It was their circumstances and the outcome of their efforts that differed. The salient characteristics common to all these movements were: awareness of the internal degeneration of Muslim society; advocacy of reconstruction through intense self-criticism; opposition to the *taqlid* of medieval authorities; insistence on *ijtihad*; elimination of superstition and obscurantism; reform of the education system; and reconciliation of religion with reason and science. The difference in their circumstances was that Sayyid Ahmad Khan and Abduh, for example, had much greater access to print media and exposure to the public in general. Certain specific instances excluded, they enjoyed, most of the time, more or less congenial relations with the colonial and indigenous authorities. Moreover, the authorities generally sympathised with their calls for reform, and sometimes even encouraged their endeavours. Many of their works were published and circulated widely during their lifetime. They were free to deliver lectures, address public meetings and attend conferences.

The work of the Bukharan reformists, on the other hand, had a very limited circulation, owing to the lack of a printing press in Bukhara, and suppression by the authorities. For example, Donish's manuscript *Navadir-ul-Voqai* was never published, and was available in manuscript form to, at most, a few dozen people during his lifetime. Though Fitrat's works were published, this was mostly outside Bukhara, and his comrades had to smuggle them into Bukhara. To evade persecution Fitrat had to remain most of the time either underground or in exile. The only public demonstration organised by the reformists in Bukhara was one to welcome the reform manifesto of the Emir. This was met by the orthodox *ulama* and the rulers with hostility and bloodshed, despite the peaceful intentions of the demonstrators. Muslim reformists in other countries, and subsequently their followers, despite many inconsistencies and failures, continued to develop and implement their ideas. Some of their successors still rule countries such as Pakistan and Egypt. *Jadidism* in Bukhara did not enjoy a similar success.

Jadidism was partly inspired by the achievements of European/Russian society. It gathered strength from the socio-economic changes caused by the Russian colonisation of much of Turkistan. However, the reactionary forces in Bukhara were too strong for it to exert much influence, and these were backed by the Czar. It was the events of 1917 in Russia which allowed Bukharan *Jadidism* to mount a serious challenge to the status quo. The *jadid* repeatedly tried to encourage the revolutionary authorities in Russia and Turkistan to help them introduce change in Bukhara. Eventually they agreed and a revolution took place; but four years later, the Bolsheviks decisively put an end to *Jadidism* and abolished Bukhara as a state. Russia did not directly rule Bukhara, thus the *jadid* did not develop an anti-Russian ideology. They looked to Russia for help, and sometimes received it, but in the end it was Bolshevik Russia that destroyed the movement.

From the beginning, the *jadid* were misunderstood. The conservative Bukharan *ulama* and rulers, deriding the reformists as Westernised infidels, denied them an opportunity to develop and implement their ideas in their own country. Later, events in Russia overtook them. The Bolsheviks considered them to be representatives of the bourgeoisie, and hence, counter-revolutionary. The Western interventionist forces in Central Asia saw them as agents of the Communists, and failed to support them, in spite of the fact that they favoured some degree of democracy and capitalism. Some of the *jadid* were forced back into revivalism and some were co-opted into Soviet Communism. They were cut off from their Islamic past. Their fifty years of Muslim reformist intellectual and political development came to an abrupt end.

The significance of Bukharan *Jadidism* is that Bukharan intellectuals, against great odds, succeeded in forming a coherent Islamic reformist ideology – a link in the greater chain of reformist movements in the Muslim world. That they were able to create an organisation committed to reforms and offering to reform the state was, in the repressive and isolated conditions of Bukhara, a tremendous achievement.

Notes

INTRODUCTION

1 Weber, M., *The Sociology of Religion*. London 1905, pp. 252–270.
2 *The Catholic Encyclopaedia*. Vol. 12, London 1911, p. 702.
3 Aini. S., *Tarikh-i Emiran-i Manghitia Bukhara*. Tashkent 1923.
4 Aini, S., *Bukhara Inqilab-i Tarikhi Uchun Materiallar*. Moscow 1926, pp. 147.
5 Khodzhaev, F., *K Istorii Revolyutsii v Bukhare*. Tashkent 1926, p. 3.
6 Khodzhaev, *K Istorii Revolutsii v Bukhare*. Also see: Khodzhaev, F., 'O Mlado Bukhartsakh'. In: *Istorik Marksist*. No. 1, 1926, pp. 123–141; 'Dzhadidy'. In: *Ocherki Revolyutsionnogo Dvizheniya v Srednei Azii*. Moscow 1937.
7 Khodzhaev, *K Istorii Revolyutsii v Bukhare*; 'O Mlado Bukhartsakh', pp. 123–141; 'Dzhadidy'; Aini 1926.
8 Umnyakov, I., 'K Istorii Novo-Metodnoi Shkoly v Bukhare'. In: *Bulletin of the Central Asian University*. No. 6. Tashkent 1927.
9 Bertels, E., 'Rukopisi Proizvedenii Akhmada Kalla'. In: *Trudy Tadzhikistanskoi Bazy*. Vol. 3, Moscow 1936, pp. 9–28.
10 *Ibid.*, p. 9.
11 *Ibid.*, p. 20.
12 Gafurov, B., and N. Prokhorov, *Padenie Bukharskogo Emirata*. Stalinabad 1940.
13 *Ibid.*, p. 39.
14 Gafurov, B., *Istoriya Tadzhikskogo Naroda*. Vol. 1, Moscow 1949, pp. 449–60.
15 Braginskii, I., *Ocherki iz Istorii Tadzhikskoi Literaturi*. Stalinabad 1956, pp. 394–409.
16 *Istoriya Uzbekskoi SSR*. Vol. 1, Part 1, Tashkent 1956, pp. 278–280, 282–286.
17 Radzhabov, Z., *Iz Istori Obshchestvenno-Politicheskoi Mysli Tadzhikskogo Naroda vo Vtoroi polovine XIX i v Nachale XX Vekov*. Stalinabad 1957.
18 Ishanov, A., *Bukharskaya Narodnaya Sovetskaya Respublika*. Tashkent 1969.
19 Iskandarov, B., *Bukhara (1918–1920)*. Dushanbe 1970.
20 Etherton, P., *In the Heart of Asia*. London 1925, pp. 168–171.
21 Park, A., *Bolshevism in Turkistan*. New York 1957.
22 *Ibid.*, p. 24.
23 *Ibid.*, pp. 22–26, 45–49.
24 Pierce. R., *Russian Central Asia, 1867–1917: A Study in Colonial Rule*. Berkeley 1960, pp. 254–255.
25 Wheeler, G., *The Modern History of Soviet Central Asia*. London 1964, p. 91.
26 Bennigsen, A., and Chantal Lemercier-Quelquejay, *Islam in the Soviet Union*. London 1967, pp. 47–48.

27 Becker, S., *Russia's Protectorates in Central Asia: Bukhara and Khiva, 1865–1924*. Cambridge 1968.
28 *Ibid.*, p. xiii.
29 Carrere d'Encausse, H., *Reforme et Revolution chez les Musulmans de l'Empire russe: Bukhara 1867–1924*. Paris 1966; *Islam and the Russian Empire Reform and Revolution in Central Asia*. London 1988, translated into English by Quintin Hoare.
30 Donish, A., *Navadir-ul-Voqai*. Unpublished manuscript.
31 Fitrat, A., *Rahbar-i-Najat*. Petrograd 1915.
32 Allworth, E., *The Modern Uzbeks*. Stanford 1990.
33 Komatsu, H. *The Evolution of Group Identity among Bukharan Intellectuals in 1911–1928: An Overview*. Tokyo 1989.
34 Adeeb, K., *The Politics of Muslim Cultural Reform: Jadidism in Tsarist Central Asia*. An unpublished PhD dissertation, The University of Wisconsin – Madison 1993.
35 In Adeeb's view, '... there appeared no arguments for reform couched in purely religious terms [in Central Asia] such as those formulated by Sayyid Ahmad Khan in India or Shaykh Muhammad 'Abduh in Egypt, or indeed Nasir Kursavi or Shihabeddin Marjani amongst the Tatars.' He thinks that Fitrat's *Rahbar-i-Najat* might fall in this category but it remained unavailable to him. Adeeb 1993, p. 227.

1 THE EMIRATE OF BUKHARA (1870–1924)

1 Coates, Z., *Soviets in Central Asia*. London 1951, p. 26.
2 Olufsen, O., *The Emir of Bukhara and His Country*. London 1911, pp. 366–367.
3 Akiner, S., 'Islam, the State and Ethnicity in Central Asia in Historical Perspective'. In: *Religion State & Society*, Vol. 24, No. 2/3, 1996.
4 Olufsen 1911, p. 369.
5 Becka, J., 'Islamic Schools in Central Asia'. In: *New Orient*, No. 2, 1967, pp. 49–56, at p. 49.
6 Shorish, M., 'Traditional Islamic Education in Central Asia Prior to 1917'. In: *Turco-Tatar Past Soviet Present*. Paris 1986, ed. Quelquejay, C. L., G. Veinstein and S. E. Wimbush, pp. 317–343, at p. 321.
7 Generally see: Ashurov, A., *Bukhara*. Tashkent 1958; Barthold, V., *Sochineniya*. Vol. 2, Part 1, Moscow 1963, pp. 25–335; Barthold, W., *Turkestan Down to the Mongol Invasion*. London 1977; Burnes, A., *Travels into Bukhara*. Karachi 1973; Holdsworth, M., *Turkistan in the Nineteenth Century*. Oxford 1959; Hutton, J., *Central Asia: from the Aryans to the Cossacks*. London 1875; Vambery, A., *Bukhara*. London 1873.
8 *Great Soviet Encyclopedia*. Vol. 4, Moscow 1970, 3rd edition, p. 164.
9 Becker 1968, p. 4.
10 Allworth, E., 'Encounter'. In: *Central Asia: 120 years of Russian Rule*. Ed. E. Allworth, Durham, NC and London 1989, p. 3.
11 Polonskaya, L. and A. Malashenko., *Islam in Central Asia*. Reading 1994, p. 36.
12 Becker 1968, p. 5.
13 *Encyclopaedia of Islam*. Vol. 1, Part 2, London 1913, p. 782.
14 Allworth, E., *The Modern Uzbeks*. Stanford, Cal. 1990, p. 13.
15 Carrere d'Encausse 1988, p. 25.
16 Holdsworth 1959, p. 4.
17 Carrere d'Encausse, H., 'Systematic Conquest, 1865 to 1884'. In: *Central Asia: 120 Years of Russian Rule*. Ed. Edward Allworth, Durham, NC and London 1989, p. 140.

18 *Arkhiv Vneshnei Politiki Rossii* ('Archives of the Foreign Policy of Russia', henceforth, AFPR), *Fond*, ('Fund', henceforth, Fund), Central Asian desk, *Delo* ('File', henceforth, F.) 298, p. 49. See also *Tsentralnyi Gosudarstvennyi Arkhiv Uzbek SSR* ('Central State Archives of the Uzbek SSR'), [presently Uzbekistan], (henceforth, CSAUz.), Fund, 5, *Opis.* ('list', henceforth, Op.) 1, F. 3, p. 2.

19 Polonskaya and Malashenko 1994, p. 39; Carrere D'Encausse 1989, p. 141.

20 CSAUz., Fund, 5, Op. 1, Book 4, F. 3435, p. 5.

21 AFPR, Fund, Central Asian desk, F. 298, p. 49.

22 *Ozbekistan SSR tarikhi.* Vol. II, Tashkent 1958, p. 235.

23 *Turkistanskaya Pravda.* 21 November 1924. Cited by Vaidyanath, R., *The formation of Soviet Central Asian Republics.* New Delhi 1967, p. 194.

24 Burnes 1973, p. 154.

25 Meiendorf, E. K., *Puteshestvie iz Orenburga v Bukharu.* Moscow 1975, p. 84.

26 Khanykov, N., *Bukhara: its Amir and its People.* Translated by Baron Clement A. De Bode, London 1845, p. 6.

27 Hutton, J., *Central Asia: from the Aryans to the Cossaack.* London 1875, p. 254.

28 Khanykov, N., *Opisanie Bukharskago Khanstva.* St. Petersburg 1843, p. 7.

29 Khanykov 1845, p. 77. Khanykov estimates the population of Bukhara at between 2 and 2.5 million. For him, 1/7 *tanab* is occupied by 25 people and his final estimate is 2,600,000. See for detail in English: Khanykov, N., *Bukhara: its Amir and its People.* London 1845, trans. by Baron Clement A. De Bode, pp. 94–95.

30 Galkin, A., 'Kratkii Ocherk Bukharskogo Khanstva'. In: *Voennyi Sbornik.* St. Petersburg 1890, No. 11, p. 191; An excellent discussion on population of Bukhara and its ethnic composition can be seen in English in an article by Kocaoglu, T., 'The Existence of a Bukharan Nationality in the Recent Past'. In: *The Nationality Question in Soviet Central Asia*, ed. Allworth, E., New York 1973, pp. 151–158.

31 Meyendorff 1975, p. 106.

32 Kislyakov, N. A., *Patriarkhalno-Feodalnye Otnosheniya Sredi Osedlogo Selskogo Naseleniya Bukharskogo Khanstva v Kontse XIX – Nachale XX Veka.* Moscow 1962, p. 20.

33 CSAUz., Fund, 3, Op. 1, F. 369, *Zapiska Voennogo Inzhinera Ermolaeva o Qarshinskoi Stepi, Sostav*, dated 10 October 1911, p. 2.

34 *Tsentralnyi Gosudarstvennyi Arkhiv Oktyabrskskoi Revolyutsii i Sotsialisticheskogo Stroitelstva Uzbek SSR* ('Central State Archives of the October Revolution and Socialist Construction of the Uzbek SSR'), (henceforth, CSAORSCUz.), Uzbekistan, Fund, 51, *Nazirat Zemledeliya BNSR.* Op. 1, F. 95, p. 300.

35 Shek, L. K., *Pobeda Narodnoi Sovetskoi Revolyutsii v Bukhare.* Tashkent 1956, p. 5. See also Semyonov, A., 'K Proshlomu Bukhary'. In: Aini, S., *Vospominaniya.* Moscow 1960, pp. 980–1015, at p. 982.

36 Ishanov, A. I., *Bukharskaya Narodnaya Sovetskaya Respublika.* Tashkent 1969, p. 25.

37 Kocaoglu 1973, p. 152.

38 *Id.*

39 Kocaoglu 1973, pp. 154–155.

40 Fomchenko, A. P., *Russkie Poselenie v Bukharskom Emirate.* Tashkent 1958, p. 12.

41 *Istoriya Uzbekskoi SSR.* Tashkent 1968. Vol. 2, p. 91.

42 Semyonov, A. A., 'Material po Istorii Tadzhikov i Uzbekov'. In: *Trudy Akademii Nauk Tadzhikskoi SSR.* Vol. 25, 2nd edition, p. 24.

43 *Tsentralnyi Gosudarstvennyi Arkhiv Oktyabrskskoi Revolyutsii i Sotsialisticheskogo Stroitelstva SSSR* ('Central State Archives of the October Revolution and Socialist Construction of the USSR'), [Russia], (henceforth, CSAORSC), Fund, 1318, Op. 1, F. 715, p. 53. Also: Khanykov 1843, p. 190.

44 Khanykov 1843, p. 190.

45 CSAUz., Fund, 1, Op. 29, F. 53, pp. 3–5; also Op. 34, F. 791, pp. 9–22.

46 Nechaev, A. V., *Po Gornoi Bukhare, Puchevye Ocherki*. St. Petersburg 1914, pp. 17–19.

47 CSWHA, Fund, 2000, *Glavnoe Upravlenie Generalnogo Shtaba*, Op. 1, F. 980, pp. 285–290.

48 Gafurov and Prokhorov 1940, p. 8.

49 *Ibid.*, p. 9. See also AFPR, Fund, Central Asian desk, F. 298, p. 54.

50 *Istoriya Uzbekskoi SSR*. Tashkent 1955, p. 134.

51 Iskandarov, B. I., *Iz Istorii Bukharskogo Emirata*. Moscow 1958, pp. 13–14.

52 In Qarategin, Darvaz, Kulyab and Kurgan-tyube *valayat*, the *mirshab* was called *kurbashi*.

53 CSAUz., Fund, 1, Op. 34, F. 724, p. 4.

54 Iskandarov 1958, p. 14.

55 Gafurov and Prokhorov, 1940, p. 9.

56 Kislyakov, N. A., 'Iz Istorii Gornogo Tadzhikistana'. In: *Izvestiya Otdeleniya Obshchestvennykh Nauk.*Vol. 4, A. N. Tadzhikskoi SSR 1953, p. 111.

57 CSAUz., Fund, 2, Op. 1, F. 251, pp. 85–97.

58 Iskandarov 1958, p. 13.

59 Khanykov 1843, p. 235.

60 Ishanov 1969, p. 56.

61 *Ibid.*, pp. 55–56.

62 CSAUz., Fund, 3, Op. 1, F. 251, pp. 59–62.

63 CSWHA, Fund, 400, F. 136, p. 37.

64 Ishanov 1969, p. 71.

65 *Tsentralnyi Gosudarstvennyi Arkhiv Sovetskoi Army SSSR* ('Central State Archives of the Soviet Army of USSR'), [Russia], (henceforth, CSASA). Fund, *Upravlenie Turkistanskim Frontom*, 1919–1920, Op. 3, F. 116, p. 91.

66 Ishanov Tashkent 1955, p. 31.

67 AFPR, Fund, *Central Asian desk*, F. 298, p. 54.

68 CSAUz., Fund, 3, Op. 2, F. 3, p. 1.

69 AFPR, Fund, *Central Asian desk*, F. 298, *From the Note of Lessar, Imperial Political Agent in Bukhara, to the Foreign Minister of Russia*, p. 54.

70 Lewis, B., *The Emergence of Modern Turkey*. London 1961, p. 16.

71 Olufsen, O. *The Emir of Bukhara and his Country*. Copenhagen 1911, pp. 370–394.

72 *Id.*

73 CSAUz., Fund, 2, Op. 2, F. 447, p. 10.

74 AFPR, Fund, Central Asian desk, F. 298, *From the Note of Lessar, Imperial Political Agent in Bukhara, to the Foreign Minister of Russia*, p. 54.

75 AFPR., Fund, Central Asian desk, F. 298, *From the Note of Lessar, Imperial Political Agent in Bukhara, to the Foreign Minister of Russia*, p. 54.

76 Semyonov 1960, pp. 980–1015, at p. 994.

77 AFPR, Fund, Central Asian desk, F. 298, *From the Note of Lessar, Imperial Political Agent in Bukhara, to the Foreign Minister of Russia*, p. 54.

78 CSAUz., Fund, 1, Op. 34, F. 791, pp. 26–31.

79 Semyonov 1960, pp. 980–1015, at p. 987.

80 CSAORSCUz., Uzbekistan, Fund, 51, *Nazirat Zemledeliya BNSR*, Op. 1, F. 95, p. 300.

81 *Bogar* (from the Tajik word *bakhor* [or *bahor*] – 'spring time') are cultivated lands dependent upon the spring rains. For further details see Khazanov, A., 'Nomads and Oases in Central Asia'. In: Hall and Jarvie (eds.), *Transition to Modernity: Essays on Power, Wealth and Belief*. Cambridge 1992, pp. 69–87.

82 Galkin, A., 'Kratkii Voenno-Statisticheski Ocherk Bukharskogo Khanstva'. In: *Geograficheskie, Topograficheskie i Statisticheskie Materialy po Azii*. 47th edition. St. Petersburg 1894, p. 15.

83 AFPR, Fund, *Central Asian desk*, F. 304, p. 9. See also Fund, *Sankt Peterburgskii Glavnyi Arkhiv*, 1–9, 1888, F. 10, p. 40; CSAUz., Fund, 3, Op. 1, F. 17, p. 7.

84 Mazov, S. I., 'Vostochnaya Bukhara, Badakhshan i Severnyi Afganistan'. In: *Turkistanskii Sbornik*. Vol. 404, no date, pp. 5–26.

85 Iskandarov, B. I., 'O Nekotorykh Izmeneniyakh v Ekonomike Vostochnoi Bukhary na Rubezhe 19–20 v v. In: *Trudy Instituta Istorii Arkhiologii i Etnografii*. Vol. LXXXIII, A. N. Tadzhikskoi SSR 1958, pp. 35–37.

86 Yusupov, S., *Ocherki Istorii Kulyabskogo Bekstvo v Kontse 19 Nachale 20 vv*. Dushanbe 1964, p. 53.

87 CSWHA, Fund, 400, Op. 261/911, 1891, SV. 108, F. 74, Part 2, *Data of Major-General Usov*. p. 31.

88 *Tsentralnyi Gosudarstvennyi Arkhiv Tadzhikistana* ('Central State Archives of Tajikistan'), (henceforth, CSAT), Fund, 21, Op. 1, F. 424, p. 18.

89 Gulishambarov 1913, p. 215.

90 CSAT, Fund, 21, Op. 1, F. 424, p. 18.

91 Radobylskii, A., *Ekonomicheskii Ocherk Bukhary i Tunisa*. St. Petersburg 1905, p. 33.

92 CSAORSCUz., Uzbekistan, Fund, 50, *Gosplan BNSR*, Op. 1, F. 7, p. 49.

93 CSAUz., Fund, 126, *Arkhiv Kushbegi Emira Bukharskogo*, Op. 1, FF. 6345, 6346, 6347.

94 CSAUz., Fund, 3, Op. 1, F. 678, pp. 300–303.

95 Madzhlisov 1967, pp. 216–225.

96 See for details, in the Institut Vostokovedeniya, A. N. Uzbekskoi SSR, Uzbekistan, F. 47, Document No. 47/143.

97 *Ibid.*, Document No. 47/147.

98 *Ibid.*, Document No. 47/141.

99 *Ibid.*, Document No. 47/171.

100 Radobylskii 1905, p. 33.

101 CSAUz., *Arkhiv Kushbegi Emira Bukharskogo*, Fund, 125, Op. 1, FF. 6303, 6308, 6311, 6312.

102 *Ibid.*, Fund, 126, Op. 1, FF. 1164–1238, 6307.

103 Fomchenko 1958, p. 32.

104 Meyendorff 1975, p. 107.

105 Khanykov 1843, p. 117.

106 Kouznietsov, P., *La lutte des civilizations et des langues dans 'Asie Centrale'*. Paris 1912, pp. 83–84.

107 Lehmann, A., *Reise nach Buchara und Samarkand in den jahren 1841 und 1842*. St. Petersburg 1852, pp. 216–217.

108 Madzhlisov, A., *Agrarnie Otnosheniya v Vostochnoi Bukhare v 19 – Nachale 20 Vekakh*. Dushanbe and Alma Ata 1967, p. 96.

109 *Ibid.*, pp. 123–125.

110 CSAUz., Fund, 3, Op. 1, F. 74, p. 400.

111 CSAUz., Fund, 2, Op. 1, F. 251, pp. 112–119.

112 CSAUz., Fund, 3, Op. 1, F. 441, p. 6.

113 *Ibid.*, F. 247, pp. 87–88.
114 CSAORSCUz., Uzbekistan, Fund, 50, *Gosplan BNSR*, Op. 1, 1923–1924, F. 7, pp. 48–50.
115 According to Major-General Usov, the cultivable area of the Emirate was 2,250,000 desiatinas. For details see: *Tsentralnyi Gosudarstvennyi Voenno-Istoricheskii Arkhiv SSSR* ('Central State War-History Archives of USSR'), [Russia], (henceforth, CSWHA) Fund, 400, Op. 261/911, 1891, *Svyazka* ('bundle', 'sheaf', henceforth, Sv.) 108, F. 73, Part 2, p. 30.
116 Remez, I. A., *Vneshnyaya Torgovlya Bukhary do Mirovoi Voiny.* Tashkent 1922, p. 6.
117 CSAUz., Fund, 50, Op. 1, F. 7, pp. 48–53.
118 Iskandarov, B. I., 'Vostochnaya Bukhara i Pamir vo Vtoroi Polovine 19 v'. In: *Trudy A. N. Tadzhikskoi SSR 1962–3.* Vol. 39, Parts 1–2, p. 79.
119 CSAORSCUz., Uzbekistan, Fund, 51, *Nazirat Zemledeliya BNSR*, Op. 1, F. 95, p. 302.
120 Carrere d'Encausse, H., *Islam and the Russian Empire: Reform and Revolution in Central Asia.* London 1988, p. 8.
121 CSAUz., Fund, 2, Op. 1, F. 10, p. 7. See also Fund, 3, Op. 1, F. 102, pp. 193–200.
122 *Ibid.*, F. 102, pp. 182–187.
123 AFPR, Fund, *Central Asian desk*, F. 404, pp. 25–26.
124 *Ibid.*, Fund, 3, Op. 1, F. 348, pp. 232–233.
125 Massalskii, V. I., *Khlopkovoe Delo v Srednei Azii (Turkistan, Zakasp. Obl. Bukhara i Khiva) i ego Budushchee.* St. Petersburg 1892, p. 145.
126 Sitnyakovskii, N. F., *Zametki o Bukharskoi Chasti Doliny Zarafshana.* Vol. 1, 2nd edition 1899, p. 135.
127 Olufsen, O., *The Emir of Bukhara and His Country.* Copenhagen 1911, pp. 490–493. See also AFPR, Fund, Sankt Peterburgskii Glavnyi Arkhiv, 1–9, F. 10, *Ocherk ob Orasichelnykh Kanalakh Bukharskogo Emirata.* pp. 101–118.
128 Khoroshkhin, A. P., 'Dolina Zarafshana'. In: *Voennyi Sbornik.* Part 54, St. Petersburg, p. 119.
129 Massalskii 1892, p. 145.
130 Gulishambarov, S., *Ekonomicheskii Obzor Turkmenskogo Kraya, Obsluzhivaemogo Sredneaziatskoi Zheleznoi Dorogi.* Parts 1–3, Ashkabad 1913, p. 198.
131 CSAUz., Fund, 1, Op. 34, F. 290, p. 43.
132 Donish, A. *Traktat Akhmada Donisha 'Istoriya Mangitskoi Dinastii'.* Dushanbe 1967, pp. 96–97. Translated into Russian by I. A. Nadzhafova.
133 Mazov, S., 'Vostochnaya Bukhara, Badakhshan i Severnyi Afghanistan'. In: *Turkistanskii Sbornik*, Vol. 404, pp. 25–26.
134 Gafurov 1955, p. 465.
135 Sukhareva, O., *K Istorii Gorodov Bukharskogo Khanstva.* Tashkent 1958, p. 90.
136 Sukhareva, O., *Pozdnefeodalnyi Gorod Bukhara Kontsa 19ogo, Nachalo 20ogo Veka.* Tashkent 1962, pp. 107–111.
137 For the regional details of domestic industry see: Narzikulov, I., 'Kratkie Svedeniya o Dorevolyutsionnoi Kustarnoi Promyshlennosti Tadzhikistana'. In: *Trudy A. N. Tadzhikskoi SSR.* Vol. 71, 1957.
138 CSAUz., Fund, 3, Op. 1, F. 840, *Naselenie Termeza i Torgovo-Promyshlennye Predpriyatiya v 1916 g*, p. 52.
139 *Ibid.*, Fund, 1, Op. 12, F. 2079, *Prilozhenie k Raportu Polit-Agenta TGG.* Dated 9 March 1916. *Spisok Khlopkoochistitelnykh Zavodov.* pp. 1–7; Fund 3, Op. 1, F. 335, p. 18.
140 *Ibid.*, F. 1063, p. 1.

141 AFPR, Fund, *Central Asian desk*, F. 208, p. 68; CSAUz., Fund, 2, Op. 1, F. 24, p. 1.
142 CSAUz., Fund, 3, Op. 1, F. 259, pp. 7–12, 21–26, 231.
143 *Ibid.*, Fund, 3, Op. 1, F. 69, *Postanovlenie o Zolotopromyshlennosti v Bukharskom Emirate, Utverzhdenie.* 24 February 1896, pp. 17–18.
144 *Ibid.*, Fund, 1, Op. 1, F. 483, *Spravka TGG. O Russkikh Kontsessiyakh v Bukhare.* Dated 5 March 1901, p. 10.
145 For the collection of taxes in the Emirate of Bukhara, see: *Vystavka Eksponatov v Bukharskom Oblastnom Muzee*; Ishanov 1969, pp. 65–69; Semyonov, A., *Ocherk po Zemelno-Podatnogo i Nalogovogo Ustroistvo Byvshego Bukharskogo Khanstva.* Vol. 1, Tashkent 1929, pp. 47–51; Semyonov 1960, pp. 998–1000; AFPR, Fund, *Central Asian desk*, F. 304, pp. 9–10; F. 92, pp. 30–67; CSAUz., *Arkhiv Kushbegi Emira Bukharskogo*, Fund, 126, FF. 6301, 6307, 6435, 6436.
146 Gafurov, B. and N. Prokhorov, *Padenie Bukharskogo Emirata.* Stalinabad 1940, p. 11.
147 AFPR, Fund, *Central Asian desk*, F. 295, pp. 200–203.
148 CSAUz., Fund, 3, Op. 1, F. 366, *Donesenie Karshinskogo Veterinarnogo Vracha*, dated 2 February 1915, p. 14.
149 Generally see: Aini, S., 'Dokhunda'. In: *Sobranie Sochinenii.* Vol. 1, Moscow 1971, pp. 123–494. Also 'Raby'. In: *Sobranie Sochinenii.* Vol. 2, Moscow 1972, pp. 7–426.
150 Gafurov, B., *Istoriya Tadzhikskogo Naroda.* Moscow 1955, p. 441.
151 The Emir often travelled to Shahr-i-Sabz and a large retinue accompanied him. Donish also wrote about the distress such expeditions could occasion. See for details, Donish 1967, pp. 82–87.
152 AFPR, Fund, *Central Asian desk*, F. 539, pp. 191–192.
153 *Id.*
154 CSAUz., Fund, 1, Op. 34, F. 724, *Otnoshenie MID-TGG.* Dated 23 January 1891. p. 21.
155 AFPR, Fund, *Central Asian desk*, F. 304, pp. 14–27; CSMHA, Fund, 400, Op. 262/912–915, Sv. 346, F. 73/98, pp. 2–11.
156 *Id.*
157 CSHA, Fund, 1276, Op. 6, 1910, F. 136, p. 56.
158 CSWHA, Fund, 400, Op. 261/911, Sv. 108, F. 73, Part 2, p. 35.
159 AFPR., Fund, Central Asian desk, F. 304, pp. 14–27; CSMHA., Fund, 400, Op. 262/912–915, Sv. 346, F. 73/98, pp. 2–11.
160 CSAUz., Fund, 2, Op. 1, F. 303, pp. 12–17.
161 CSWHA, Fund, 400, Op. 262/912–915, Sv. 346, F. 73/98, pp. 2–11.
162 CSAUz., Fund, 3, Op. 1, F. 74, p. 400.
163 Aini 1923, p. 88.
164 Logofet, D., *Strana Bespraviya, Bukharskoe Khanstvo i ego Sovremennoe Polozhenie.* St. Petersburg 1909, p. 55.
165 AFPR, Fund, Central Asian desk, F. 304, pp. 14–27; CSWHA, Fund, 400, Op. 262/912–915, Sv. 346, F. 73/98, pp. 2–11.
166 CSAUz., Fund, 3, Op. 1, F. 74, *Otnoshenie Polit-Agenta-TGG.* Dated 8 December 1894, p. 400.
167 Logofet 1909, p. 46.
168 CSAUz., Fund, 3, Op. 1, F. 197, p. 103.
169 *Ibid.*, Fund, 3, Op. 1, F. 909, pp. 229–233.
170 AFPR, Fund, *Central Asian desk*, F. 304, pp. 14–27; CSMHA, Fund, 400, Op. 262/912–915, Sv. 346, F. 73/98, pp. 2–11.

171 Aini 1926, p. 281.

172 AFPR, Fund, *Central Asian desk*, F. 305, p. 7.

173 Aini 1926, p. 283.

174 AFPR, Fund, *Central Asian desk*, F. 304, pp. 14–27; CSWHA, Fund, 400, Op. 262/912–915, Sv. 346, F. 73, pp. 2–3.

175 Adeeb, K., *The Politics of Muslim Cultural Reform: Jadidism in Tsarist Central Asia*. An unpublished PhD dissertation, University of Wisconsin, Madison 1993, p. 40.

176 Adeeb 1993, p. 40.

177 Stremukhov, N., 'Poezdka v Bukharu'. In: *Russkii Vestnik*, 117, 1875, p. 667; Sukhareva, O. A., *Bukhara XIX- Nachalo XX v (Pozdnefeodal'nyi Gorod i ego Naselenie)*. Moscow 1966, pp. 238–240.

178 Donish *Navadir-ul-Voqai*, p. 3.

179 The Quran, II: 256.

180 For details see: Aini, S., *Yaddashtha*. Book 1, 2, Vol. 1, 2, 3, 4, Stalinabad 1954–55; *Vospominaniya*. Moscow 1960; Fitrat, A., *Munazara*; *Bayanat-i-Sayyah-i-Hindi*; *Rahbar-i-Najat*.

181 Aini, S., *Yaddashtha*. Book 1, 2, Vol. 1, 2, 3, 4, Stalinabad 1954–55; *Vospominaniya*. Moscow 1960.

182 Aini, S., *Maktab-i Kuhnah*. Dushanbe 1966; translated into Russian as *Staraya Shkola*. Dushanbe 1966; also in *Sobranie Sochinenii*. Vol. 3, Moscow 1973, pp. 154–182.

183 See: Kaufman, K. P., 'Proekt vcepoddanneishevgo otchyota general ad'yutanta K. P. Kaufmana po grazhdanskomu upravleniyu i ustroistvu v oblastyakh Turkistanskogo general-gubernatorstva'. Cited by, Bendrikov, K., *Ocherki po Istirii Narodnogo Obrazovaniya v Turkestane (1865-1924 gody*. Moscow 1960, p. 27; Schuyler, E., *Turkistan*. Vol. 2, London 1876; Vambery, A, *Sketches of Central Asia*. London 1868; Skrine, F. and Edward Ross, *The Heart of Asia*. London 1889.

184 Khanykov, N., *Opisanie Bukharskago Khanstva*. St. Petersburg 1843; *Bukhara: its Amir and its People*. London 1845, translated into English by Baron Clement A. De Bode.

185 Kaufman, K. P., 'Proekt vcepoddanneishevgo otchyota general ad'yutanta K. P. Kaufmana po grazhdanskomu upravleniyu i ustroistvu v oblastyakh Turkistanskogo general-gubernatorstva'. Cited by, Bendrikov, K., *Ocherki po Istirii Narodnogo Obrazovaniya v Turkestane (1865-1924 gody*. Moscow 1960, p. 27; Schuyler, E., *Turkistan*. Vol. 2, London 1876, pp. 88–93; Vambery, A., *Sketches of Central Asia*. London 1868. pp. 181, 199.

186 Khanykov, N., *Bukhara: its Amir and its People*. Translated by Baron Clement A. De Bode, London 1845, pp. 293–294.

187 Allworth, E., 'The Changing Intellectual and Literary Community'. In: *Central Asia: 130 Years of Russian Dominance, A Historical Overview*. Durham and London 1994, pp. 349–396.

188 Cited by, Bendrikov, p. 45; Becka, J., 'Islamic Schools in Central Asia'. In: *New Orient*, No. 6, 1966, pp. 186–190, at p. 186.

189 Vambery, A., *Sketches of Central Asia*. London 1868, p. 186.

190 *Ibid.*, pp. 187–188.

191 Vambery 1868, p. 188.

192 *Ibid.*, p. 190.

193 Skrine, F. and Edward Ross, *The Heart of Asia*. London 1889, p. 375.

194 Schuyler, E., *Turkistan*. Vol. 1, London 1876, p. 172.

195 Fitrat *Razskazy*, pp. 20–22.

196 Becka 1967, p. 49.
197 Fitrat *Razskazy*. pp. 19–20.
198 Khanykov 1845, pp. 246–276.
199 Medlin, W. K., Cave, W. M., and Finley Carpenter, *Education and Development in Central Asia*. Lieden 1971, p. 28.
200 Olufsen 1911, pp. 387–388.
201 Aini 1966, pp. 8–13; Aini 1973, pp. 158–162; See also Becka 1966, pp. 186–190.
202 For details see: Shorish 1986, pp. 332–333.
203 To poularise Islam this text was originally compiled in Farsi/Tajiki by Sharafuddin al-Bukhari in the ninth century. Fariduddin Attar in the late twelfth century supplemented it.
204 Cited by Adeeb 1993, p. 50.
205 Cited by Bendrikov, p. 19; Becka 1966, p. 188.
206 Aini, 1960, p. 198.
207 Shorish 1986, p. 337.
208 Aini 1960, p. 198.
209 Shorish 1986, p. 337.
210 For a complete list of subjects and books taught in *maktab* and *madrasa* of Bukhara, see: Khanykov, N., *Bukhara: its Amir and its People*. Translated by Baron Clement A. De Bode, London 1845, pp. 274–293.
211 Khanykov, p. 292.
212 Shorish 1986, p. 337.
213 Becka 1967, p. 50.
214 Medlin, pp. 39–40.
215 *Ibid.*, p. 40.
216 *Razskazy*, p. 2.
217 Khanykov, p. 293.
218 Fitrat *Razskazy*, p. 24.
219 Fitrat *Razskazy*, p. 2.
220 *Ibid.*, p. 26.
221 Medlin 1971, p. 42.
222 Hadizade, R., 'Akhmad Donish i ego Tvorchestvo'. In: *Puteshestvie iz Bukhary v Peterburg*. Stalinabad 1960, p. 16; Aini 1960, pp. 399–400. Becker 1968, p. 202.
223 *Tsentralnyi Gosudarstvennyi Istoricheskii Arkhiv Leningrad* ('Central State Historical Archives Leningrad (St. Petersburg), (henceforth, CSHA), Fund, 954, *Von Kaufman*, Op. 1, F. 156, 1870. p. 1.
224 Becker 1968, p. 127.
225 CSAUz., Fund, 2, Op. 1, F. 278, *Russko-Bukharskii Dogovor*. 25 June 1885, p. 3. AFPR, Fund, *Sankt. Peterburgskii Glavnyi Arkhiv* 1–9, 1888, F. 10, p. 278.
226 *Id.*
227 CSAUz., Fund, 3, Op. 1, F. 197, p. 103.
228 *Ibid.*, F. 224, pp. 2–3.
229 *Ibid.*, Fund, 3, Op. 1, F. 446, *Tekst Dogovora*. Dated 15 June 1912, p. 27, F. 448, p. 38.
230 *Istoriya Uzbekskoi SSR*. Tashkent 1955, p. 134.
231 Pahlen, K., *Mission to Turkistan*. London 1964, p. 19. Translated by N. Couriss.
232 Lenin, V. I., *Collected Works*. Vol. 5, Moscow 1977 p. 82.
233 CSAUz., Fund, 3, Op. 1, F. 21, pp. 1–24; Fund, 1, Op. 29, F. 850, pp. 12–13, 25–26.

234 CSAUz., Fund, 3, Op. 1, F. 166, *Zhurnal Soveshchaniya po Khlopkovomu Delu v Bukharskom Emirate*. Dated 19 January 1899, p. 2.
235 *Ibid.*, pp. 2–4.
236 Ishanov 1969, p. 85.
237 CSAUz., Fund, 3, Op. 1, F. 189, pp. 88–91.
238 *Ibid.*, F. 166, pp. 16, 25.
239 *Ibid.*, p. 25.
240 *Ibid.*, pp. 2–4, 15–21, 25–28.
241 *Ibid.*, F. 165, pp. 20–23, 71.
242 *Ibid.*, Fund, 3, Op. 1, F. 165, p. 99.
243 *Ibid.*, pp. 99–102.
244 CSAUz., F, 794, *Letter From the Imperial Political Agent in Bukhara to the Russian Foreign Ministry*. Dated 22 December 1915. pp. 185–188.
245 Massalskii 1892, p. 141.
246 Dobson, G., *Russia's Railway Advance into Central Asia*. London 1890, p. 207.
247 Yuferov, V. I., *K Izucheniyu Ekonomiki Khlopkovogo Proizvodstva v Rossii*. Tashkent 1914, p. 3.
248 *Id.*
249 CSAUz., Fund, 3, Op. 1, F. 368, p. 78; F. 919, pp. 17–18.
250 *Ibid.*, Fund, 3, Op. 2, F. 620a, p. 17; Fund, 3, Op. 1, F. 919, *Dokladnaya Zapiska Chlenov Vostochno-Bukharskogo Tovarishchestva po Skupke Khlopka*. Dated 28 November 1916, pp. 17–18.
251 *Ibid.*, Fund, 3, Op. 1, F. 368, *Data of Political Agent*. Dated, 2 August 1913, p. 116.
252 Gulishambarov 1913, p. 209.
253 Remez 1922, p. 49.
254 *Ibid.*, p. 68.
255 CSWHA, Fund, 400, Op. 261/911, Sv. 108, 1891, F. 73, Parts 1–4.
256 CSAUz., Fund, 3, Op. 1, F. 47, pp. 64–68, 136–137.
257 CSWHA, Fund, 400, Op. 261/911, Sv. 108, 1891, F. 73, Part 2, p. 179.
258 CSAUz., Fund, 3, Op. 1, F. 92, *Otnoshenie Kushbegi Polit-Agentu*. Dated 6 August 1898, p. 16.
259 *Ibid.*, Fund, 1, Op. 29, F. 28, pp. 1–2; F. 625, pp. 37–38; Fund, 3, Op. 1, F. 171, pp. 189–190; F. 307, p. 2.
260 *Ibid.*, Fund, 3, Op. 1, F. 21, pp. 1–3.
261 CSAUz., Fund, 2, Op. 1, F. 251, pp. 112–119.
262 CSWHA, Fund, 400, Op. 262/912–915, 1909, Sv, 293, F. 90/77, *Dannye Ministerstva Inostrannykh Del*. Dated 28 January 1910, p. 81.
263 *Id.*
264 Ishanov 1969, p. 83.
265 CSAUz., Fund, 3, Op. 1, F. 368, pp. 28–32, 124–125.
266 Ryabinskii, A. M., *Istoriya Kolonialnogo Poraboshcheniya Bukharskogo Khanstva Tsarskoi Rossii*. Vol. 4, Moscow 1940, p. 179.
267 Ryabinskii, A. M., 'Tsarskaya Rossiya i Bukhara v Epokhu Imperialisma'. In: *Istorik Marksist*. No. 4, 1941, p. 5.
268 CSAUz., Fund, 3, Op. 1, F. 465, p. 17.
269 CSAUz., Fund, 1, Op. 17, F. 795, p. 50; Fund, 3, Op. 1, F. 21, p. 1; F. 556, p. 17; F. 919, pp. 17–18.
270 *Ibid.*, F. 300, *Obrashchenie Polit-Agenta k Russkim Firmam, Tovarishchestvam i Chastnym litsam pod Nazvaniem 'Sirkularno'*. 1907, pp. 179–180, 204–206, 230.
271 *Id.*

2 AHMAD MAKHDOOM DONISH

1 Hadi-Zade, R. *Istochniki k Izucheniyu Tadzhikskoi Literatury Vtoroi Poloviny XIX Veka.* Stalinabad 1956, pp. 70–80, 120–121.
2 Kostenko, L., *Puteshestvie v Bukharu Russkoi Missii v 1870 g.* St. Petersburg 1871.
3 Donish was known as Mir Ahmad and sometimes Mirza Ahmad amongst the Bukharans and Russian officials, although he himself gives his full name as Ahmad ibn Nasir al-Siddiqi al-Hanafi al-Bukhari. Donish, A., *Navadir-ul-Voqai.* p. 2.
4 Kostenko 1871, pp. 72–75.
5 *Golos.* St. Petersburg, 15 February 1874; *Novoe Vremya.* St. Petersburg, 16 March 1874.
6 Sadradin Aini (1878–1954) was born in the village of Sektar in the Ghijduvan region of the Emirate of Bukhara. A graduate of a Bukharan *madrasa*, Aini became a teacher, taught in *jadid* schools in Bukhara, and wrote textbooks, poetry and stories. He took part in the struggle for reform in the Emirate of Bukhara, for which in April 1917 he was brutally punished by the Emir and received 75 lashes, a punishment few men survived. During the Soviet period he became an eminent writer, poet and academician. He became the first President of the Tajik Academy of Sciences in 1951.
7 Aini writes that 'before reading *Navadir-ul-Voqai*, I could not conceive that the world could be progressively transformed. After reading Donish, I began to think of reforming the world'. Aini, S., *Sobranie Sochinenii.* Vol. 5, Moscow 1974, pp. 306–307.
8 The journal *Shu'ala-i Inqilab* was published in Samarkand, in Russian-controlled Turkistan. Aini's work *Tarikh-i Emiran-i Manghitia Bukhara* was serialised in Nos. 50–53, 56–60, 62, 63, 66, 68, 70, 72, 74, 76, 77, 79, 82–85, 89–99. The timing of the publication of Aini's articles on the Manghit Emirs of Bukhara, which included references to Donish, is significant. Aini himself gives us a very naive explanation. He writes that he gave up teaching in Samarkand in 1919, owing to poor health, and became a journalist. He worked for *Shu'ala-i Inqilab*, published in Tajiki, and for the newspaper *Golos Trudyashchikhsiya* ('Voice of the Working People'), published in Uzbeki. The shortage of material meant that he had to write everything himself, using pseudonyms. He wrote poetry and articles in both languages. 'In the journal *Shu'ala-i Inqilab* I began to publish an historical essay entitled 'History of the Manghit Emirs of Bukhara'. A series of these articles were to provide a summary of Bukharan history. In these essays, not only did I expose the last Emir and his courtiers, but the heinous crimes and tyranny of all the former Manghit Emirs, who had ruled Bukhara for 150 years, were unmasked'. Aini, S., *Sobranie Sochinenii.* Vol. 1, Moscow 1971, pp. 111–112. In reality, these articles were published precisely at the time when, after their unsuccessful uprising against the Emir of Bukhara, most of the *jadid* leaders were living in Bolshevik-controlled Turkistan, and seeking help from the Bolsheviks to overthrow the Emir. The Bolsheviks, too, were interested in the downfall of the Emir. Since Donish had been a fearless critic of the Emirs and their system, and not only advocated the introduction of reforms but even called for the overthrow of the Emir, both *jadid* and Communists were attracted by his ideas and works.
9 Aini, S., *Tarikh-i Emiran-i Manghitia Bukhara.* Tashkent 1923.
10 Aini, S., 'Tarikh-i Emiran-i Manghitia Bukhara'. In: *Sobranie Sochinenii.* Vol. 10, Dushanbe 1966, pp. 99–100.

11 Aini, S., *Bukhara Inqilab-i Tarikhi Uchun Materiallar.* Moscow 1926, pp. 25–28.
12 Aini, S., *Namuna Adabiat-i Tajiki.* Moscow 1926, pp. 287–301.
13 Aini, S., *Sobranie Sochinenii.* Vol. 5, Moscow 1974, pp. 305–319. Also see: Aini, S., *Vospominaniya.* Moscow and Leningrad 1960, pp. 252–266, 385–414, 771–798.
14 Aini 1960, p. 789.
15 Bertels, E., 'Rukopisi Proizvedenii Akhmada Kalla'. In: *Trudy Tadzhikistanskoi Bazy Akademii Nauk SSR.* Vol. 3, Moscow 1936, pp. 9–28.
16 *Ibid.*, p. 11.
17 *Ibid.*, p. 9.
18 *Ibid.*, p. 23. This latter work of Donish has been given different titles by several translators/editors. Professor Edward Bertels refers to this work as *Traktat <<Risolaji tarjumaji ahvoli amironi Bukhoroji Sharif>>* (*Zhizneopisaniya emirov svyashennoi Bukhary*), Bertels 1936, p. 11.
19 Bertels 1936, p. 20.
20 Ulugh-Zade, S., *Ahmad Donish.* Stalinabad 1959.
21 *Ibid.*, pp. 31, 86.
22 *Ibid.*, pp. 85–86.
23 Gafurov, B., *Istoriya Tadzhikskogo Naroda.* Moscow 1949, p. 432.
24 This manuscript is held in the St. Petersburg branch of the Institute of Oriental Studies, Academy of Sciences of Russia.
25 Mirzoev, A. 'Pervaya Redaktsiya *Navadir-ul-Voqai* i Vremya eyo Sostavleniya', In: *Sbornik Statei po Istorii i Filologii Narodov Srednei Azii.* Stalinabad 1953, pp. 151–161.
26 Hadi-Zade, R., *Istochniki k Izucheniyu Tadzhikskoi Literatury Vtoroi Poloviny XIX Veka.* Stalinabad 1956. See also: Hadi-Zade, R., 'Akhmad Donish i ego Tvorchestvo', the introduction to a Russian translation of extracts from Donish's work. In: *Puteshestvie iz Bukhary v Peterburg.* Stalinabad 1960, pp. 5–29; Hadi-Zade, R., 'Peshguftar'. In: Donish, A., *Risala Dar Nazm-i Tamaddun vo Ta'vun.* Dushanbe 1976.
27 Mominov, I., *Izbrannye Proizvedeniya.* Vol. 2, Tashkent 1976, p. 126.
28 Donish, A., *Traktat Akhmada Donisha, 'Istoriya Mangitskoi Dinastii'.* Dushanbe 1967. Translated into Russian by I. A. Nadzhafova.
29 Nadzhafova, I. A., 'Predslovie'. In: Donish 1967, p. 16.
30 Radzhabov, Z., *Iz Istorii Obshchestvenno-Politicheskoi Mysli Tadzhikskogo Naroda v Vtoroi Polovine XIX i v Nachale XX Vekov.* Stalinabad 1957, p. 205.
31 *Id.*
32 *Ibid.*, pp. 435–436.
33 Radzhabov, Z., *O Politicheskom Traktate Akhmada Donisha.* Dushanbe 1976.
34 *Ibid.*, pp. 103–104.
35 *Ibid.*, p. 98.
36 Donish, A., *Navadir-ul-Voqai.* Unpublished manuscript, Manuscript Collection, Institute of Language and Literature, Academy of Sciences of Tajikistan, Dushanbe. p. 54.
37 Aini 1960, p. 403.
38 Razaev, A. K., and D. Tashkulov, *Tusi, Donish.* Moscow 1990, p. 70.
39 Donish 1960, pp. 212–213.
40 Vambery, A., *Sketches of Central Asia.* London 1868, p. 181.
41 Donish 1960, p. 213.
42 *Id.*
43 Razaev and Tashkulov 1990, p. 71.
44 Hadi-Zade 1960, p. 9.

45 Aini 1960, p. 403.
46 Donish 1960, p. 222.
47 Aini 1926, pp. 23–24; Aini 1960, p. 255.
48 Donish 1967, p. 54.
49 Razaev and Tashkulov 1990, p. 78.
50 Donish 1967, pp. 40–41; Donish, A., *Risala Ya Mukhtasari az Tarikh-i Saltanat-i Khonadan-i Manghitia*. Stalinabad 1960, pp. 35–36.
51 Donish 1960, p. 274.
52 Razaev and Tashkulov 1990, p. 81.
53 Hadi-Zade 1960, p. 14.
54 Donish 1960, p. 139.
55 Hadi-Zade 1960, p. 14.
56 *Golos*. St. Petersburg, 15 February 1874.
57 *Novoe Vremya*. St. Petersburg, 16 March 1874.
58 Hadi-Zade 1960, p. 15.
59 *Ibid.*, p, 16.
60 Donish, A., *Risala ya Mukhtasari az Tarikh-i Saltanat-i Khanadan-i Manghitia*. Stalinabad 1960, edited and introduced by Abdulghani Mirzaef.
61 Mirzoev 1953, pp. 151–161.
62 Mominov 1976, p. 107.
63 *Ibid.*, pp. 107–108.
64 Radzhabov 1957, p. 13.
65 Mominov 1976, p. 108.
66 Donish, A., *Parchaho az Navadir-ul-Voqai*. Stalinabad 1957.
67 Donish, A. *Risala Dar Nazm-i Tamaddun vo Ta'vun*. Dushanbe 1976, compiled by Nazruula Rustamov and edited by R. Hadi-Zade.
68 Donish *Navadir-ul-Voqai*, pp. 6–113.
69 *Ibid.*, pp. 14–33.
70 *Ibid.*, pp. 33–63.
71 *Ibid.*, pp. 63–80.
72 Donish *Navadir-ul-Voqai*, pp. 5–6.
73 Rosenthal, E., *Political Thought in Medieval Islam*. Part 2, Cambridge 1958, pp. 113–223.
74 Kai Kaus ibn Iskandar, *Qabusnama: A Mirror for Princes*. Translated and edited by R. Levy, London 1951.
75 Nizam al-Mulk, *Siyasatnama*. Text edited by M. Modarresi Chahardehi, Tehran 1956.
76 Ghazali, A. *Counsel for Kings (Nasihat Al-Muluk)*. Translated by F. R. C. Bagley, London 1964.
77 Donish *Navadir-ul-Voqai*, p. 3.
78 *Id.*
79 Bertels 1936, p. 13.
80 Bertels 1936, p. 11.
81 Mirzaef, A., 'Muqaddima'. In: Donish, A., *Risala ya Mukhtasari az Tarikhi Sultanati Khanadani Manghitia*. Stalinabad 1960, pp. I-V.
82 Donish, A., 'Tarikhcha'. In: *Asarhoi Muntakhab*. Stalinabad 1959, pp. 16–115, (edited by Hadi-Zade, R., and K. Aini).
83 Donish, A., *Risala ya Mukhtasari az Tarikhi Sultanati Khanadani Manghitia*. Stalinabad 1960. (Hereafter, *Risala Mukhtasari*).
84 Donish, A., *Puteshestvie iz Bukhary v Peterburg*. Tajikistan 1960, pp. 33–122.
85 Donish, A., *Traktat Akhmada Donisha, 'Istoriya Mangitskoi Dinastii'*. Dushanbe 1967.

86 *Risala Mukhtasari*, pp. 3–173.
87 *Risala Mukhtasari*, p. 4.
88 *Ibid.*, pp. 4–5.
89 *Ibid.*, pp. 5–6.
90 *Risala Mukhtasari*, p. 11; Donish 1967, pp. 20–26.
91 *Risala Mukhtasari*, pp. 11–12; Donish 1967, p. 26.
92 *Risala Mukhtasari*, pp. 12–173;
93 Donish *Navadir-ul-Voqai*, pp. 7–8.
94 *Ibid.*, p. 11.
95 Rahman 1966, p. 104.
96 *Ibid.*, pp. 104–105.
97 Donish *Navadir-ul-Voqai*, p. 11.
98 Rahman 1966, p. 99.
99 Donish, A., 'Dar Vasoyoi Farzondon va Bayoni Haqiqati Kasabhao Peshahao'. In: *Asarhoi Muntakhab*. Stalinabad 1959, pp. 230–231; 'V Nazidanie Detyam o Polze Remesl i Zanyatii'. In: *Puteshestvie iz Bukhary v Peterburg*. p. 253.
100 Donish *Navadir-ul-Voqai*, p. 14.
101 *Ibid.*, p. 15.
102 *Ibid.*, p. 16.
103 *Ibid.*, pp. 16–17.
104 The battle of Badr in 624, the Prophet Muhammad's first military success over the Meccans.
105 The angel who brought God's revelation and messages to the Prophet Muhammad.
106 Donish *Navadir-ul-Voqai*, p. 17.
107 *Id.*
108 *Id.*
109 *Ibid.*, p. 18.
110 *Risala Mukhtasari*, pp. 107–108; Donish 1967, pp. 81–82.
111 *Ibid.*, pp. 108–109.
112 Donish *Navadir-ul-Voqai*, p. 18.
113 *Id.*
114 *Id.*
115 Geier, I., *Turkistan*. Tashkent 1909, p. 190; Aini 1926, pp. 23–24.
116 Donish *Navadir-ul-Voqai*, p. 18.
117 *Ibid.*, pp. 18–19.
118 *Ibid.*, p. 19.
119 Semyonov, A., *Ocherk Ustroistva Tsentralnogo i Administativnogo Upravleniya Bukharskogo Khanstva Pozdneishego Vremeni*. Stalinabad 1954, p. 22.
120 Donish *Navadir-ul-Voqai*, pp. 20–21.
121 *Ibid.*, p. 21.
122 The *Shari'a* and *sunna*, for Donish, are 'a collection of *amr vo novahi* ['do's and don'ts'], laid down by the Prophet. The *avlia* ['holy men'] alone can understand the hidden meaning of *amr vo novahi*, and it is the duty of rulers to implement the *Shari'a*.' *Ibid.*, p. 13.
123 Donish, A., 'Dar Vasoyoi Farzondon va Bayoni Haqiqati Kasabhao Peshahao'. In: *Asarhoi Muntakhab*. Stalinabad 1959, pp. 169–236, at p. 225; 'V Nazidanie Detyam o Polze Remesl i Zanyatii'. In: *Puteshestvie iz Bukhary v Peterburg*. pp. 203–258, at p. 249.
124 Donish *Navadir-ul-Voqai*, p. 21.
125 *Ibid.*, pp. 21–22.
126 *Ibid.*, p. 22.

127 *Id.*
128 *Ibid.*, p. 23.
129 *Ibid.*, p. 25.
130 *Ibid.*, pp. 25–26.
131 *Ibid.*, p. 28.
132 *Ghulam*, ('lad'): used for slave-boys employed as pages and messengers, and also for slave soldiers. Barthold, W., *Turkestan Down to the Mongol Invasion.* London 1928, p. 227.
133 Donish *Navadir-ul-Voqai*, pp. 28–29.
134 *Ibid.*, p. 29.
135 *Ibid.*, pp. 30–31.
136 *Ibid.*, p. 31.
137 See: Ghazali 1964, pp. 14–31; Donish *Navadir-ul-Voqai*, pp. 14–33.
138 Donish *Navadir-ul-Voqai*, p. 37.
139 Ghazali 1964, p. xxxix.
140 Donish, A., 'Dar Vasoyoi Farzondon va Bayoni Haqiqati Kasabhao Peshahao'. In: *Asarhoi Muntakhab.* Stalinabad 1959, pp. 171–236.
141 Donish, A., 'Dar Vasoyoi Farzondon va Bayoni Haqiqati Kasabhao Peshahao'. In: *Asarhoi Muntakhab.* Stalinabad 1959, pp. 225–226; 'V Nazidanie Detyam o Polze Remesl i Zanyatii'. In: *Puteshestvie iz Bukhary v Peterburg.* pp. 248–249.
142 Donish *Navadir-ul-Voqai*, p. 34.
143 Ibid., pp. 34–35.
144 *Ibid.*, pp. 92–93.
145 *Ibid.*, pp. 95–96.
146 *Ibid.*, p. 91.
147 Shubinskii, P., *Ocherki Bukhary.* St. Petersburg 1892, p. 6.
148 Galkin, M., *Etnograficheskie i Istoricheskie Materialy po Srednei Azii i Orenburgskomu Krayu.* St. Petersburg 1868, p. 229.
149 Snesarev, A., *Vostochnaya Bukhara.* St. Petersburg 1906, p. 72.
150 A, P., 'Administrativnoe Ustroistva Gissarskogo Bekstva'. In: *Turkistanskie Vedomosti*, 27 March 1908.
151 Donish *Navadir-ul-Voqai*, p. 106.
152 *Ibid.*, p. 46.
153 *Ibid.*, pp. 106–107.
154 *Ibid.*, p. 58.
155 *Id.*
156 *Ibid.*, p. 41.
157 *Ibid.*, p. 44.
158 Donish 1960, pp. 224–227.
159 Donish *Navadir-ul-Voqai*, p. 44.
160 Burnes, A., *Travels into Bukhara.* Vol. 1, Karachi 1973, p, 307.
161 Vambery, A., *Puteshestvie po Srednei Azii.* St. Petersburg 1865, pp. 181–182.
162 Krestovskii, V., *V Gostiyakh u Emira Bukharskogo.* St. Petersburg 1887, p. 346.
163 Donish, A., 'Dar Vasoyoi Farzondon va Bayoni Haqiqati Kasabhao Peshahao'. In: *Asarhoi Muntakhab.* Stalinabad 1959, pp. 225–226; 'V Nazidanie Detyam o Polze Remesl i Zanyatii'. In: *Puteshestvie iz Bukhary v Peterburg.* pp. 204–206, 225–226.
164 Donish *Navadir-ul-Voqai*, p. 60.
165 *Id.*
166 *Ibid.*, p. 35.
167 *Ibid.*, pp. 63–64.

168 *Ibid.*, p. 66.
169 *Ibid.*, p. 81.
170 *Ibid.*, pp. 65–66.
171 *Ibid.*, p. 68.
172 *Id.*
173 *Ibid.*, pp. 68–69.
174 Burnes 1973, pp. 283–284.
175 Donish *Navadir-ul-Voqai*, p. 68.
176 *Ibid.*, pp. 69, 77.
177 *Ibid.*, p. 76.
178 *Ibid.*, p. 82.
179 *Risala Mukhtasari*, pp. 109–116; Donish 1967, pp. 82–86.
180 Donish *Navadir-ul-Voqai*, p. 38.
181 *Ibid.*, pp. 118–121.
182 *Ibid.*, p. 81.
183 Ibid., p. 80.
184 *Ibid.*, p. 79.
185 *Id.*
186 *Id.*
187 *Ibid.*, p. 89.
188 *Ibid.*, p. 80.
189 *Ibid.*, pp. 126–127.
190 *Risala Mukhtasari*, pp. 132–133; Donish 1967, pp. 96–97.
191 Kostenko 1871, pp. 72–75.
192 Donish *Navadir-ul-Voqai*, p. 37.
193 *Ibid.*, p. 38.
194 *Ibid.*, pp. 50–55.
195 Donish *Navadir-ul-Voqai*, pp. 6–7.
196 The exact work Donish used is *Nasihatgar* ('a person notorious for giving advice'), *Risala Mukhtasari*, p. 155; Donish 1967, p. 111.
197 Donish 1967, p. 111, *Risala Mukhtasari*, p. 155; Donish 1959, p. 109.
198 *Risala Mukhtasari*, p. 31; Donish 1967, pp. 39–40.
199 *Risala Mukhtasari*, p. 32; Donish 1967, p. 39.
200 The work *Rozat-ul-Safa* was written originally by Mirkhond in 15th century AD. The work cited by Donish is continuation of the same work (Vol. 8–9) by Raza Quli Khan published in Tehran in 1275 AH. *Risala Mukhtasari*, p. 33; Donish 1967, p. 39.
201 *Risala Mukhtasari*, p. 33; Donish 1967, p. 39.
202 *Risala Mukhtasari*, pp. 35–36; Donish 1967, p. 40–41.
203 *Risala Mukhtasari*, p. 36; Donish 1967, p. 41.
204 *Risala Mukhtasari*, p. 157; Donish 1967, p. 113.
205 *Risala Mukhtasari*, pp. 157–158; Donish 1967, p. 113.
206 *Risala Mukhtasari*, pp. 164–165; Donish 1967, pp. 116–117.
207 *Risala Mukhtasari*, p. 172; Donish 1967, p. 123.
208 *Risala Mukhtasari*, p. 172; Donish 1967, p. 124.
209 *Risala Mukhtasari*, pp. 172–173; Donish 1967, p. 124.
210 *The Quran.* XXXIV: 9.
211 *The Quran.* VII: 179; *Risala Mukhtasari*, p. 174; Donish 1960, p. 121; Donish 1959, p. 114; Donish 1967, p. 125.
212 Donish 1959, pp. 114–115; *Risala Mukhtasari*, p. 174; Donish 1960, p. 121; Donish 1967, p. 125.

3 MUSLIM REFORMISM IN BUKHARA: *JADIDISM*

1 Esposito, J., *Islam: The Straight Path.* New York 1988, p. 33; Gibb, H. A. R., *Studies on the Civilization of Islam.* London 1962, p. 5.

2 *The Quran.* III: 110. All quotations from English translation of the Quran *The Meanings of the Glorious Quran.* New Delhi 1993, 5th Reprint. Translated by M. M. Pickthal.

3 Donohue, J. J., and J. L. Esposito, (eds.), *Islam in Transition.* New York 1982, p. 4.

4 Esposito 1988, p. 77, Rahman, F., *Islam.* Chicago 1979, p. 69.

5 Rahman 1979, p. 70.

6 Gibb 1962, p. 16.

7 The four orthodox schools of law are known as Hanafi, Maliki, Shafi'i, and Hanbali after the four jurists of the second and third centuries who are regarded their founders. They differ on relatively minor points of law and ritual, the Hanbalis, however, with their more intense opposition to all innovations (*Bidda*), theoretically reject *Ijma* in all but its narrowest sense. Gibb, H. A. R., *Modern Trends in Islam.* New York 1972, p. 14.

8 A theoretical foundation was provided for *ijma* by a saying of the Prophet, 'My community shall never agree on an error'.

9 Rahman 1979, p. 76.

10 Gibb, 1972, p. 13.

11 Rahman 1979, p. 77.

12 Bennigsen, A., and Lemercier-Quelquejay, *Islam in the Soviet Union.* London 1967, p. 31; Carrere D'Encausse 1988, pp. 54–58; Esposito 1988, p. 116; Rahman 1979, p. 212; Kerr, H. M., *Islamic Reform.* Berkeley and Los Angeles 1966, pp. 16–17.

13 Rahman 1979, pp. 197–198.

14 Gibb, 1972, p. 27.

15 For details see: Smith, C. W., *Modern Islam in India.* London 1946; Ahmad, A., *Islamic Modernism in India and Pakistan, 1857–1964.* London 1967; Troll, W. C., *Sayyid Ahmad Khan: A Reinterpretation of Muslim Theology.* New Delhi 1978; Lelyveld, D., *Aligarh's First Generation: Muslim Solidarity in British India.* Princeton 1978; Hourani, A., *Arabic Thought in the Liberal Age.* London 1962; Keddie, R. N., (ed., transl.,) *An Islamic Response to Imperialism: Political and Religious Writings of Sayyid Jamal al-Din 'al-Afghani'.* Berkeley 1968; also *Sayyid Jamal al-Din 'al-Afghani': A Political Biography.* Berkeley 1972; Kerr, H. M., *Islamic Reform: The Political and Legal Theories of Muhammad Abduh and Rashid Rida.* Berkeley 1966; Lazzerini, J., *Ismail Bay Gaspirinski And Muslim Modernism in Russia.* Michigan 1991.

16 Aini, S., *Vospominaniya.* Moscow 1960, pp. 252–265.

17 Khodzhaev, *K Istorii...*, p. 5; Umnyakov 1927, p. 82.

18 *Tarjuman* ('The Translator'), a Tatar newspaper brought out from 1883–1914 by the famous reformist Ismail Gasprinskii of Bakhchi Sarai.

19 *Vaqt* ('The Times'), a Tatar literary and political daily published in Orenburg in 1905.

20 *Mulla Nasiruddin*, a progressive satirical journal published in Azerbaijan from 1906 to 1931.

21 Umnyakov 1927, p. 83; Khodzhaev, *K Istorii...*, p. 5.

22 Aini 1926, pp. 32–39.

23 Babakhanov, M., *Iz Istorii Periodicheskoi Pechatu Turkistana.* Dushanbe 1987, pp. 13–91.

24 Ibid, pp. 74–80.
25 *Taraqqi*. 1906, 17 June; 13, 20 July; 12 August.
26 Behbudi, M., 'Ta'mini Istiqlal' (Guarantee of Independence), and 'Khosiyat-i-Ilm' (Benefits of Science). In: *Taraqqi*, 1906, 1 July.
27 Aini 1926, pp. 32–39.
28 Khodzhaev, *K Istorii...*, p. 5.
29 *Ibid.*, pp. 5–6.
30 Khodzhaev, *K Istorii...*, p. 6.
31 *Id.*
32 Lazzerini, J., *Ismail Bay Gasprinskii And Muslim Modernism in Russia*. UMI Dissertation Information Service, Michigan 1991, pp. 183–186.
33 Umnyakov 1927, p. 83.
34 *Ibid.*, pp. 83–84.
35 Shukurov. M., *Istoriya Kulturnoi Zhizni Sovetskogo Tadzhikistana*. Dushanbe 1970, p. 33. Also see: Lazzerini 1991, pp. 29–39.
36 Aini 1926, pp. 32–39.
37 Aini reports that the elder son of *mulla* Ikram, who was 33, learned to read and write in 40 days as a pupil of a new-method school in Bukhara. This partly accounted for *mulla* Ikram's support for the movement for *jadid* schools. See Aini 1926, p. 93.
38 Umnyakov 1927, p. 85.
39 Khodzhaev, *K Istorii...*, p. 15. The position taken by the conservative *ulama* and their arguments against new-method schools are illustrated by Fitrat in his work *Munazara*. The book also provides a rebuttal of the objections of the *ulama* against new-method schools and explains the position of the *jadid*. (For details see Chapter Four).
40 Aini, S., *Sobranie Sochinenii*. Vol. 1. Moscow 1971, p. 83.
41 On 17 December 1908, the Turkish Parliament was opened with a speech from the throne proclaiming the Constitution anew. A huge majority of the Members of Parliament belonged to the Party of Union and Progress. For history of modernism in Turkey see: Lewis, B., *The Emergence of Modern Turkey*. London 1961; Mardin, S., *The Genesis of Young Ottoman Thought: A Study in the Modernization of Turkish Political Ideas*. Princeton 1962.
42 The Iranian revolution of 1905–1911 which led to the formation of the *Majlis* (Parliament). For history of modernism in Iran see: Algar, H., *Mirza Malkum Khan: A Study in the History of Iranian Modernism*. Berkeley 1973.
43 Khodzhaev, *K Istorii ...*, p. 6.
44 Aini 1926, p. 36; Also see: Allworth, E. (ed.), *Central Asia: 120 years of Russian Rule*. Durham, NC and London, 1989, pp. 195–196.
45 Allworth 1989, p. 196.
46 The statutes and by-laws are printed in A. Arsharuni and Kh. Gabidullin, *Ocherki Panislamisma i Pantyurkisma v Rossii*. Moscow 1931, pp. 131–135. An English translation may be found in Carrere D'Encausse 1988, pp. 194–196.
47 *Tsentralnyi Partiinnyi Arkhiv Instituta Marksizma Leninizma* ('Central Party Archives of the Institute of Marxism-Leninism', henceforth, CPAIML), Fund, 61, Op. 1, F. 122, p. 3; Umnyakov 1927, p. 88.
48 Umnyakov reports that the Society successfully managed to run a secret school in the house of Mukammil-ud-din Makhzum until the death of the Emir Abd-al Ahad in December 1910. Umnyakov 1927, p. 88.
49 Becker 1968, p. 206.
50 Aini 1971, p. 84.

51 Some 153 issues were published between 11 March 1912 and 2 January 1913. Babakhanov, M., *Iz Istorii Periodicheskoi Pechati Turkistana*. Dushanbe 1987, p. 102.
52 *Id.*, 49 issues appeared between 14 July 1912 and 1 January 1913.
53 Samoilovich, A., 'Pechat, Russkikh Musulman'. In: *Mir Islama*, 1, (1912), 478n. Cited by Adeeb 1993, p. 353.
54 CPAIML, Fund, 61, Op. 1, F. 122, p. 3.
55 AFPR, Fund, *Central Asian Desk* (B). F. b, pp. 119–120; Umnyakov 1927, p. 89.
56 Umnyakov 1927, p. 90.
57 Khodzhaev, *K Istorii...*, p. 12.
58 Fitrat was son of a merchant who had travelled extensively in the Ottoman empire, Iran and Chinese Turkistan. Cited by Adeeb 1993, p. 173.
59 Khodzhaev, *K Istorii...*, p. 12.
60 *Ibid.*, pp. 13–14.
61 AFPR, Fund, *Central Asian desk*, F. 301, pp. 14–17.
62 CSAUz., Fund, 3, Op. 1. F. 370, p. 8.
63 Khodzhaev, *K Istorii...*, p. 12.
64 Khodzhaev, F., *Izbrannye Trudy*. Vol. 1, Tashkent 1970, p. 92.
65 Babakhanov 1987, p. 102.
66 Radzhabov, Z., 'Po Ctranitsam Zhyrnala <> [Ayna]'. In: *Izvestiya* A N Tajik SSR, No. 4, 1984, p. 3; also see: Dada Mirza Qari, 'Mu'allim wa shagirdlar', In: *Ayna*, 14 December 1913, p. 184; Mulla Ishaq Jan, 'Jawab', In: *Ayna*, 4 January 1914, p. 258.
67 *Ayna*, 1915, No. 14, p. 379.
68 Khodzhaev, *K Istorii...*, p. 15; Umnyakov 1927, p. 87.
69 Khodzhaev, *K Istorii...*, p. 15.
70 Umnyakov 1927, p. 87.
71 Khodzhaev, *K Istorii...*, p. 16.
72 *Id.*
73 *Ibid.*, p. 18.
74 CSAUz., Fund, 3, Op. 1, F. 555, p. 4.
75 Khodzhaev, *K Istorii...*, p. 18.
76 *Ibid.*, p. 17.
77 *Id.*
78 *Ibid.*, p. 18.
79 *Ibid.*, pp. 18–19; Radzhabov 1957, p. 429. Also see: Iskandarov, B., *Bukhara (1918–1920 gg)*. Dushanbe 1970, p. 31.
80 Khodzhaev *K Istorii...*, p. 19; Radzhabov 1957, p. 430.
81 Khodzhaev, *K Istorii...*, p. 19.
82 *Ibid.*, p. 20.
83 *Ibid.*, p. 22.
84 See illustration of the manifesto, p. 104.
85 Khodzhaev, *K Istorii...*, p. 20.
86 *Ibid.*, pp. 22–23.
87 *Ibid.*, p. 23.
88 *Ibid.*, pp. 23–24.
89 Carrere d'Encausse 1988, p. 134.
90 Khodzhaev, *K Istorii...*, p. 24.
91 Iskandarov 1970, p. 34.
92 Khodzhaev, *K Istorii...*, p. 26.
93 Aini 1971, pp. 107–108.

94 Carrere d'Encausse 1988, p. 136.
95 Khodzhaev, *K Istorii...*, p. 28.
96 Khodzhaev, 'O Mlado Bukhartsakh'. p. 139.
97 Khodzhaev, *K Istorii...*, p. 29.
98 *Id.*
99 *Ibid.*, p. 30.
100 *Ibid.*, p. 32.
101 *Ibid.*, p. 36.
102 *Ibid.*, p. 40; Fitrat wrote about the Bolshevik revolution in November 1917, 'A new calamity has befallen Russia, the Bolsheviks have taken over.' See: Fitrat, A., 'Siyasi Hallar'. *Hurriyat*, 7 November 1917.
103 Ishanov 1969, p. 120.
104 CSAUz., Fund, 25, Op. 1, F. 566, pp. 36–44.
105 CSAOR Russia, Fund, 130, Op. 2, F. 669, pp. 1–2.
106 Ishanov 1969, p. 121.
107 Vaidyanath, R., *The Formation of the Soviet Central Asian Republics*. New Delhi 1967, pp. 80–81.
108 Khodzhaev, *K Istorii...*, pp. 40–41.
109 Usupov, E., 'Faizulla Khodzhaev'. In: *Revolyutsiei Prizvannye*. Tashkent 1987, pp. 243–244.
110 Iskandarov 1970, pp. 56–57; Ishanov 1969, p. 122.
111 Khodzhaev, *K Istorii...*, p. 42.
112 Vaidyanath 1967, p. 83.
113 Ishanov 1969, p. 123.
114 Khodzhaev, *K Istorii...*, p. 47.
115 Carrere d'Encausse 1988, pp. 155–156.
116 Iskandarov 1970, pp. 63–67.
117 Khodzhaev, *K Istorii...*, p. 43.
118 Kamilov, K., 'V Borbe s Reaktsiei'. In: *Za Sovetskii Turkistan*. Tashkent 1963, p. 444.
119 Iskandarov 1970, p. 65.
120 Khodzhaev, *K Istorii...*, p. 55.
121 Radzhapova, P., 'Petr Alekseevich Kobozev'. In: *Revolyutsiei Prizvannye*. Tashkent 1987, pp. 93–94.
122 *Ibid.*, p. 95.
123 Carrere d'Encausse 1988, p. 163.
124 Khodzhaev, *K Istorii...*, p. 58; Dervish, 'Bukharskaya Sovetskaya Narodnaya Respublika'. In: *Zhizn Natsionalnosti*, 1, 1937, p. 197.
125 The organ of the Central Committee of the Bukharan Communists was published in Uzbeki and Tajiki twice a week at *Novaya* Bukhara. It was smuggled into Bukhara and other cities of the Emirate.
126 The organ of the Revolutionary Young Bukharans appeared for the first time on 15 April 1920. It was published in Uzbeki at Tashkent, twice a month. In all, 8 issues were brought out. A maximum of 5,000 copies were published, which were mostly smuggled into the Emirate.
127 Khodzhaev, F., *Izbrannye Trudy*. Vol. I, Tashkent 1970, pp. 163–166.
128 Usupov, E., 'Faizulla Khodzhaev' In: *Revolyutsiei Prizvannye*. Tashkent 1987, p. 244.
129 Khodzhaev, *K Istorii...*, p. 71.
130 Park, A., *Bolshevism in Turkistan 1917–1927*. New York 1957, p. 46.
131 Khodzhaev, *K Istorii...*, p. 72.
132 *Ibid.*, p. 71.

133 The members of the Turkistan Commission were S. Z. Eliava, Y. Z. Rudzutak, M. V. Frunze, F. Goloshchokov and V. V. Kuibyshev. They were appointed by the Russian Communist Party to oversee the affairs of Turkistan.

134 Khodzhaev, *K Istorii...*, p. 73.

135 Vaidyanath 1967, p. 126.

136 Park 1957, p. 47. The conference took place in Chaharjui from 16 to 18 August 1920. The Communist Party had a membership of 5,000 and 20,000 sympathisers. After the merger of the two groups on 11 September 1920, their joint membership exceeded 15,000. Khodzhaev 1970, p. 465.

137 Carrere d'Encausse 1988, p. 164.

138 'Direktiva voiskam Turkistanskogo fronta', No. 3667, 25 August 1920. In: Frunze, M. V., *Izbrannye Proizvedeniya*. Vol. 1, Moscow 1957, pp. 339–341.

139 Becker 1968, p. 294.

140 *Istoriya Uzbekskoi SSR*, Tashkent 1958, pp. 31, 87.

141 Vaidyanath 1967, p. 128.

142 *Ibid.*, pp. 128–131.

143 Arkhipov, 'Bukharskaya narodnaya sovetskaya respublica'. In: *Sovetskoe Pravo*. Vol. 1, 1923, p. 134.

144 *Ibid*, pp. 134–136.

145 *Ibid*, p. 135.

146 *Ibid*, pp. 136–137.

147 Carrere d'Encausse 1988, pp. 172–173.

148 Gordienko, A. A., *Sozdinie sovetskoi nationalnoi gosudarstvennosti v Srednoi Azii*. Moscow 1959, p. 125.

149 Skalov, G., 'Ekonomicheskoe obedenenie Sredne Aziatskikh respublik kak faktor natsionalnoi politiki'. In: *Zhizn Natsionalnostei*, Vol. 5, 1923, p. 42.

150 Ishanov, A. I., 'Bukharskaya narodnaya sovetskaya respublica'. In: *Uchenie Zapiski Tashkentskogo yuridicheskogo instituta*. Tashkent 1955, Vol. 1, p. 49.

151 Carrere d'Encausse 1988, pp. 177, 233; Vaidyanath 1967, p. 134.

4 ABDAL RAUF FITRAT

1 Shukurov, M., 'Fitrat i Tadzhikskaya Literatura'. Unpublished article by Mohammadzhan Shukurov, a member of the Academy of Sciences of Tajikistan. Dushanbe 1992, p. 6.

2 'Rang-i adabiat-i nau giriftani zabon-i Tajiki dar nasr az Abdurrauf Fitrat aghoz myobad'. See: Aini, S., *Namuna-i Adabiat-i Tajiki*. Moscow 1926, p. 531.

3 Fitrat, A., *Qayamat*. Moscow 1923. (The book was originally written in Uzbeki and later translated into Russian and Tajiki.)

4 Fitrat, A., *Strashnyi Sud*. Dushanbe 1964. Transl. by K. Nasirov, p. 2.

5 Qosimov, B., 'Fitrat.' In: *Sharq Yulduzi*, No. 10, 1992, p. 170.

6 For Fitrat's whereabouts in Isanbul see: 'Gulja i'anasidan yubarligan Aynalar'. In: *Ayna*, 17 May 1914, p. 588, cited by Adeeb 1993, p. 191.

7 Carrere D'Encausse, 'Social and Political Reform'. In: *Central Asia: A Century of Russian Rule*. ed. E. Allworth, London 1967, p. 197. For details of the conflict see: Becker, S., *Russia's Protectorates in Central Asia: Bukhara and Khiva, 1865–1924*. Cambridge, Mass. 1968, pp. 218–221.

8 Carrere D'Encausse 1988, p. 92.

9 Fitrat's *Munazara* is often cited as *The Dispute* in modern literature in English. In our view, a more accurate translation would be *The Debate*, which is also more consistent with the Russian translation, *Spor*. Moreover, *Munazara* is an established term for a debate between member of the *ulama*.

10 Fitrat, A., *Munazara-i Mudarris-i Bukhara-i ba yak Nafar-i Farangi dar Hindustan dar bara-i Maktab-i Jadid*. Istanbul 1327 AH (1909–10 AD), 61 pp.

11 Fitrat, A., *Spor Bukharskogo Mudarrisa s Evropetsom v Indii o Novometodnykh Shkolakh*. Tashkent 1911, 56 pp. Translated into Russian by Colonel Yagello. (Henceforth, *Spor.*)

12 Fitrat, A., *Hindustan bir Farangi ile Bukharalik bir Mudarrisning birnecha masalalar ham usul-i Jadida khususida qilghan Munazarasi*. Tashkent 1331 AH (1913 AD), 41 pp. Translated into Uzbeki by Haji Muin ibn Shukrullah Samarkandi.

13 Allworth, E., *The Modern Uzbeks*. Stanford, Cal. 1990, p. 144.

14 Aini. S., *Tarikh-i Inqilab-i Bukhara*. Dushanbe 1987, p. 102.

15 Fitrat, A., *Bayanat-i-Sayyah-i-Hindi*. Istanbul 1330 AH (1911 AD).

16 Fitrat, A., *Razskazy Indiiskago Puteshestvennika (Bukhara, Kak ona est)*. Samarkand 1913, 98 pp. Translated into Russian by A. Kondrateva. (Henceforth, *Razskazy*).

17 Fitrat, A., 'Rasskazy Indiiskogo Puteshestvennika: Bukhara, Kak ona est'. Ed. H. Ismailov. In: *Zvezda Vostoka*. No 7, Tashkent 1990.

18 Aini, S., *Sobranie Sochinenii*. Vol. 1, Moscow 1971, p. 94: Usopov, E., and E. Karimov, 'Nastala Pora Obektivnykh Otsenok'. In: *Kommunist Uzbekistana*. No. 12, December 1988, p. 69.

19 Fitrat, A., *Rahbar-i-Najat*. Petrograd 1915, 224 pp. (Henceforth, *Rahbar.*)

20 Fitrat, A., *Mukhtasar Tarikh-i Islam*. Samarkand 1333 AH (1915). 36 pp.

21 Fitrat, A., *Aila*. Baku 1915. Khalid Adeeb cites this book of Fitrat as, A'ila, yakhud waza'if-i khanadari (Bukhara, 1916). Fitrat, according to Adeeb, lays out the rules for the proper conduct, from the point of view of the *Shari'a*, of family relations, beginning with choosing a wife, through the wedding ceremony, to child rearing. The book also covers the rights of parents, orphans, and servants. Adeeb 1993, p. 234. Also see: *Hurriyat* 22 September 1917 and 28 November 1917.

22 Fitrat, A., *Saiha*. Istanbul 1913.

23 Khodzhaev, F., *Izbrannye Trudy*. Vol. 1, Tashkent 1970, p. 92.

24 Aini 1987, p. 102.

25 'Inqilab dar afkar avurd'. Aini 1926, p. 533.

26 See the newspaper *Kizl Uzbekistan*, Nos. 215–216, 1929, and the journal *Dialog*, No. 7, 1991, p. 76; for Fitrat's connection with Islamic circles in Turkey especially, *Sirat-i Mustaqim*, see Hisau Komatsi, 'Fitrat'. In: *Munazar'si uzerine bazi notlar*, Doghu Dilleri, 2 (1981), pp. 161–102.

27 Aini 1971, p. 94.

28 Khodzhaev 1926, p. 35; Khodzhaev 1970, pp. 454–455.

29 Komatsu, H. *The Evolution of Group Identity among Bukharan Intellectuals in 1911–1928: An Overview*. Tokyo 1989, pp. 123–124.

30 Hayit, B., *Soviet Russian Colonialism and Imperialism in Turkistan as an Example of the Soviet Type of Colonialism of an Islamic People in Asia*. p. 54.

31 Khodzhaev, *K Istorii...*, p. 59.

32 Fitrat, A., *Sharq Siyasati*. (n.p., n.d. [1919]).

33 *Ibid.*, pp. 14–40.

34 Usupov and Karimov report that Fitrat joined the Bukharan Communist Party in 1918 and became a member of its Central Committee in June 1919. Usupov and Karimov 1988, p. 72.

35 Khodzhaev 1970, p. 455. Usupov and Karimov 1988, p. 72.

36 Komatsu 1989, p. 123.

37 Usupov and Karimov 1988, p. 72.
38 Ismailov 1990, p. 130.
39 *Id.*
40 Fitrat, A., *Qayamat.* Moscow 1923. (Originally written in Chaghatay/Uzbeki, Fitrat himself translated it into Tajiki in the 1930s. This book was also translated into Russian.)
41 Fitrat, A., *Uzbek Adabiat-i Namunalari.* Tashkent and Samarkand 1928.
42 Fitrat, A., *Shorash-i-Vosey.* Dushanbe 1927.
43 Allworth 1990, p. 228.
44 *Rahbar,* p. 5.
45 *Ibid.,* p. 17.
46 *Ibid.,* pp. 14–15.
47 *Ibid.,* p. 15; Also see: Fitrat, 'Hayat va Ghaya-i Hayat'. In: *Ayna.* 14 December 1913, pp. 196–197, and 21 December 1913, pp. 220–222.
48 *Id.*
49 *The Quran.* XLV: 13.
50 *Rahbar,* p. 17.
51 *Ibid.,* p. 18.
52 *Id.*
53 *The Quran.* XCV: 4.
54 *Rahbar,* p. 19.
55 *Ibid.,* p. 20.
56 *The Quran.* II: 201.
57 *The Quran.* II: 202.
58 *Rahbar,* p. 30.
59 *Id.*
60 *Ibid.,* p. 31.
61 *Ibid.,* p. 32.
62 *Ibid.,* p. 39.
63 *Ibid.,* p. 33.
64 *Ibid.,* p. 34.
65 *Id.*
66 *The Quran.* II: 221.
67 *The Quran.* II: 219.
68 *The Quran.* XXX: 24.
69 *The Quran.* III: 3–4.
70 *Rahbar,* p. 35.
71 *Ibid.,* pp. 36–37.
72 *Ibid.,* p. 37.
73 *Id.*
74 *Ibid.,* p. 38.
75 *Ibid.,* p. 39.
76 *Ibid.,* p. 40.
77 *The Quran.* XXXIX: 9.
78 *The Quran.* XXXV: 28.
79 *The Quran.* XX: 114.
80 *Rahbar,* p. 41.
81 *Id.*
82 *Id.*
83 *Id.*
84 *Id.*
85 *Ibid.,* p. 42.

86 *Id.*
87 *Ibid.*, p. 43.
88 *Ibid.*, pp. 63, 77.
89 *Ibid.*, p. 63.
90 *Id.*
91 *Ibid.*, p. 43.
92 *Ibid.*, pp. 59–63.
93 *Ibid.*, p. 87.
94 *Ibid.*, pp. 42–43.
95 *Ibid.*, p. 44.
96 *Ibid.*, pp. 44–45.
97 *Ibid.*, p. 45.
98 *Ibid.*, p. 47.
99 *Ibid.*, pp. 47–51.
100 *Ibid.*, p. 51.
101 *Ibid.*, p. 52.
102 *Ibid.*, p. 58.
103 *Ibid.*, p. 59.
104 *Ibid.*, p. 94.
105 *Ibid.*, p. 6.
106 *Ibid.*, p. 10.
107 Fitrat, 'Quran'. In: *Ayna*, 15 June 1915, p. 443.
108 *Rahbar*, p. 7.
109 *Ibid.*, p. 8.
110 *The Quran.* III: 165.
111 *Rahbar*, p. 8.
112 *The Quran.* IV: 79.
113 *Rahbar*, p. 4.
114 *Id.*
115 *The Quran.* XIII: 11.
116 *Spor*, pp. 45–46.
117 *Rahbar*, p. 5.
118 *Ibid.*, pp. 5–6.
119 *The Quran.* XXXIX: 9.
120 *Razskazy*, pp. 23–24.
121 *Ibid.*, p. 23.
122 *Rahbar*, pp. 2–3.
123 *Razskazy*, p. 24.
124 *Rahbar*, p. 11.
125 *Id.*
126 *Id.*
127 *Ibid.*, pp. 11–12.
128 *Ibid.*, p. 19.
129 *The Quran.* II: 200.
130 *Rahbar*, pp. 20, 23.
131 *The Quran.* II: 29.
132 *The Quran.* XXXI: 20.
133 *The Quran.* XLV: 13.
134 *Rahbar*, p. 24.
135 *The Quran.* II: 3.
136 *The Quran.* II: 5.
137 *Rahbar*, p. 24.

138 *Ibid.*, pp. 24–25.
139 *Ibid.*, p. 20.
140 *Ibid.*, p. 21.
141 *Id.*
142 *Ibid.*, pp. 25–26.
143 *The Quran.* III: 159.
144 *Rahbar*, p. 26.
145 *Id.*
146 *The Quran.* XXIX: 22.
147 *Rahbar*, p. 28.
148 *Razskazy*, pp. 11–12.
149 *Rahbar*, p. 28.
150 *Ibid.*, p. 29.
151 *The Quran.* X: 18.
152 *The Quran.* XXXIX: 44.
153 *Rahbar*, pp. 29–30.
154 *Ibid.*, p. 26.
155 *The Quran.* VIII: 53.
156 *Rahbar*, p. 7.
157 *The Quran.* X: 45.
158 *The Quran.* XLII: 30.
159 *Spor*, pp. 22–23.
160 *Ibid.*, p. 25.
161 *Rahbar*, p. 9.
162 *The Quran.* XVII: 16.
163 *The Quran.* XXII: 48.
164 *The Quran.* XXII: 49.
165 *The Quran.* XLIII: 55.
166 *The Quran.* XLIII: 56.
167 *Rahbar*, p. 10.
168 *Ibid.*, p. 2.
169 *Razskazy*, pp. 23–24.
170 *Ibid.*, pp. 19–20.
171 *Ibid.*, pp. 20–22.
172 *Ibid.*, p. 22.
173 *Ibid.*, p. 23.
174 *Ibid.*, p. 26.
175 *Spor*, p. 14.
176 *Razskazy*, p. 26.
177 *Spor*, p. 18.
178 *Ibid.*, p. 17.
179 *Razskazy*, p. 2.
180 *Id.*
181 *Spor*, p. 18.
182 *Razskazy*, pp. 36–39.
183 *Spor*, p. 19.
184 *Ibid.*, p. 20.
185 *Razskazy*, p. 26.
186 *Ibid.*, p. 2.
187 *Ibid.*, pp. 26–27.
188 *Spor*, pp. 46–47.
189 *Ibid.*, p. 8.

190 *Alim* sometimes added a few extra names of non-existent students to the list while distributing the *vaqf* money; in this way they embezzled up to 10,000 *tenga* over and above their alloted fee of 2,000 *tenga*.

191 *Spor*, pp. 10–11.

192 *Ibid.*, pp. 11–12.

193 *Razskazy*, p. 27.

194 *Spor*, p. 47.

195 *Razskazy*, p. 77.

196 *The Quran.* XCV:4.

197 *The Quran.* XLV:13.

198 *Razskazy*, p. 77.

199 *Ibid.*, p. 29.

200 *Ibid.*, pp. 26–27.

201 *Ibid.*, p. 2.

202 *Ibid.*, p. 76.

203 *Spor*, p. 52.

204 Becker 1968, p. 200.

205 AFPR, Fund, *Central Asian desk* (B), F. b, pp. 119–120.

206 *Razskazy*, pp. 31–32.

207 *Ibid.*, p. 32.

208 Fitrat quotes a long passage from 'the great French professor' about the glories of medieval Muslim civilisation, *Razskazy*, pp. 32–37. According to Adeeb Fitrat's library contained a Turkish translation of Charles Seignobos's *Histoiere politiqque de l 'Europe*. See: Adeeb 1993, p. 225.

209 *Razskazy*, p. 33.

210 *Ibid.*, pp. 33–34.

211 *Ibid.*, p. 33.

212 *Spor*, p. 55.

213 *Ibid.*, pp. 55–56.

214 Fitrat *Spor*, p 28.

215 *Ibid.*, p. 34.

216 *Ibid.*, p. 38.

217 *Ibid.*, pp. 41–43.

218 *Ibid.*, p. 47.

219 *Ibid.*, p. 31.

220 *Spor*, pp. 42–43.

221 *Ibid.*, p. 38.

222 *Ibid.*, pp. 43–44.

223 *Ibid.*, p. 44.

224 *Ibid.*, p. 44.

225 *Ibid.*, pp. 47–48.

226 *Ibid.*, p. 32.

227 It is strange that the year for the opening of the school in Madina is given as 1329 AH, i.e. 1912, in the Russian translation, while the original *Munazara* gave 1328. See: *Spor*, p. 36; *Munazara* p. 41. Both the original *Munazara* and its Russian translation were published before that year. Neither is any record available to us to confirm the year in which the school in Madina was opened, nor does Fitrat quote any source.

228 *Spor*, pp. 35–36.

229 The four orthodox schools of law are known as Hanafi, Maliki, Shafi'i, and Hanbali after the four jurists of the second and third centuries who are regarded their founders. They differ on relatively minor points of law and

ritual, the Hanbalis, however, with their more intense opposition to all innovations (*Bidda*), theoretically reject *ijma* in all but its narrowest sense. Gibb, H. A. R., *Modern Trends in Islam*. New York 1972, p. 14.
230 A theoretical foundation was provided for *Ijma* by a saying of the Prophet, 'My community shall never agree on an error'.
231 *Spor*, p. 16.
232 *Spor*, p. 6.
233 *Spor*, p. 46.
234 *Razskazy*, pp. 8–9, 46–52.
235 *Ibid.*, p. 9.
236 *Ibid.*, pp. 53–54.
237 *Ibid.*, p. 51.
238 *Ibid.*, pp. 51–52.
239 *Ibid.*, p. 52.
240 *Ibid.*, p. 54.
241 *Ibid.*, pp. 55–57.
242 *Ibid.*, pp. 63–64.
243 *Ibid.*, p. 60.
244 *Ibid.*, p. 61.
245 *Ibid.*, pp. 63–64.
246 *Ibid.*, p. 88.
247 *Ibid.*, pp. 88–90.
248 *Ibid.*, p. 92.
249 *Ibid.*, pp. 92–93.
250 *Ibid.*, pp. 93–94.
251 *Ibid.*, pp. 95–96.
252 *Ibid.*, pp. 97–98.
253 Khodzhaev, *K Istorii...*, pp. 34–40; D'Encausse 1988, pp. 199–206; 'Partiya Mlado-Bukhartsev' in *Programmnye Dokumenty Musulmanskikh Partii 1917–1920 gg.* Oxford 1985, pp. 54–69.
254 *Razskazy*, p. 29.
255 *Spor*, p. 52.
256 *Razskazy*, pp. 75–76.
257 *Ibid.*, p. 78.

CONCLUSIONS

1 The Quran. 4:59.
2 Fitrat, *Spor*. p. 20.

Appendix One

EXTRACTS FROM DONISH'S *NAVADIR-UL-VOQAI*

(a) Illustrations of Precept No. 4

... 'Somebody committed a crime and fled. His brother was arrested and brought to Mamun. Mamun threatened to kill him if he did not produce his brother. The person said, "O commander of the believers! if you ordered your subordinate not to kill me would he obey?" Mamun said, "yes". The [accused] man said "I have brought you an order from God who has made you the ruler of this world", and recited this verse of the Quran: "And no burdened soul can bear another's burden". (Source: *The Quran*. XXXV: 18). Mamun set him free and said "he has delivered the reason".'

'Mamun dismissed Ahmad bin Arvo from the rulership of Ahwaz. Being displeased with him, Mamun was counting his failures and crimes. Ahmad said, "on the Day of Judgement you will face similar interrogation and your failures will be counted: would you wish to be pardoned in that situation?" Mamun replied in the affirmative. Ahmad begged for forgiveness, and Mamun pardoned him and restored his job.'

'Masa'b bin Zubair, after defeating Mukhtar, ordered his death. Mukhtar said, "look at your beautiful face in the mirror. On the Day of Judgement, I will complain against you. It is a pity that such a beautiful face should be punished for the sake of such an insignificant person as me". Masa'b thought for a while and then pardoned him. Mukhtar said that life without wealth is even worse than death. Masa'b returned him all of his confiscated property.'

'Once, Mamun was riding a horse in the streets of Baghdad. A man suddenly appeared who wanted to hand him a petition. Mamun's horse, frightened by the man's sudden movement, jumped back and threw Mamun down. Mamun's officials wanted to punish the man, who was waiting in fear for the executioner. However, Mamun sat back on his horse, took the petition, and ordered that his problem be solved.'

'Once, in the summer, Hajjaj went out of the city and reached a farm. A farmer was busy sowing. He asked him whether he knew Hajjaj. The farmer replied that he was the most corrupt, cruel, unjust and oppressive person. Hajjaj asked, "do you know me?" The farmer said, "No". "I am Hajjaj", retorted Hajjaj. The farmer said, "do you know me?" Hajjaj said, "No". The farmer said, "I am the slave of the descendants of Zubair. I become insane three days a month: today is one of those days." Hajjaj laughed and did not harm him.'

(Source: Donish *Navadir-ul-Voqai*, pp. 19–20)

(b) Illustrations of Precept No. 7

... God's Prophet stated that 'on the Resurrection day holders of authority will be brought in and told, "you were shepherds of my sheep". "Why did you award a penalty and inflict a punishment on so-and-so in excess of I bade you?" He will reply, "O Lord God, in wrath because they were offending against you"; and he will be told, "Why should your wrath exceed Mine?" Another will be asked, "Why did you inflict a punishment falling short of what I bade you?" He will reply, "O Lord God, I did so out of compassion"; and he will be told, "Why should you be more compassionate than I am?" Then God on High will order them to be shown the corners of Hell.'

'Hudaifah [ibn al-Yaman] used to say, "I never praise any holder of authority, whether virtuous or wicked." When asked why, he replied that it was because he had heard God's Prophet declare: "On the day of Resurrection, all holders of authority will be brought in, whether unjust or just. All will be stationed at the bridge called *sirat*, and God on High will inspire the *sirat* to shake them off in one sharp shake, for there will not be a single one among them who has not judged unjustly, taken a bribe when trying a case, or lent his ear overmuch to one contestant. All will fall off the *sirat*, and all will go down to Hell for seventy years, at the end of which time they will reach their final resting place".'

'It is related in the Traditions that David used to go out at night and ask all whom he met their secret opinion about his character. On one occasion Gabriel came up to him in the form of a man. David put the same question to him, and he replied, "David is a good man, except that he gets his living from the public treasury and not from the toil of his own hands." David then went into the mosque and wept, saying, "O Lord God, teach me a trade so that I may live by the toil of my own hands." Then God on High taught him the trade of armourer.'

'Umar [ibn al-Khattab] used to substitute for his own night-watchman and go out on the beat, so that if he saw anything amiss he might have it attended to. "If a mangy goat", he said, "were to be left by the side of an irrigation ditch and not rubbed with ointment, I would fear lest I be questioned about it on the day of Resurrection".'

'Abd Allah ibn Umar said: I used to pray to God that He would let me see Umar in our dreams, and after twelve years I saw him. It was as though he had just bathed and had a loin-cloth tied around his waist. I asked him, "How have you found your Lord, and for what good works has He recompensed you?" "O Abd Allah", he replied, "how long is it since I departed from you?" "Twelve years", I said. "Since I have departed from you", he continued, "I have been in the process of being called to account, and I was afraid lest I should perish. But God is forgiving and compassionate, bountiful and generous." Such was the case of Umar, who during his lifetime used no instrument of government except his whip. The Caesar of the Romans sent several emissaries to observe what sort of a man he was and what sort of life he led. On arriving at Madina they asked, "Where is your king?" and were answered, "We have no king, but an Emir, who has gone out of the city gate." The emissaries went out to the city gate and saw him sleeping on the ground in the sun, with a whip placed beneath his head and so much sweat flowing from his brow that the ground had become moist. When they saw Umar thus, their hearts were filled with great astonishment that a man in awe of whom the world's kings trembled should be sleeping in such surroundings. Then they said: "he has ruled justly; of course he can sleep in safety. Our king has ruled unjustly; he is always apprehensive. We testify that your religion is the right religion, and even though this was not the purpose of our mission, we have become inwardly Muslim here and now. We shall return soon and publicly make ourselves Muslims." Such, then are the dangers of authority.'

(*Ibid.*, pp. 23–25)

(c) Illustrations of Precept No. 8

… 'Harun al-Rashid once went with Abbas to visit Fudayl ibn Iyad. When he reached the door of the house, Fudayl was reciting the verse: "Or do those who commit ill-deeds suppose that We shall make them as those who believe and do good works, the same in life or death? Bad is their judgement!" (*The Quran*. XLV: 21) meaning: "Do those who do evil deeds suppose that We shall treat them equally with those who believe and do good deeds? They judge ill." Harun said, "If we have come to seek advice, this is enough". Then he bade his companion knock on the door. Abbas knocked at the door and cried out, "Homage to the Prince of the Believers! Open the door for him". It was night-time, and Fudayl set down a lantern and opened the door. Harun groped in the darkness until his hand touched Fudayl's hand. "Alas for so soft a hand," exclaimed Fudayl, "unless it gets salvation from God!" Then he said, "O Prince of the Believers, prepare to answer God on the day of Resurrection! For you will be made to stand with every Muslim, one by one, and be questioned about the justice of your conduct towards each of them." Harun wept. "Hush", said Abbas; "you might kill the Prince of the Believers". "O Haman," replied Fudayl, "you and your clique have already destroyed him, and you tell me that I might kill him!" Harun said to Abbas, "They call you Haman because you have turned me into a Pharaoh." Then Harun laid a thousand Dinars before Fudayl, saying: "This is lawful. It is from my mother's dowry and inheritance." "I bid you", rejoined Fudayl, "keep what you hold. Take refuge in the Lord; in so doing you will give it back to me." Then he rose and left him, having accepted nothing.'

'Umar ibn Abd al-Aziz asked Muhammad ibn al-Ka'b to describe justice to him. He replied, "To every Muslim who is younger than you, be a father, and to every Muslim who is older than you, be a son; and to every Muslim of the same age, be a brother. Punish every offender in proportion to his crime; and beware lest you inflict a whipping in anger, for your place will then be in Hell".'

'One day when Marwan ibn al-Hakam was Caliph, he thought to himself: "I have been blessed with wealth in this world for such and such [a length of time]. How shall I fare at the day of Resurrection?" He sent one of his servants to Abu Hazim, an *alim* and ascetic of the time, with a message saying: "Send me some of the food which you will take when you finish fasting." Abu Hazim sent him a small portion of cooked bran, with a message saying: "This is what I shall eat for supper." Marwan wept on seeing it; it made a deep impression on his heart, and he fasted for three days, eating nothing whatever. On the third night he broke his fast with the bran. They say that during that night he had intercourse with his spouse, who conceived Abd al-Aziz [the father of Umar ibn Abd al-Aziz], who [Umar ibn Abd al-Aziz] was unique in the world and resembled Umar ibn al-Khattab in the justice of his rule. They say it was because of the blessing which resulted from Marwan's sincere intention when he ate that food. Umar ibn Abd al-Aziz was asked what was the cause of his repentance. "One day", he replied, "I was beating a page-boy." He said to me, "Remember the night whose morrow will be the day of Resurrection"; and those words troubled my heart.'

(*Ibid.*, pp. 26–28)

(d) Illustrations of Precept No. 9

... 'It is written in the Torah that an unjust act by an official which the ruler notices but passes over in silence is an unjust act committed by the ruler himself, and will be counted against him as such. A ruler should understand that there is no greater dupe and fool than he who sells his religion and future life to another for the sake of this life. His officials and servants will all work for the sake of their own interests in this life. They will cause injustice to appear good in the eyes of the ruler, and thus send him to Hell, in order to attain their own ends. What greater enemy is there than one who promotes your total destruction for the sake of a few unlawful *dirhams*. Justice consists in restraining tyrannous instincts, passions and anger in order to make them the prisoners of reason. Justice springs from the perfection of reason, and the perfection of reason means that one sees things as they are and perceives the facts of their inner reality without being deceived by their outward appearance. For instance, if you oppress people for the sake of this world, then you should consider what your aim in this world is. If your aim is to eat good food, you should understand that this is an animal passion in human form, for the brute beasts eat gluttonously. If your aim is to wear finery, you are a woman in the form of a man, for self-adornment is an activity of women. If your aim is to vent your wrath against your enemies, you are a beast of prey in human form, for the violent excess of wrath is characteristic of beasts of prey. If your aim is that people should serve you, then you are an ignorant man in the form of an intelligent man, for if you were intelligent you would know that those who serve you are only servants and slaves to their own bellies and passions, and that they have been using you as a net with which to catch what they desire, and that their subservience and prostration are for their own benefit, not yours. A sure sign of this would be if they were to hear rumours that authority might be taken from you and given to another; they would turn away from you with one accord and seek the other ruler. They will bow down and serve that person who can deliver money to them. In reality this is not service but mockery. The intelligent man is one who sees the spirit and reality of things and is not deceived by their outward form. The real nature of the above-mentioned activities is as we have described and explained. A man who will not let himself be assured of this is not intelligent; and a man who is not intelligent will not be just, and his last abode will be Hell-fire. The capital from which all forms of happiness are derived is reason'.

(*Ibid.*, pp. 29–30)

(e) Illustrations of Precept No. 10

... 'A certain man was described to God's Prophet as an exceedingly strong man. "In what way?" asked the Prophet. "Any man whom he wrestles with", they replied, "he throws down. He prevails over all". God's prophet declared: "The strong and virile man is one who prevails over his own anger, not one who throws other men down." God's Prophet also said that if any man can achieve three things, his faith will be perfect. They are: not to form a wrong intention when angered, not to set aside what is right when pleased and not to take more than what is right when powerful.'

'Ali bin Hussain, blessings upon him, went one day to the mosque, where a man insulted him. His attendants made ready to kill the man, but he said: "Keep your hands off him!" Then he said to the man: "What you do not know about us far exceeds what you do know. Have you any request which could be satisfied by our hands?" The man was ashamed. Ali then gave his own cloak and a thousand Dinars to the man, who started to go, saying: "I testify that there is no true scion of the Prophet except him".'

'Another story told of Abu Dard [Ali Zayn al-Abidin] is that he twice summoned a slave but got no answer. "Did you not hear me call?" he asked him. "I did hear", he replied. "Why did not you answer?" "You are so good-tempered", he said, "that I was confident that you would not be annoyed with me." "Thanks be to God", said his master, "that my slave has confidence in me"; and he set him free. Another slave, belonging to Zayn al-Abidin, once broke the leg of one of his master's sheep. "Why did you do it?", asked Zayn al-Abidin. "I did it on purpose", he replied, "to anger you". "Then I will anger the person who gave you the idea, namely the devil", rejoined Zayn al-Abidin; and he set this slave free also. Another man used to insult him [Zayn al-Abidin]. To this man he said: "Gallant sir, between Heaven and Hell there is a narrow pass. If I cross it I shall not fear these words of yours; if I cannot cross it, I shall be worse than you have said".'

'God's Prophet said, "There may well be persons who through forbearance and forgiveness attain the same degree of purity as those who keep the fast and perform the prayer; and there may well be persons whose names will be inscribed in the register of the mighty even though they hold no authority except over their own household." Another saying of God's Prophet is that Hell has a gate through which only those will enter who give vent to their anger in ways contrary to God's law. It is related that the Devil came to Moses and said: "O Moses, three things will I teach you; then you should seek a favour for me from the Lord. Beware of quick temper, for the quick tempered-man is light-headed and I can play with him. Beware of the tongue, for on none of the traps which I have set for humans do I rely so much as on the tongue. Beware of avarice, for I deprive miser of both religion and the world".

God's Prophet declared: 'Whoever suppresses anger and has strength enough to set it aside will be clad by the True God on High in beatific raiment; and "Woe to him who grows angry and forgets God's anger against him." A certain person asked God's Prophet, "Teach me some action whereby I may enter Heaven!" "Never become angry", the Prophet told him; "and furthermore, never ask anybody for anything that is heaven to you." "Teach me more", requested the man; and the Prophet told him, "Following the afternoon prayer, beg God's pardon seventy times, so that He may forgive your sins of seventy years." "I have not been sinning for seventy years", rejoined the man. "Then your mother's", said the Prophet. "My mother has not been sinning so long", rejoined the man. "Then your father's", said the Prophet. "My father has not been sinning so long", rejoined the man. "Then your brethren's", said the Prophet. Abd Allah ibn Masud relates that once, when God's Prophet was apportioning a property, a man said, "This apportionment is not for God", meaning that it was not equitable. Ibn Masud repeated the story to God's Prophet. The latter grew angry, and his blessed face flushed; but all he said was, "God have mercy on my brother Moses. People caused him greater annoyance than this, but he kept his patience".'

(Ibid., pp. 31–33)

Appendix Two

(a) Traditions quoted by Fitrat to emphasise the virtue of *aql*

According to Qorat bin Habira, the Prophet said, 'those would be saved, whom Allah granted intellect'. According to Vabisa, the Prophet said, 'You should seek *fatva* from reason even if the *mufti* has pronounced the *fatva* already. Meaning, do not blindly submit to the *fatva* pronounced by the *mufti.*' According to Abi Sa'lba, the Prophet said that 'any act is permissible if it is in conformity with reason and your conscience is satisfied. Sin is that which reason does not condone and hurts your conscience. Even if the *mufti* have pronounced *fatva*'.

(b) Analogies from Fitrat's work to explain *tawakkal*

Another analogy Fitrat employed was that of a certain youth who has ability and financial resources and wants to become a great *alim*. Now if the young man, instead of going to school and reading books, went to a mausoleum and prayed to God for knowledge, his prayers would not be granted and he would remain ignorant until death. But if he went to school and worked hard it would not necessarily follow that he would become a scholar, because he might fall ill or involve himself in sensuous desires and discontinue his studies. Hence, one should pray to avoid unseen hurdles, and such prayers may be granted.

Fitrat pointed out, the Prophet had himself acted in this way. On the day of *Badr*, he prepared the weapons, gathered the army, faced the infidels, and only then prayed for victory. '... Allah is swift at reckoning', [*The Quran.* II: 202] wrote Fitrat, implying that God will not ignore a single deed, but will consider all the actions and efforts of those who pray, and will only answer the prayers of those who make an effort towards their goal.

(Source: *Rahbai-i-Najat*, pp. 35–36)

Appendix Three

LIST OF TAXES PAID BY THE BUKHARANS

1 *Kharaj*:   Land tax.

2 *Zakat*:   Obligatory alms paid by Muslims on various forms of property for purposes outlined in the Quran. A tax of 2.5% was collected on sale of goods. Tax collected on cattle was called *zakat savoem*: on 40 head of cattle, one head was levied, on 40 to 120, two head, on 120 to 300, three head, and on each following hundred, one head.

3 *Aminona*:   A bazaar tax, 1.5% of the price of a commodity; thus, on every pud (1 pud = 16.38 kg.) of cotton, 15 copecks were levied as *aminona*. On wool worth 150 roubles, the tax was 2 roubles.

4 *Pul-i-takhta-joi*:   Tax for space in the market for goods or cattle.

5 *Tarozu-puli*:   Tax on weighing in the market.

6 *Dalloli-puli*:   Brokerage money.

7 *Mirabona*:   Tax for the irrigation administration.

8 *Bokia-puli*:   Tax for other irrigation needs.

9 *Chigir puli*:   Tax to the local administration for the water-raising wheel.

10 *Labaki puli*:   Tax for digging irrigation ditches.

11 *Jazya*:   Tax on the non-Muslim population e.g. Jews, Hindus.

12 *Avorizot*:   Emergency war tax.

13 *Kara-chirik*:   Tax for the irregular army.

14 *Farsakh puli*:   Road tax.

15	*Asia puli:*	Tax on water-milling.
16	*Yaksara or kosh puli:*	Tax on a pair of oxen.
17	*Haveli puli:*	Chimney tax.
18	*Objuvoz puli:*	Tax on rice husking.
19	*Khas puli:*	Tax on the sale of bush wood.
20	*Ojas puli:*	Tax on kitchen gardens.
21	*Sanjit puli:*	Tax on Sanjit (a tree).
22	*Chorbogh puli:*	Tax on fruit trees.
23	*Chob puli:*	Tax on wood.
24	*Aliaf puli:*	Tax on clover fields.
25	*Kharbuz puli:*	Tax on melons and water melons.
26	*Kimey puli:*	Tax on passage.
27	*Mohrana:*	Stamp tax for the *qazi, mufti, rais* and other officials.
28	*Khizmatona:*	Tax when a matter was examined by the *qazi, bek* or other officials.
29	*Kafshan puli:*	Tax on the yield of a *dehqan* for the *bek, amlakadar, mirshab, mirza* and other officials.
30	*Vasiqa puli:*	Tax on land transfer deeds.

Sources: *Vystavka Eksponatov v Bukharskom Oblastnom Muzee*; Ishanov 1969, pp. 65–69; Semyonov, A., *Ocherk po Zemelno-Podatnogo i Nalogovogo Ustroistvo Byvshego Bukharskogo Khanstva*. Vol. 1, Tashkent 1929, pp. 47–51; Semyonov 1960, pp. 998–1000; AFPR, Fund, *Central Asian desk*, F. 304, pp. 9–10; F. 92, pp. 30–67; CSAUz., *Arkhiv Kushbegi Emira Bukharskogo*, Fund, 126, FF. 6301, 6307, 6435, 6436.

Glossary

Akhund	title of revered holy man.
Alacha	Bukharan hand-made cloth.
Aliaf puli	tax on clover fields.
Amin	head of a *kent* (small administrative unit).
Aminona	a bazaar tax, 1.5% of the price of a commodity.
Amlakadar	ruler of an *amlakadari*.
Amlakadari	administrative sub-unit of a *valayat*.
Ammaldor	class of people in civil and military service.
Aql	intellect/reason.
Aql-i-Sharifa	noble intellect, reason.
Aqsaqal	lit. 'white beard', head of a village. (Uzbeki)
Arbob	head of a village (Tajiki).
Arbobstvo	village (used in Russian sources dealing with Tajiki-speaking areas).
Ariq	canal.
Asia puli	tax on water milling.
Ataliq	guardian.
Avlia	holy men.
Avorizot	emergency war tax.
Azanchi	one who chants the call to obligatory prayers.
Bai	big landowner.
Bara	half-platoon.
Barshina	corvee.
Batman	1 Batman = 8 puds or 131.1 kg.
Batrak	pauper.

Begar	unwaged labour.
Bek	the ruler of a *valayat* (Uzbeki).
Beklik	principality (Uzbeki).
Bekstvo	principality (in Russian sources).
Bewatan	landless farm worker.
Bokia-puli	subsidiary tax for irrigation needs.
Bunak	credit advanced to Bukharan *dehqan* for purchase of cotton or *karakul*.
Chairikar	share-cropper.
Charek	1 Charek = 5 lbs or 2.048 kg.
Chehraogasi	Sergeant-Major.
Chigir puli	tax paid to the local administration for water-raising wheels.
Chob puli	tax on wood.
Chorbogh puli	tax on fruit trees.
Dah-boshi	officer in charge of the police station, also lance-corporal.
Dalloli-puli	brokerage money.
Dasta	(military) company.
Datkho	battalion commander.
Dehqan	farmer.
Divonbegi	head of the civil bureaucracy.
Domulla	teacher, one who is in charge of a *maktab*.
Dzharib	police station.
Emir	lit. 'Commander'.
Emir al-Momineen	'Commander of the Faithful'.
Farsakh puli	road tax.
Fatva	legal opinion or edict given by a *mufti*.
Fuqara	rabble.
Furqan	distinguisher, criterion of right and wrong (Quran)
Ghaya	objective or purpose.
Hadith	Tradition of the Holy Prophet Muhammad.
Hadji	from *Hodja* ('master' or 'owner'), descendants of Arab conquerors who settled in Bukhara in the seventh century.
Haj	pilgrimage to Mecca.

Hakim	ruler of a *valayat* (Arabic, used in some *valayat* of eastern Bukhara).
Hashar	unpaid labour by a *dehqan*.
Haveli puli	chimney tax.
Hukmana	tax paid to a *qazi* for pronouncing a judgement.
Ijaridar	leading cotton or *karakul* broker, working for Russian companies in Bukhara.
Ijma	consensus.
Ijtihad	systematic original thinking.
Imam	one who leads the obligatory prayers.
Iman	faith.
Ishan	mystic, sufi teacher.
Ishan Rais	the official who enforced the Islamic code of ethics and correct weights and measures in Bukhara's markets.
Jadid	new, modern/reformist (Arabic); here also used to refer to members of reformist movements in Turkistan and Bukhara.
Jadidism	modernism/reformism.
Jamoa	gathering or assembly.
Jazya	tax on non-Muslim population (e.g. Jews, Hindus).
Jul	a discretionary tax.
Kafir	infidel.
Kafshan puli	tax on the yield of a *dehqan* for the *bek*, *amlakadar*, *mirshab*, *mirza* and other officials.
Kara-chirik	tax for the irregular army.
Karakul	lambs fleece.
Kent	administrative sub-unit of an *amlakadari* (Uzbeki).
Khalat	robe.
Khan	oldest member of the ruling house.
Khanqa	mausoleum.
Kharaj	land tax.
Kharbuz puli	tax on melons, water melons.
Kharcha	'pocket money' given to a landless *dehqan* who worked for a *bai*.
Khas puli	tax on sale of kindling.
Khatmona	tax on circumcision of a male child.

Khizmatona	tax when a matter was examined by *qazi*, *bek* or other officials.
Kimey puli	toll on transporting goods.
Kosh	a pair of oxen.
Kosib	artisan.
Krai	territory (Russian).
Labaki puli	tax on *dehqan* to pay for digging irrigation ditches.
Madrasa	lit. 'lesson giving place', college of religious learning.
Maktab	elementary Quranic school.
Mavat lands	dead lands, uncultivated for whatever reason.
Mawra al-Nahr	lit. 'beyond the river', the part of Central Asia between the Amu Darya and Syr Darya.
Mazar	'tomb', (holy place).
Mir	the ruler of a *valayat* (Tajiki).
Mira'b	the official in charge of the distribution and use of water.
Mirabona	tax on *dehqan* to pay for the irrigation administration.
Mirkhazar	head of a *kent*.
Mirkhazarstvo	*kent* (in Russian sources).
Mirshab	the chief of the night police.
Mirza	secretary, clerk.
Mirzobashi	Head clerk, Secretary.
Mohrana	stamp tax for *qazi*, *mufti*, *rais* and other officials.
Mudarris	teacher, one who is in charge of a *madrasa*.
Mufti	jurisconsult, one who is qualified to pronounce a *fatva*.
Mujtahid	lit. 'renewer', a great scholar, the head of the *Shi'a* religious officials in Bukhara.
Mulazim	personnel who execute justice.
Mulk-hurr-khalis	tax-free lands belonging to private individuals.
Mulk Kharaj	tax paying lands belonging to private individuals.
Mulla	a lower-grade member of the religious class.
Mullabachai	students.
Nafs	self.

Nafs-i-Kasif	lower self.
Nikohona	tax on marriage.
Nim Dasta	(military) half-company.
Novaya	new (Russian).
Objuvoz puli	tax on removing husk from rice.
Oblast	region (Russian).
Obrok	a discretionary tax.
Obshchestvo	society, company (Russian).
Ojas puli	tax on kitchen gardens.
Pakhtakash	small cotton or *karakul* buyer working for an *ijaridar*.
Pud	1 pud = 16.38 kg.
Pul-i-takhta-joi	tax for space in the market.
Qadim	old (Arabic).
Qari	one who recites the Quran.
Qazi	Judge.
Qazi-i-Kalan	Chief Justice.
Qias	analogical reasoning.
Qishlaq	village (Uzbeki).
Qushbegi-i-Bala	grand master of the bek, Prime Minister.
Qushbegi-Payan	junior *Qushbegi*.
Quwa	power, faculty.
Rais	chief local official of a town.
Rasad	platoon.
Rivayat	religious opinion formed on the basis of a Tradition.
Saad	smaller administrative unit of an *amlakadari* (Tajiki).
Sa'dat-i-Darain	the pursuit of happiness in this world as well as in the world hereafter.
Sadzhen	1 Sadzhen = 1.83 metres.
Sahranashin Chorvodar	nomadic livestock-breeders.
Sanjit puli	tax on the Sanjit tree.
Sarbaz	soldier.
Sarbazkhona	army barracks.
Sayyid	descendants of the Prophet Muhammad through his daughter Fatima and son-in-law Ali.

Shabgardam	policemen.
Shah	the ruler of a *valayat* (Tajiki).
Shaharnashin	town-dwellers.
Sharakat	cooperation between *dehqan*.
Shari'a	the divinely ordained pattern of human conduct.
Sheikh-ul-Islam	supreme religious leader, leader of the *sayyid* and *hadji*.
Shodeona	tax on the birth of a child.
Sipoi	army.
Sultan	ruler.
Sunna	the conduct and words of the Prophet Muhammad.
Tafsir	Quranic exegesis.
Taloqona	tax on dissolution of marriage.
Tanab	a *tanab* varied from area to area, generally, 1 tanab = 3,600 square steps, or 2,730 sq. m.
Tankhva land	land granted for military service.
Taqlid	acceptance of the authority of earlier schools, blind following.
Tarozudar	weighers, meaning commission agents.
Tarozu-puli	tax on weighing in the market.
Tawakkal	trust in God.
Tenga	1 Silver *tenga* = 76 Kopecks.
Tillai	1 Gold *tillai* = 16 Roubles.
Toksabo	commander of a squadron.
Toksan-Tartuk	presents sent to the Emir every year by local officials such as the *bek*.
Topchi-Boshi Lashkar	Commander-in-Chief of the army.
Tovarishchestvo	partnership, company (Russian).
Tujjor	merchants.
Tumen	smaller unit of a *valayat*, also called *amlakadari*.
Ulama	the collective term for all religious functionaries, including teachers and interpreters of the sacred law.
Ulum	sing. *Ilm*, science, knowledge.
Uraq	a high religious title granted to some *sayyid*.
Usul-i-Jadid	new method (of education).

Uzboshi	junior lieutenant.
Valayat	principality (Tajiki).
Vaqf lands	properties whose revenues were spent on a charitable institution such as a school, mosque or mausoleum.
Vasiqa documents	land transfer deeds.
Vasiqa puli	tax on land transfer.
Vazaif	sing. *vazifa*, duty.
Vazir	minister.
Yaksara or Kosh puli	tax on a pair of oxen.
Zakat	obligatory alms paid by Muslims on various forms of property for purposes outlined in the Quran.
Zakatchi Kalan	grand collector of the *Zakat*.
Zamin Amlak	state lands.
Zindan	jail.

Bibliography

UNPUBLISHED PRIMARY SOURCES

Donish, A. *Navadir-ul-Voqai*. Unpublished manuscript, Manuscript Collection, of the Institute of Language and Literature, Academy of Sciences of Tajikistan, Dushanbe.

ARCHIVE DOCUMENTS

Archives of the Foreign Policy of Russia. Fund, *Sankt. Peterburgski Glavnyi Arkhiv* 1–9, dated 1888, F. 10. *Ocherk ob Orositelnykh Kanalakh Bukharskogo Emirata.*

Archives of the Foreign Policy of Russia. Fund, *Central Asian desk*, F. 301.

Archives of the Foreign Policy of Russia. Fund, *Central Asian desk*, F. 404.

Archives of the Foreign Policy of Russia. Fund, 3, Op. 1, F. 348.

Archives of the Foreign Policy of Russia. Fund, *Central Asian desk*, F. 304.

Archives of the Foreign Policy of Russia. Fund, *Central Asian desk*, F. 92.

Archives of the Foreign Policy of Russia. Fund, *Central Asian desk*, F. 295.

Archives of the Foreign Policy of Russia. Fund, *Central Asian desk*, F. 539.

Archives of the Foreign Policy of Russia. Fund, *Central Asian desk*, F. 298. *From the Note of Lessar, Imperial Political Agent in Bukhara, to the Foreign Minister of Russia.*

Archives of the Foreign Policy of Russia. Fund, *Central Asian desk*, F. 208.

Archives of the Foreign Policy of Russia. Fund, *Central Asian desk*, F. 305.

Central Party Archives of the Institute of Marxism-Leninism. Fund, 61, Op. 1, F. 122.

Central State Archives of Tajikistan. Fund, 21, Op. 1, F. 424.

Central State Archives of the Uzbek SSR (Uzbekistan). *Arhhiv Kushbegi Emira Bukharskogo*, Fund, 126, FF. 6301, 6307, 6435, 6436.

Central State Archives of the Uzbek SSR (Uzbekistan). *Arkhiv Kushbegi Emira Bukharskogo*, Fund, 125, Op. 1, FF. 6303, 6308, 6311, 6312.

Central State Archives of the Uzbek SSR (Uzbekistan). *Arkhiv Kushbegi Emira Bukharskogo*, Fund, 126, Op. 1, FF. 1164–1238, 6307.

Central State Archives of the Uzbek SSR (Uzbekistan). *Arkhiv Kushbegi Emira Bukharskogo*, Fund, 126, Op. 1, FF. 6345, 6346, 6347.

Central State Archives of the Uzbek SSR (Uzbekistan). Fund, 5, Op. 1, Book 4, F. 3435.

Central State Archives of the Uzbek SSR (Uzbekistan). Fund, 3, Op. 1, F. 74.

Central State Archives of the Uzbek SSR (Uzbekistan). Fund, 2, Op. 1, F. 251.
Central State Archives of the Uzbek SSR (Uzbekistan). Fund, 3, Op. 1, F. 441.
Central State Archives of the Uzbek SSR (Uzbekistan). F. 247.
Central State Archives of the Uzbek SSR (Uzbekistan). Fund, 50, Op. 1, F. 7.
Central State Archives of the Uzbek SSR (Uzbekistan). Fund, 1, Op. 34, F. 290.
Central State Archives of the Uzbek SSR (Uzbekistan). Fund, 3, Op. 1, F. 17.
Central State Archives of the Uzbek SSR (Uzbekistan). Fund, 3, Op. 1, F. 678.
Central State Archives of the Uzbek SSR (Uzbekistan). Fund, 3, Op. 1, F. 366.
   Donesenie Karshinskogo Veterinarnogo Vracha, dated 2 February 1915.
Central State Archives of the Uzbek SSR (Uzbekistan). Fund, 1, Op. 34, F. 724.
   *Otnoshenie Ministerstvo Innostrannykh Del Tashkentskogo Generala Guber-
   natorstva (MID-TGG)*, dated 23 January 1891.
Central State Archives of the Uzbek SSR (Uzbekistan). Fund, 1, Op. 29, F. 53.
Central State Archives of the Uzbek SSR (Uzbekistan). Fund, 1, Op. 34, F. 791.
Central State Archives of the Uzbek SSR (Uzbekistan). Fund, 2, Op. 1, F. 251.
Central State Archives of the Uzbek SSR (Uzbekistan). Fund, 3, Op. 2, F. 3.
Central State Archives of the Uzbek SSR (Uzbekistan). Fund, 2, Op. 2, F. 447.
Central State Archives of the Uzbek SSR (Uzbekistan). Fund, 3, Op. 1, F. 251.
Central State Archives of the Uzbek SSR (Uzbekistan). Fund, 2, Op. 1, F. 278.
   Russko-Bukharskii Dogovor, dated 25 June 1885.
Central State Archives of the Uzbek SSR (Uzbekistan). Fund, 3, Op. 1, F. 197.
Central State Archives of the Uzbek SSR (Uzbekistan). Fund, 3, Op. 1, F. 224.
Central State Archives of the Uzbek SSR (Uzbekistan). Fund, 3, Op. 1, F. 446, *Tekst
   Dogovora*, dated 15 June 1912.
Central State Archives of the Uzbek SSR (Uzbekistan). Fund, 3, Op. 1, F. 448.
Central State Archives of the Uzbek SSR (Uzbekistan). Fund, 3, Op. 1, F. 21.
Central State Archives of the Uzbek SSR (Uzbekistan). Fund, 1, Op. 29, F. 850.
Central State Archives of the Uzbek SSR (Uzbekistan). Fund, 3, Op. 1, F. 166.
   Zhurnal Soveshchaniya po Khlopkovomu Delu v Bukharskom Emirate, dated
   19 January 1899.
Central State Archives of the Uzbek SSR (Uzbekistan). Fund, 3, Op. 1, F. 189.
Central State Archives of the Uzbek SSR (Uzbekistan). Fund, 3, Op. 1, FF. 165, 166.
Central State Archives of the Uzbek SSR (Uzbekistan). F. 794. *Letter of the Imperial
   Political Agent in Bukhara to the Russian Foreign Ministry*, dated 22 December
   1915.
Central State Archives of the Uzbek SSR (Uzbekistan). Fund, 3, Op. 1, F. 368.
Central State Archives of the Uzbek SSR (Uzbekistan). Fund. 3, Op. 2, F. 620 a.
Central State Archives of the Uzbek SSR (Uzbekistan). Fund, 3, Op. 1, F. 919.
   *Dokladnaya Zapiska Chlenov Vostochno-Bukharskogo Tovarishchestva po
   Skupke Khlopka*, dated 28 November 1916.
Central State Archives of the Uzbek SSR (Uzbekistan). Fund, 3, Op. 1, F. 368. *Data
   of Political Agent*, dated 2 August 1913.
Central State Archives of the Uzbek SSR (Uzbekistan). Fund, 3, Op. 1, F. 465.
Central State Archives of the Uzbek SSR (Uzbekistan). Fund, 1, Op. 17, F. 795.
Central State Archives of the Uzbek SSR (Uzbekistan). FF. 556, 919.
Central State Archives of the Uzbek SSR (Uzbekistan). F. 300. *Obrashchenie Polit-
   Agenta k Russkim Firmam, Tovarishchestvam i Chastnym Litsam Pod
   Nazvaniem 'Sirkularno'*. 1907.
Central State Archives of the Uzbek SSR (Uzbekistan). Fund, 3, Op. 1, F. 840.
   Naselenie Termiza i Torgovo-Promyshlennye Predpriyatiya v 1916 g.
Central State Archives of the Uzbek SSR (Uzbekistan). Fund, 1, Op. 12, F. 2079.
   Prilozhenie k Raportu Polit-Agenta TGG, dated 9 March 1916.

Central State Archives of the Uzbek SSR (Uzbekistan). Fund, 3, Op. 1, F. 335. *Spisok Khlopko-Ochischitelnykh Zavodov.*
Central State Archives of the Uzbek SSR (Uzbekistan). Fund, 3, Op. 1, F. 1063.
Central State Archives of the Uzbek SSR (Uzbekistan). Fund, 2, Op. 1, F. 24.
Central State Archives of the Uzbek SSR (Uzbekistan). Fund, 3, Op. 1, F. 259.
Central State Archives of the Uzbek SSR (Uzbekistan). Fund, 3, Op. 1, F. 69. *Postanovlenie o Zolotopromyshlennosti v Bukharskom Emirate, Utverzhdenie,* dated 24 February 1896.
Central State Archives of the Uzbek SSR (Uzbekistan). Fund, 3, Op. 1, F. 483. *Spravka TGG o Russkikh Kontsessiyakh v Bukhare,* dated 5 March 1901.
Central State Archives of the Uzbek SSR (Uzbekistan). Fund, 3, Op. 1, F. 47.
Central State Archives of the Uzbek SSR (Uzbekistan). Fund, 3, Op. 1, F. 92. *Otnoshenie Kushbegi- Polit-Agentu,* dated 6 August 1898.
Central State Archives of the Uzbek SSR (Uzbekistan). Fund, 3, Op. 1, F. 302.
Central State Archives of the Uzbek SSR (Uzbekistan). Fund, 1, Op. 29, FF. 28, 625.
Central State Archives of the Uzbek SSR (Uzbekistan). Fund, 3. Op. 1, FF. 171, 307.
Central State Archives of the Uzbek SSR (Uzbekistan). Fund, 3, Op. 1, F. 21.
Central State Archives of the Uzbek SSR (Uzbekistan). Fund, 2, Op. 1, F. 303.
Central State Archives of the Uzbek SSR (Uzbekistan). Fund, 3, Op. 1, F. 74, *Otnoshenie Polit-Agenta – TGG,* dated 8 December 1894.
Central State Archives of the Uzbek SSR (Uzbekistan). Fund, 3, Op. 1, F. 909.
Central State Archives of the Uzbek SSR (Uzbekistan). Fund. 3, Op. 1, F. 370.
Central State Archives of the Uzbek SSR (Uzbekistan). Fund, 3, Op. 1, F. 555.
Central State Archives of the Uzbek SSR (Uzbekistan). Fund, 25, Op. 1, F. 566.
Central State Archives of the Uzbek SSR (Uzbekistan). Fund, 5, Op. 1, F. 3.
Central State Archives of the Uzbek SSR (Uzbekistan). Fund, 3, Op. 1, F. 369. *Zapiska Voennogo Inzhenera Ermolaeva o Karshinskoi Stepi, Sostav.* dated 10 October 1911.
Central State Archives of the Uzbek SSR (Uzbekistan). Fund, 3, Op. 1, F. 368.
Central State Archives of the Uzbek SSR (Uzbekistan). Fund, 2, Op. 1, F. 10. Central State Archives Uzbekistan. Fund, 3, Op. 1, F. 102.
Central State Archives of the October Revolution and Socialist Construction of the USSR (Russia). Fund, 1318, Op. 1, F. 715.
Central State Archives of the October Revolution and Socialist Construction of the Uzbek SSR, Uzbekistan. Fund, 51, *Nazirat Zemledeliya BNSR,* Op. 1, F. 95.
Central State Archives of the October Revolution and Socialist Construction of the Uzbek SSR, Uzbekistan. Fund, 50, *Gosplan BNSR.* Op. 1 (1923–1924), F. 7.
Central State Archives of the October Revolution and Socialist Constructon of the Uzbek SSR, Uzbekistan. Fund, 130, Op. 2, F. 669.
Central State Archives of the Soviet Army, USSR. Fund, *Upravlenie Turkistanskim Frontom,* 1919–1920, Op. 3, F. 116.
Central State Historical Archives, Leningrad (St. Petersburg). Fund, 1276, Op. 6 (1910), F. 136.
Central State Historical Archives, St. Petersburg. Fund, 954, *Fon Kaufman,* Op. 1, F. 156, 1870.
Central State War-History Archives, USSR. Fund, 400, Op. 261/911 (1891), Sv. 108, F. 74, Part 2. *Data of Major General Usov.*
Central State War-History Archives, USSR. Fund, 400, Op. 261/911 (1891), Sv. 108, F. 73, Part 2.
Central State War-History Archives, USSR. Fund, 2000. *Glavnoe Upravlenie Generalnogo Shtaba,* Op. 1, F. 980.
Central State War-History Archives, USSR. Fund, 400, F. 136.

Central State War-History Archives, USSR. Fund, 400, Op. 261/911, Sv. 108 (1891), F. 73, Parts 1–4.
Central State War-History Archives, USSR. Fund, 400, Op. 262/912–915 (1909), Sv. 293, F. 90/77, *Dannye Ministerstva Innostrannykh Del*, dated 28 January 1910.
Central State War-History Archives, USSR. Fund, 400, Op. 262/912–915, Sv. 346, F. 73/98.
Institut Vostokovedeniya, A. N. Uzbekistana. F. 47, Document Nos. 47/143, 47/147, 47/141, 47/171.
State Archives of Orenburg Oblast. Fund, 6, Op. 10, FF. 7238, 1856.
Vystavka Eksponatov v Bukharskom Oblastnom Muzee.

UNPUBLISHED PHD DISSERTATION

Adeeb, K. [1993] *The Politics of Muslim Cultural Reform: Jadidism in Tsarist Central Asia*. An unpublished PhD dissertation, University of Wisconsin, Madison.

PUBLISHED BOOKS

Ahmad, A. [1967]: *Islamic Modernism in India and Pakistan, 1857–1964*. London.
Aini, S. [1923]: *Tarikh-i Emiran-i Manghitia Bukhara*. Tashkent.
Aini, S. [1926]: *Bukhara Inqilab-i Tarikhi Uchun Materiallar*. Moscow.
Aini, S. [1926]: *Namuna-i Adabiat-i Tajiki*. Moscow.
Aini, S. [1960]: *Vospominaniya*. Moscow and Leningrad.
Aini, S. [1966]: *Maktab-i Kuhnah*. Dushanbe.
Aini, S. [1966]: *Sobranie Sochinenii*. Vol. 10. Dushanbe.
Aini, S. [1966]: *Staraya Shkola*. Dushanbe.
Aini, S. [1971]: *Sobranie Sochinenii*. Vol. 1. Moscow.
Aini, S. [1974]: *Sobranie Sochinenii*. Vol. 5. Moscow.
Aini. S. [1987]: *Tarikh-i Inqilab-i Bukhara*. Dushanbe.
Algar, H. [1973]: *Mirza Malkum Khan: A Study in the History of Iranian Modernism*. Berkeley.
Allworth, E. [1989]: *Central Asia: 120 Years of Russian Rule*. Durham, NC and London.
Allworth, E. [1990]: *The Modern Uzbeks*. Stanford, Cal.
Arsharuni, A. and Kh. Gabidullin. [1931]: *Ocherki Panislamisma i Pantyurkisma v Rossii*. Moscow.
Ashurov, A. [1958]: *Bukhara*. Tashkent.
Babakhanov, M. [1987]: *Iz Istorii Periodicheskoi Pechati Turkistana*. Dushanbe.
Barthold, W. [1928]: *Turkestan Down to the Mongol Invasion*. London.
Barthold, W. [1963]: *Sochineniya*. Vol. 2. Part, 1. Moscow.
Barthold, W. [1977]: *Turkestan Down to the Mongol Invasion*. London.
Becker, S. [1968]: *Russia's Protectorates in Central Asia: Bukhara and Khiva, 1865–1924*. Cambridge, Mass.
Bennigsen, A., and Lemercier-Quelquejay, [1967]: *Islam in the Soviet Union*. London.
Braginskii, I. [1956]: *Ocherki iz Istorii Tadzhikskoi Literaturi*. Stalinabad.
Burnes, A. [1973]: *Travels into Bukhara*. Karachi.
Carrere d'Encausse, H. [1988]: *Islam and the Russian Empire: Reform and Revolution in Central Asia*. London.
Coates, Z. [1951]: *Soviets in Central Asia*. London.

Dobson, G. [1890]: *Russia's Railway Advance into Central Asia*. London.

Donohue, J. and J. Esposito, [1982]: *Islam in Transition*. New York.

Donish, A. [1957]: *Parchaho az Navadir-ul-Voqai*. Stalinabad.

Donish, A. [1960]: *Puteshestvie iz Bukhary v Peterburg*. Dushanbe.

Donish, A. [1967]: *Risala-i Ahmad Donish, Tarikh-i-Sultanat-i-Manghitia*. Dushanbe.

Donish. A. [1967]: *Traktat Akhmada Donisha, 'Istoriya Mangitskoi Dinastii'*. Dushanbe. Translated into Russian by I. A. Nadzhafova.

Donish, A. [1976]: *Risala Dar Nazm-i Tamaddun vo Ta'vun*. Dushanbe, compiled by Nazruula Rustamov and edited by R. Hadi-Zade.

Donish, A., *Risala ya Mukhtasari az Tarikhi Saltanati Khanadani Manghitia*. Stalinabad 1960, edited and introduced by Abdulghani Mirzaef.

Encyclopaedia of Islam. [1913]: Vol. 1. Part 2. London.

Esposito, J. [1988]: *Islam: The Straight Path*. New York.

Etherton, P. [1925]: *In the Heart of Asia*. London.

Fitrat, A. [1327 AH, 1909–10 AD]: *Munazara-i Mudarris-i Bukhara-i ba yak Nafar-i Farangi dar Hindustan dar bara-i Maktab-i Jadid*. Istanbul.

Fitrat, A. [1910]: *Saiha*. Istanbul.

Fitrat, A. [1911]: *Bayanat-i-Sayyah-i-Hindi*. Istanbul.

Fitrat, A. [1911]: *Spor Bukharskogo Mudarrisa s Evropetsom v Indii o Novometodnykh Shkolakh*. Tashkent. Translated into Russian by Colonel Yagello.

Fitrat, A. [1331 AH (1913 AD)], *Hindustan bir Farangi ile Bukharalik bir Mudarrisning birnecha masalalar ham usul-i Jadida khususida qilghan Munazarasi*. Tashkent 41 pp. Translated into Uzbeki by Haji Muin ibn Shukrullah Samarkandi.

Fitrat, A. [1913]: *Razskazy Indiiskogo Pucheshestvennika: Bukhara, Kak ona est*. Samarkand. Translated by A. Kondrateva.

Fitrat, A. [1915]: *Mukhtasar Tarikh-i Islam*. Samarkand.

Fitrat, A. [1915]: *Oila*. Baku.

Fitrat, A. [1915]: *Rahbar-i-Najat*. Petrograd.

Fitrat, A. [1919]: *Sharq Siyasati*. (n.p., n.d.).

Fitrat, A. [1923]: *Qayamat*. Moscow.

Fitrat, A. [1927]: *Shorish-i Vosey*. Dushanbe.

Fitrat, A. [1928]: *Uzbek Adabiat-i Namunalari*. Tashkent and Samarkand.

Fitrat, A. [1964]: *Strashnyi Sud*. Dushanbe. Translated by K. Nasirov.

Fomchenko, A. P. [1958]: *Russkie Poseleniya v Bukharskom Emirate*. Tashkent.

Gafurov, B. [1949]: *Istoriya Tadzhikskogo Naroda*. Vol. 1. Moscow.

Gafurov, B. [1955]: *Istoriya Tadzhikskogo Naroda*. Moscow.

Gafurov, B. and N. Prokhorov. [1940]: *Padenie Bukharskogo Emirata*. Stalinabad.

Galkin, M. [1868]: *Ethnograficheskie i Istoricheskie Materyaly po Srednei Azii i Orenburgskomu Krayu*. St. Petersburg.

Geier, I. [1909]: *Turkestan*. Tashkent.

Ghazali, A. [1964]: *Counsel for Kings (Nasihat al-Muluk)*. London. Translated by F. Bagley.

Gibb, H. A. R. [1972]: *Modern Trends in Islam*. New York.

Gordienko, A. A. [1959]: *Sozdinie sovetskoi nationalnoi gosudarstvennosti v Srednoi Azii*. Moscow.

Great Soviet Encyclopaedea. [1970]: Vol. 4. 3rd edition. Moscow.

Gulishambarov, S. [1913]: *Ekonomicheskii Obzor Turkistanskogo Kraya, Obsluzhivaemogo Sredno Aziatskoi Zheleznoi Dorogi*. Parts. 1–3, Ashkabad.

Hadi-Zade, R. [1956]: *Istochniki k Izucheniyu Tadzhikskoi Literatury Vtoroi Poloviny XIX Veka*. Stalinabad.

Hanbly, G. [1969]: *Central Asia*. London.

Holdsworth, M. [1959]: *Turkistan in the Nineteenth Century*. Oxford.

Hourani, A. [1962]: *Arabic Thought in the Liberal Age*. London.

Hutton, J. [1875]: *Central Asia: from the Aryans to the Cossack*. London.

Ishanov, A. I. [1955]: *Sozdanye Bukharskoi Narodnoi Sovetskoi Respubliki*. Tashkent.

Ishanov, A. I. [1969]: *Bukharskaya Narodnaya Sovetskaya Respublika*. Tashkent.

Iskandarov, B. I. [1958]: *Iz Istorii Bukharskogo Emirata*. Moscow.

Iskandarov, B. [1970]: *Bukhara (1918–1920)*. Dushanbe.

Istoriya Uzbekskoi SSR. [1955]: Tashkent.

Istoriya Uzbekskoi SSR. Vol. 1. Part. 1, [1956]: Tashkent.

Istoriya Uzbekskoi SSR. Vol. 2. [1968]: Tashkent.

Kai Kaus ibn Iskandar. [1951]: *Qabus Nama: A Mirror for Princes*. London. Translated and edited by R. Levy.

Keddie, R. N., (ed., transl.,). [1968]: *An Islamic Response to Imperialism: Political and Religious Writings of Sayyid Jamal al-Din 'al-Afghani'*. Berkeley.

Keddie, R. N. [1972]: *Sayyid Jamal al-Din 'al-Afghani': A Political Biography*. Berkeley.

Kerr, H. M. [1966]: *Islamic Reform: The Political and Legal Theories of Muhammad Abduh and Rashid Rida*. Berkeley.

Khanykov, N. [1843]: *Opisanie Bukharskogo Khanstva*. St. Petersburg.

Khanykov, N. [1845]: *Bukhara: its Amir and its People*. London. Translated by Baron Clement A. De Bode,

Khodzhaev, F. [1926]: *K Istorii Revolyutsii v Bukhare*. Tashkent.

Khodzhaev, F. [1970]: *Izbrannye Trudy*. Vol. I. Tashkent.

Kislyakov, N. A. [1962]: *Patriarkhalno-Feodalnie Otnosheniya Sredi Osedlogo Selskogo Naseleniya Bukharskogo Khanstva v Kontse 19 – Nachale 20 Vekov*. Moscow.

Komatsu, H. [1989]: *The Evolution of Group Identity among Bukharan Intellectuals in 1911–1928: An Overview*. Tokyo.

Kostenko, L. [1871]: *Puteshestvie v Bukharu Russkoi Missii v 1870 g*. St. Petersburg.

Kouz"nietsov, P. [1912]: *La lutte des civilisations et des langues dans Asie Centrale*. Paris.

Krestovskii, V. [1886]: *V Gostiyakx u Emira Bukharskogo*. St. Petersburg.

Lazzerini, J. [1991]: *Ismail Bay Gasprinskii And Muslim Modernism in Russia*. Michigan.

Lehmann, A. [1852]: *Reise nach Buchara und Samarkand in den Jahren 1841 und 1842*. St. Petersburg.

Lelyveld, D. [1978]: *Aligarh's First Generation: Muslim Solidarity in British India*. Princeton.

Lenin, V. I. [1977]: *Collected Works*. Vol. 5, Moscow.

Lewis, B. [1961]: *The Emergence of Modern Turkey*. London.

Logofet, D. [1909]: *Strana Bespraviya, Bukharskoe Khanstvo i ego Sovremennoe Polozhenie*. St. Petersburg.

Madzhlisov, A. [1967]: *Agrarnie Otnosheniya v Vostochnoi Bukhare v 19 – Nachale 20 Vekakh*. Dushanbe and Alma Ata.

Mardin, S. [1962]: *The Genesis of Young Ottoman Thought: A Study in the Modernization of Turkish Political Ideas*. Princeton.

Massalskii, V. I. [1892]: *Khlopkovoe Delo v Srednei Azii (Turkistan, Zakasp. Obl. Bukhara i Khiva) i ego Budushchee*. St. Petersburg.

Medlin, W. K., Cave, W. M., and Finley Carpenter, [1971]: *Education and Development in Central Asia*. Lieden.

Meyendorff, E. K. [1975]: *Puteshestvie iz Orenburga v Bukharu*. Moscow.
Mominov, I. [1976]: *Izbrannye proezvedeniya*. Vol. 2, Tashkent.
Nechaev, A. V. [1914]: *Po Gornoi Bukhare*. St. Petersburg.
Nizam al-Mulk, [1956]: *Siyasat Nama*. Tehran. Text, ed. by M. Modarresi Chahardehi,
Olufsen, O. [1911]: *The Emir of Bukhara and His Country*. Copenhagen.
Ozbekistan SSR tarikhi. Vol. II, [1958] Tashkent.
Pahlen, K. [1964]: *Mission to Turkistan*. London. Translated by N. Couriss.
Park, A. [1957]: *Bolshevism in Turkistan*. New York.
Polonskaya, L. and Alexei Malashenko. [1994]: *Islam in Central Asia*. Reading.
Radobylskii, A. [1905]: *Eknomicheskii Ocherk Bukhary i Tunisa*. St. Petersburg.
Radzhabov, Z. [1957]: *Iz Istorii Obshchestvenno-Politicheskoi Mysli Tadzhikskogo Naroda v Vtoroi Polavine XIX i v Nachale XX Vekov*. Stalinabad.
Radzhabov, Z. [1976]: *O Politicheskom Traktate Akhmada Donisha*. Dushanbe.
Rahman, F. [1979]: *Islam*. Chicago and London. 2nd Edition.
Razaev, A. K., and D. Tashkulov, [1990]: *Tusi, Donish*. Moscow.
Remez, I. A. [1922]: *Vneshnaya Torgovlya Bukhary do Mirovoi Voiny*. Tashkent.
Revolyutsiei Prizvannie. [1987]: Tashkent.
Rosenthal, E. [1958]: *Political Thought in Medieval Islam*. Part II. Cambridge.
Ryabinskii, A. M. [1940]: *Istoriya Kolonialnogo Poraboshcheniya Bukharskogo Khanstva Tsarskoi Rossii*. Vol. 4, Moscow.
Semyonov, A. [1929]: *Ocherk po Zemelno-Podatnogo i Nalogovogo Ustroistva Byvshchego Bukharskogo Khanstva*. Vol. 1. Tashkent.
Semyonov, A. [1954]: *Ocherk Ustroistva Tsentralnogo i Administativnogo Upravleniya Bukharskogo Khanstva Pozneshchevogo Vremini*. Stalinabad.
Shek, L. K. [1956]: *Pobeda Narodnoi Sovetskoi Revolyutsii v Bukhare*. Tashkent.
Shubinskii, P. [1892]: *Ocherki Bukhary*. St. Petersburg.
Shukurov, M. [1970]: *Istoriya Kulturnoi Zhizni Sovetskogo Tadzhikistana*. Dushanbe.
Sitnyakovskii, N. F. [1899]: *Zametki o Bukharskoi Chasti Daliny Zarafshana*. Vol. 1, 2nd edition.
Smith, C. W. [1946]: *Modern Islam in India*. London.
Snesarev, A. [1906]: *Vostochnaya Bukhara*. St. Petersburg.
Sukhareva, O. [1958]: *K Istorii Gorodov Bukharskogo Khanstva*. Tashkent.
Sukhareva, O. [1962]: *Pozdne Feodalnyi Gorod Bukhara Kontsa 19 ogo Nachalo 20 ogo Veka*. Tashkent.
Sukhareva, O. A., *Bukhara XIX – Nachalo XX v (Pozdnefeodal'nyi Gorod i ego Naselenie)*. Moscow 1966.
The Catholic Encyclopaedia. [1912]: Vol. 12. London.
Troll, W. C. [1978]: *Sayyid Ahmad Khan: A Reinterpretation of Muslim Theology*. New Delhi.
Ulugh-Zade, S. [1946]: *Ahmad Donish*. Stalinabad.
Vaidyanath, R. [1967]: *The Formation of the Soviet Central Asian Republics*. New Delhi.
Vambery, A. [1865]: *Puteshestvie po Srednei Azii*. St. Petersburg.
Vambery, A. [1868]: *Sketches of Central Asia*. London.
Vambery, A. [1873]: *Bukhara*. London.
Weber, M. [1905]: *The Sociology of Religion*. London.
Yuferov, V. I. [1914]: *K Izucheniyu Ekonomiki Khlopkovogo Proizvodstva v Rossii*. Tashkent.
Yusupov, S. [1964]: *Ocherki Istorii Kulyabskogo Bekstvo v Kontse 19 nachale 20 Vekov*. Dushanbe.

ARTICLES IN NEWSPAPERS, JOURNALS AND BOOKS

Aini, S. 'Dokhunda'. In: *Sobrannie Sochinenii*. Vol. 1, Moscow. 1971. 'Rabi'. In: *Sobrannie Sochinenii*. Vol. 2, Moscow. 1972.

Akiner, S. [1996]: 'Islam, the State and Ethnicity in Central Asia in Historical Perspective'. In: *Religion State & Society*. Vol. 24, No. 2/3, 1996.

A. P. [1908]: 'Administrativnoe Ustroistvo Gissarskogo Bekstvo'. In: *Turkistanskie Vedomosti*. (27 March 1908).

Arandarenko, G. [1881]: 'Bukharskie Voiska v 1880 g'. In: *Voennyi Sbornik*. (1881).

Arkhipov. [1923]: 'Bukharskaya narsonaya sovetskaya respublica'. In: *Sovetskoe Pravo*. Vol. 1, 1923.

Ayna, 17 May 1914; 1915, No. 14.

Becka, J. [1966]: 'Islamic Schools in Central Asia'. In: *New Orient*, No. 6.

Becka, J. [1967]: 'Islamic Schools in Central Asia'. In: *New Orient*, No. 2.

Behbudi, M. [1906]: 'Ta'mini Istiqlal', and 'Khosiyat-i- Ilm'. In: *Taraqqi*, 1906, 1 July.

Bertels, E. [1933]: 'Rukopisi Proizvedenii Akhmada Kalla'. In: *Trudy Tadzhikistanskoi Bazy*. Moscow and Leningrad. (1936).

Carrere d'Encausse, H. [1967]: 'Social and Political Reform'. In: *Central Asia: A Century of Russian Rule*. Ed. E. Allworth, London. (1967).

Carrere d'Encausse, H. [1989]: 'Systematic Conquest, 1865 to 1884'. In: *Central Asia: 120 years of Russian Rule*. Ed. E. Allworth, Durham, NC and London. (1989).

Dada Mirza Qari. [1913]: 'Mu'allim wa shagirdlar'. In: *Ayna*, 14 December 1913.

Dervish. [1937]: 'Bukharskaya Sovetskaya Narodnaya Respublika'. In: *Zhizn Natsionalnosti*, 1.

'Direktiva voiskam Turkistanskogo fronta', No. 3667, [25 August 1920]: In: Frunze, M. V., *Izbrannye Proizvedeniya*. Vol. 1, Moscow 1957.

Donish, A. [1895–97?]: 'Tarikhcha'. In: *Asarhoi Muntakhab*. Stalinabad 1959, edited by Hadi-Zade, R., and K. Aini.

Donish, A. [n.d.]: 'Dar Vasoyoi Farzondon va Bayoni Haqiqati Kasabhao Peshahao'. In: *Asarhoi Muntakhab*. Stalinabad 1959.

Donish, A. 'V Nazidanie Detyam o Polze Remesl i Zanyatii'. In: *Puteshestvie iz Bukhary v Peterburg*. Dushanbe 1960.

Dialog. [1991]: No. 7.

Fitrat, A. 'Hayat va Ghaya-i Hayat'. In: *Ayna*. 14 December 1913, and 21 December 1913.

Fitrat, A. 'Quran'. In: *Ayna*, 15 June 1915.

Fitrat, A. [1913]: 'Rasskazy Indiiskogo Puteshestvennika: Bukhara, Kak ona est'. In: *Zvezda Vostoka*. No. 7. 1990 Tashkent. Ed. by H. Ismailov.

Fitrat, A. [1917]: 'Siyasi Hallar'. In: *Hurriyat*, 7 November 1917.

Galkin, A. [1890]: 'Kratkii Ocherk Bukharskogo Khanstva'. In: *Voennyi Sbornik*. No. 11. (1890), St. Petersburg.

Galkin, A. [1894]: 'Kratkii Voenno-Statisticheskii Ocherk Bukharskogo Khanstva'. In: *Geograficheskie, Topograficheskie i Statisticheskie Materyaly po Azii*. 47th edition. (1894), St. Petersburg.

Golos. [15 February 1874]. St. Petersburg.

Hadi-Zade, R. [1960]: 'Akhmad Donish i evo Tvorchestvo'. In: *Puteshestvie iz Bukhary v Peterburg*. (1960), Stalinabad.

Hurriyat. 22 September 1917, 28 November 1917.

Ishanov, A. I. [1955]: 'Bukharskaya narsonaya sovetskaya respublica'. In: *Uchenie Zapiski Tashkentskogo yuridicheskogo instituta*. Vol. 1, Tashkent 1955.

Iskandarov, B. I. [1958]: 'O Nekotorykh Izmeneniyakh v Ekonomike Vostochnoi Bukhary na Rubezhe 19–20 v v'. In: *Trudy Instituta Istorii Arkhiologii i Etnografii*. A. N. Tadzhik SSR. Vol. LXXXIII.

Iskandarov, B. I. [1962–3]: 'Vostochnaya Bukhara i Pamir vo Vtoroi Polovine 19 v'. In: *Trudy A. N. Tadzhik SSR*. Vol. 39, Parts 1–2. (1962–3).

Kamilov, K. [1963]: 'V Borbe c Reaktsei'. In: *Za Sovetskii Turkistan*. Tashkent.

Khazanov, A. [1992]: 'Nomads and Oases in Central Asia'. In: *Transition to Modernity Essays on Power Wealth and Belief*. Hall and Jarvie (eds.), Cambridge (1992).

Khodzhaev, F. [1926]: 'O Molodo Bukhartsakh'. In: *Istorik Marksist*. No. 1 (1926).

Khodzhaev, F. [1937]: 'Dzhadidy'. In: *Ocherki Revolyutsionnogo Dvizheniya v Sarednei Azii*. Moscow (1937).

Khoroshkhin, A. P. 'Dalina Zarafshana'. In: *Voennyi Sbornik*. Part 54, St. Petersburg.

Kislyakov, N. A., [1953]: 'Iz Istorii Gornovo Tadzhikistana'. In: *Trudy A. N. Tadzhik SSR*. Vol. 4.

Kizl Uzbekistan. [1929]: Nos. 215–216.

Kocaoglu, T., [1973]: 'The Existence of a Bukharan Nationality in the Recent Past'. In: *The Nationality Question in Soviet Central Asia*. ed. Allworth, E., New York.

Komatsu, H. [1981]: 'Fitrat'. In: *Munazar'si uzerine bazi notlar*. Doghu Dilleri, 2.

Mazov, S. I. 'Vostochnaya Bukhara, Badakhshan i Severnyi Afghanistan'. In: *Turkistan Sbornik*. Vol. 404, n. y.

Mirzaef, A. [1960]: 'Muqaddima'. In: Donish, A., *Risala ya Mukhtasari az Tarikhi Sultanati Khanadani Manghitia*. Stalinabad.

Mirzoev, A. [1953]: 'Pervaya Redaktsiya *Navadir-ul-Voqai* i Vremya eyo Sostovleniya'. In: *Sbornik Statiei po Istorii i Filologii Narodov Srednei Azii*. Stalinabad.

Mulla Ishaq Jan. [1914]: 'Jawab', In: *Ayna*, 4 January 1914.

Narzikulov, I. [1957]: 'Kratkie Svedeniya o do Revolyutsionnoi Kustarnoi Promyshlennosti Tadzhikistana'. In: *Trudy A. N. Tadzhik SSR*. Vol. 71.

Novoe Vremya. St. Petersburg. [16 March 1874].

'Partiya Mlado-Bukhartsev'. [1985]: In *Programmnye Dokumenty Musulmanskikh Partii 1917–1920 gg*. Oxford.

Qosimov, B., [1992]: 'Fitrat'. In: *Sharq Yulduzi*, No. 10.

Radzhabov, Z. [1984]: 'Po Ctranitsam Zhyrnala <<Oyna>> [Ayna]'. In: *Izvestiya A. N. Tajik SSR*, No. 4.

Radzhapova, P. [1987]: 'Petr Alekseevich Kobozev'. In: *Revolyutsiei Prizvannye*. Tashkent.

Ryabinskii, A. M. [1941]: 'Tsarskaya Rossiya i Bukhara v Epokhu Imperializma'. In: *Istorik Marksist*. No. 4.

Semyonov, A. A. 'Material po Istorii Tadzhikov i Uzbekov'. In: *Trudy Akademii Nauk Tadzhik SSR*. Vol. 25, 2nd edition.

Semyonov, A., [1960]: 'K Proshlomy Bukhary'. In: *Vospominaniya*. Moscow. (1960).

Shorish, M. [1986]: 'Traditional Islamic Education in Central Asia Prior to 1917'. In: *Turco-Tatar Past Soviet Present*. Paris, editors. Quelquejay, C. L., G. Veinstein and S. E. Wimbush.

Shua'la-i Inqilab. Samarkand. No. 50–53, 56–60, 62, 63, 66, 68, 70, 72, 74, 76, 77, 79, 82–85, 89–99.

Shukurov, M. [1992]: 'Fitrat i Tadzhikskaya Literatura'. An unpublished article by Shukurov, a member of the Academy of Sciences of Tadjikistan, Dushanbe. (1992).

Skalov, G. [1923]: 'Ekonomicheskoe obedenenie Sredne Aziatskikh respublik kak faktor natsionalnoi politiki'. In: *Zhizn Natsionalnostei*, Vol. 5, 1923.

Stremukhov, N. [1875]: 'Poezdka v Bukharu'. In: *Russkii Vestnik*, 117, 1875.

Taraqqi. 1906, 17 June; 13, 20 July; 12 August

Turkistanskaya Pravda. 21 November 1924.

Umnyakov, I. [1927]: 'K Istorii Novo-Metodnoi Shkoly v Bukhare'. In: *Bulletin of the Central Asian University*. No. 6, Tashkent.

Yusupov, E. [1987]: 'Faizulla Khodzhaev'. In: *Revolyutsiei Prizvannye*. Tashkent (1987).

Yusupov, E., and E. Karimov, [1988]: 'Nastala Pora Obektivnykh Otsenok'. In: *Kommunist Uzbekistana*. No. 12 (1988).

Index

219